LEGAL
NEGOTIATION
THEORY AND APPLICATIONS

By

Donald G. Gifford
Dean and Professor of Law
University of Maryland

WEST GROUP

Bancroft-Whitney • Banks-Baldwin • Clark Boardman Callaghan
Lawyers Cooperative Publishing • WESTLAW® • West Publishing

COPYRIGHT © 1989 By WEST PUBLISHING CO.
        610 Opperman Drive
        P.O. Box 64526
        St. Paul, MN 55164–0526

All rights reserved
Printed in the United States of America

Library of Congress Cataloging-in-Publication Data

Gifford, Donald G., 1952–
    Legal negotiation : theory and applications / by Donald G. Gifford.
        p.   cm.
    Includes index.
    ISBN 0–314–50511–3
    1. Compromise (Law)—United States. 2. Attorney and client—
United States. 3. Negotiation. I. Title.
    KF9084.G54 1989
    347.73′77—dc19
    [347.30777]   88–26877
                                                        CIP

ISBN 0–314–50511–3

 TEXT IS PRINTED ON 10% POST
CONSUMER RECYCLED PAPER

Gifford-Legal Neg. Misc.
5th Reprint—1998

*To my wife Nancy,
and Our Daughters Rebecca and Caroline*

*

Preface

This book presents a comprehensive overview of legal negotiation for law students and lawyers studying their negotiating behavior. The analysis presented often is derived from the research of social scientists, but the book is specifically designed to teach the reader how to negotiate more effectively in the actual practice of law. Examples of specific negotiation techniques are included throughout the text, and theoretical models of social scientists are discussed only when the conclusions derived from them are directly relevant to legal negotiation. At the same time, the book avoids the mundane mechanics of both local negotiation practice and "pop-psychology."

Included within this single book are analysis of both competitive negotiation tactics and more collaborative approaches, such as problem-solving and cooperative tactics. No single negotiation strategy works best in all negotiations. Accordingly the lawyer should be able to use a variety of approaches and know when to choose each tactic.

Most lawyers not only change their tactics from one negotiation to another, but also use a combination of varying tactics—for example, problem-solving and competitive tactics—within a single negotiation. For this reason, this text divides the negotiation process into six components or subprocesses: negotiation planning, initial orientation, initial proposals, information bargaining, narrowing of differences and closure. This organization allows discussion in a single chapter of how the different approaches to negotiation—competitive, cooperative or problem-solving—address varying aspects of the negotiation process.

The book focuses on negotiation as client representation. The lawyer's role as an advocate changes the negotiation process in a number of ways that often are not considered in general negotiation texts written by social scientists and others. This book includes separate chapters on Negotiation Planning and Negotiation Counseling, and the impact of the client is stressed throughout the text.

Both the generosity of others who contributed to this book and the value of their input have been overwhelming. Their collaboration made writing this book worthwhile. My colleagues and friends Larry Dessem, Nancy Gifford, Peter Hoffman, Bob Moberly, Al Neely and Mike Oberst read virtually every word of this text and offered detailed and insightful comments. Irv Horowitz read it and provided the expertise of a social psychologist; Bill Bryant and Mike Lipson offered their comments from their perspectives as practicing attorneys. Susan Martyn contributed her knowledge and guidance on the difficult professional responsiblility issues surrounding negotiation. Don Peters, Doug Ray, Bill Richman and Anne Spitzer read specific chapters of the text, and the final product is significantly improved because of their comments. Conversations with Bill Richman and with Dave Binder assisted me in refining the major organizing concepts presented in the book.

The University of Florida College of Law supported my research and writing in a variety of ways, and I gratefully acknowledge the encouragement and assistance of Dean Jeffrey E. Lewis and former Dean Frank T. Read. My research assistant Peggy Lyon worked tirelessly for eighteen months and has proven the value of hiring a former reference librarian as a research assistant. I also want to thank Carol Marcinkiewicz and Noreen Fenner for their patient and competent secretarial assistance.

Finally, I want to express my gratitude to my wife Nancy and my daughters Rebecca and Caroline for all those contributions too important to detail here.

DONALD G. GIFFORD

Gainesville, Florida
January, 1989

Summary of Contents

*

Table of Contents

LEGAL NEGOTIATION

THEORY AND APPLICATIONS

*

Chapter One

NEGOTIATION AS CLIENT REPRESENTATION

A. LEARNING NEGOTIATION SKILLS

Early in the practice of law, the lawyer is sure to be asked, "Do you think we could settle this thing?" or "Could our clients work out a deal here?" Away from judicial chambers and the courtroom, the lawyer is thus initiated into the negotiation process, the single most prevalent and important legal decision-making system.

How can you prepare yourself for this moment? Certainly, knowledge of the substantive law affecting your client's situation will be important, as will your ability to analyze the legal issues. And nothing is more important to your success as a negotiator than preparation—your understanding of the relevant facts and law and of your client's interests. Additional factors—your personality or your past relationship with the other lawyer—also may play a role.

How well you serve your client's interests when you respond to that inquiry depends upon at least one other factor. Practicing attorneys know that a few among them are always able to get a good deal for their clients through skillful negotiation. They also know that skilled negotiators are not born. The ability to negotiate competently is not a trait like blue eyes, quick reflexes or the ability to roll one's tongue. All individuals "learn" to negotiate from infancy as they develop their abilities to influence Mom or Dad, or classmates or teachers, to do what they want them to do. Beginning lawyers learn about "legal" negotiation by watching more experienced attorneys negotiate with them or against them. Eventually negotiating techniques are acquired—but often slowly and erratically. Some novice lawyers are fortunate enough to be working with capable negotiators; others are not.

This book provides both the necessary theoretical background and the specific techniques to make you a better negotiator. The prospect of *learning* to become a more effective negotiator should not be a startling one. Few law students and lawyers today would quarrel with the assertion that trial practice courses and texts can teach effective

1

cross-examination skills, however novel that idea may have been a generation or two ago. Part of what is taught as the "art" of cross-examination depends upon the law of evidence, but the most important underpinnings of cross-examination skills lie in the behavioral reactions of the witness and the jurors to the type and pacing of questions. The art and science of negotiation similarly depend upon predictions as to how the other lawyer will respond to your strategic moves as a negotiator—your demands or proposals, arguments and questions. While the interactions of negotiators are less stylized than those of attorney and witness in the courtroom, they can be analyzed and understood so that you can become a more capable negotiator.

This is a practical text, designed to assist the law student or lawyer in becoming a better negotiator. It is not merely a theoretical overview of the social psychology of negotiation or of game theory. On the other hand, it is not a cook book or a mechanics' manual. To be sure, it describes a number of specific negotiating techniques, but the effective legal negotiator cannot be programmed in advance like a computer or trained like a seal. For the lawyer to know when to choose a particular technique, when to extrapolate from a described tactic and when to improvise totally, she [1] needs a fuller understanding of the psychology of legal negotiation. Therefore, the knowledge and theories of social psychologists and others who have studied negotiation will be described and analyzed when they provide helpful insights for the negotiating lawyer.

B. WHAT IS NEGOTIATION?

Everyone knows what negotiation is. Two parties face each other and haggle, whether over the price of an automobile, the terms of a commercial lease or the control of a corporation. Adjudication, on the other hand, appears to be its polar opposite. Opposing advocates present evidence and arguments to a third party, either judge or jury, and await a binding decision.

The demarcation between these two processes, however, sometimes is obscure. If the prosecutor, in plea bargaining, makes the defendant a "take it or leave it offer" in a case in which the defendant otherwise faces certain conviction on higher charges, is that negotiation or is the prosecutor in reality functioning as a judge? If the parties in a complicated business dispute agree to participate in a "mini-trial," [2] a formalized presentation of evidence to a third party, and they ask the third party to render a decision but stipulate that it is non-binding, is that an adjudication, or a part of the negotiation process, or both?

---

1. Anyone writing about negotiation or other multiple party human interactions in a modern context realizes the difficulty of pronoun selection. I refer to the principal negotiator as "she" throughout this text; her client and her negotiating counterpart typically are referred to as "he."

2. For a discussion of mini-trials, see *infra* Chapter Twelve, *Alternative Dispute Resolution and Negotiation,* at 218.

For the purposes of this book, *negotiation* can be defined as a process in which two or more participants attempt to reach a joint decision on matters of common concern in situations where they are in actual or potential disagreement or conflict.[3] The factor distinguishing negotiation from adjudication is that the parties themselves—not someone else—determine the result, and they must consent to the outcome for it to be operative. Even when the prosecutor possesses overwhelming bargaining power, the plea bargain still requires the defendant's consent. Plea bargaining, therefore, remains negotiation. The "mini-trial" too is a negotiation technique. Although it looks like adjudication, the parties remain free to accept or reject the results of the "mini-trial" and decide the outcome.

Throughout this book the term "bargaining" will be used interchangeably with "negotiation," although many social scientists use it in a more restrictive sense to refer to the presentation and exchange of proposals for the terms of agreement on specific issues.[4]

C. THE CLIENT AND NEGOTIATION

If everyone negotiates constantly, what makes legal negotiation different? The most important distinction is that while the lawyer sometimes negotiates on her own behalf, such as when she negotiates her own salary or her office lease, the essence of legal negotiation is the lawyer's role as a representative of her client. Legal negotiations involve not only a relationship between the two negotiating attorneys, but also relationships between each lawyer and her respective client. The interactions between lawyer and client as a part of the negotiation process will be explored in a comprehensive manner in Chapter Eleven, *Negotiation Counseling,* and the effects of the client on the negotiation process will be considered throughout this book. For now, three differences between legal negotiation and other negotiation must be highlighted.

First, the client, and not the negotiator herself, should make the important substantive decisions in negotiation, such as whether to make or accept specific offers. The American Bar Association's Model Rule of Professional Conduct 1.2 provides that "a lawyer shall abide by a client's decision whether to accept an offer of settlement of a matter."[5] The rule requires that the lawyer "abide by the client's decisions concerning the objectives of the representation" and to "consult with the client as to the means by which they are to be pursued."[6]

3. *See* P. Gulliver, Disputes and Negotiations: A Cross–Cultural Perspective xiii (1979).

4. *E.g., id.* at 71.

5. Model Rules of Professional Conduct Rule 1.2(a) (1983). Similarly, *Ethical Consideration* 7–7 of the *Model Code of Professional Responsibility* provides that in most instances "the authority to make decisions is exclusively that of the client and, if made within the framework of the law, such decisions are binding on the lawyer." Model Code of Professional Responsibility EC 7–7 (1987). EC 7–7 specifically identifies the decision whether or not to accept a settlement offer as an example of a decision to be made by the client.

6. *Id.*

Caselaw [7] and commentators [8] frequently refer explicitly to the lawyer as "an agent" for the client in negotiations.

The quality of a negotiated agreement is measured by the extent to which it meets the client's interests, both long term and short term. If the lawyer is to achieve better negotiation results, therefore, she must be able to ascertain the client's true interests and priorities and to counsel the client effectively regarding the alternatives available to him and the consequences of each option.

A negotiated agreement is never any better than the extent to which it serves the client's interests. The lawyer may believe that if she continues her hard-nosed, aggressive bargaining she will be able to extract a better compensation package for a new partner in a group of physicians. Only her client could decide, however, if the additional compensation is sufficiently important to him to risk the potential jealousy and resentment of his partners. Similarly, a plaintiff's personal injury attorney may believe that her client has an excellent chance of receiving a verdict in excess of $800,000 if the case proceeds to trial. But only the paraplegic client can choose between a certain settlement offer of $300,000 and the riskier, albeit more lucrative, prospects at trial. Some of us play the lottery; some of us don't. Because each individual has his own level of risk-tolerance, the client should decide for himself whether the settlement is a "good deal."

On the other hand, the client's decision to accept or reject a negotiated agreement should be a fully informed one. Two separate rules of the Model Rules of Professional Conduct address the lawyer's obligation to assist the client in making an informed decision. First, Model Rule of Professional Conduct 1.4(a) requires the lawyer to "keep a client reasonably informed about the status of a matter." [9] Thus, the lawyer should continually update the client as the negotiations progress. Further, Model Rule 1.4(b) specifically directs the lawyer to "explain a matter to the extent reasonably necessary to permit the client to make informed decisions." [10] The comment to the rule indicates that the lawyer shall promptly inform her client of settlement offers, inform the client of communications from the other attorney

7. *See* Moving Picture Mach. Operators Union Local No. 162 v. Glasgow Theaters, Inc., 6 Cal.App.3d 395, 86 Cal.Rptr. 33 (1970) (principles of agency applied when attorney is involved in labor dispute negotiations); Dillon v. City of Davenport, 366 N.W.2d 918 (Iowa 1985) (agency principles applied when attorney is negotiating a settlement on a workman's compensation claim); Southwestern Bell Tel. Co. v. Roussin, 534 S.W.2d 273 (Mo.App.1976) (principles of agency applied when attorney is negotiating a settlement of an easement dispute); Mattco, Inc. v. Mandan Radio Ass'n, Inc., 246 N.W.2d 222 (N.D.1976) (principles of agency applied when attorney is renegotiating terms of an existing contract); Johnson v. Tesky, 57 Or.App. 133, 643 P.2d 1344 (1982) (agency principles applied when attorney is negotiating a settlement agreement in a negligence action).

8. *See e.g.,* L. Patterson, Legal Ethics: The Law of Professional Responsibility 75–76 (2d ed. 1984).

9. Model Rules of Professional Conduct Rule 1.4(a) (1983); *see also* C. Wolfram, Modern Legal Ethics 163–65 (1985); Martyn, *Informed Consent in the Practice of Law,* 48 Geo.Wash.L.R. 307 (1980).

10. Model Rules of Professional Conduct Rule 1.4(b) (1983).

during negotiation and provide the facts relevant to the matter being negotiated.[11]

The lawyer's proper professional rule as counselor involves more than merely keeping the client informed, however. Model Rule of Professional Conduct 2.1 requires the lawyer to "exercise independent professional judgment and render candid advice." [12] The rule further suggests that the lawyer's advice include not only legal factors, but also "other considerations such as moral, economic, social and political factors." [13] The paraplegic client ultimately may decide to accept the $300,000 settlement, but his lawyer has the responsibility to assure that he understands that there is a good chance of an even larger verdict at trial and that he appreciates the other consequences of accepting such a settlement. Is he fully aware of how his injury will affect his life and his finances, or is he reacting impulsively to what is for him a previously unheard of sum of money?

A second difference between the legal negotiation process and other negotiations is the lawyer's role as an intermediary or buffer between her client's interests and the interests of the other party and his attorney. The lawyer's undivided loyalty to her client's interests often conflicts with the pressures she experiences as a negotiator. On one hand, she is professionally obligated to obtain the most favorable settlement possible during negotiation, while on the other, she is subject to professional pressure to pursue settlements that are just and fair to both parties.

The responsiveness of the negotiator to both her client and to the other negotiator, and her position as an intermediary between these competing influences, exemplify what social scientists call *boundary-role conflict*.[14] When negotiating, opposing lawyers attempt to achieve an agreement, while maintaining valuable continuing professional relationships with each other. The lawyers' lack of a substantial emotional stake in the dispute, and the traditions of courtesy and fair play among members of the bar, enable them to reach mutually satisfactory solutions in many cases when the parties themselves cannot. Often, however, there is only a fine distinction between the lawyer legitimately seeking to reconcile conflicting interests and the lawyer wrongfully yielding to peer pressure to accommodate. In extreme cases, the lawyer "sells-out" the interests of the client in order to achieve settlement.

A third difference between legal negotiations and other negotiations also relates to the client's effect on them. Repeated counseling

11. *Id.*, Rule 1.4 comment.

12. Model Rules of Professional Conduct Rule 2.1 (1983). *Ethical Considera-tion* 7–8 of the *Model Code of Professional Responsibility* specifically provides that "[a] lawyer should exert his best efforts to insure that decisions of his client are made only after the client has been informed of

relevant considerations." Model Code of Professional Responsibility, EC 7–8 (1987).

13. *Id.*

14. *See* D. Pruitt, Negotiation Behavior 41–44 (1981); R. Walton & R. McKersie, A Behavioral Theory of Labor Negotiations: An Analysis of a Social Interaction System 282–302 (1965).

sessions between clients and their lawyers punctuate the negotiation process, and negotiations may involve many bargaining sessions and last for years. The length of legal negotiations and the number of exchanges between the lawyers, of course, vary greatly with the type and importance of the transaction or case being negotiated. A routine misdemeanor plea bargaining conference may take as little as twenty or thirty seconds; a sophisticated corporate merger or divestiture might go on for months or even years. For example, the antitrust action against American Telephone and Telegraph settled after six years of settlement negotiations.[15] It is probably the exception, and not the rule, however, when legal negotiations are concluded within a single negotiation session. This realization is important, because most research involves study of simulated negotiations that begin and end in one encounter. Indeed, most simulated negotiations conducted in law school courses include only one meeting between the negotiating students. In practice, however, written correspondence and telephone communications supplement face-to-face encounters and dramatically increase the number of negotiation proposals exchanged between the parties. Legal negotiation is rarely a one-night stand; the process usually consists of alternating counseling sessions between the lawyers and their clients, and bargaining sessions between the lawyers.

This aspect of the legal negotiation process thus resembles the *cyclical process* of negotiation described by the social anthropologist P.H. Gulliver who studied dispute resolution in two native African cultures.[16] According to Gulliver, the *cyclical process* is one of two separate processes which occur simultaneously during negotiation. It consists of the recurrent cycle of exchange of information between parties, its assessment by the parties, and their adjustments of expectations and preferences as a result of the new knowledge. Gulliver's *cyclical process* accurately reflects the interplay between client counseling and bargaining sessions in the negotiation process. When the lawyer initially discusses with the client the possibility of pursuing a negotiation alternative, the information available to her is usually incomplete. If the client is involved in actual or potential litigation, the lawyer frequently cannot predict with accuracy the eventual trial outcome. In other contexts, if the client's matter does not involve litigation, but instead a sale of assets or a merger of two businesses, the lawyer can offer at best only an educated guess regarding the other party's response to specific negotiation proposals.

Initially, the client is often unable to articulate fully his own goals and preferences. Typically, the client "wants it all" before the negotiations, and unrealistically assesses the likely outcomes of pursuing any of the available alternatives. The client has not decided how much risk he is willing to assume and which of his multiple objectives is his

15. *See* Axinn & Stoll, *AT & T: Do U.S. Actions Compute? The Settlement and Dismissal,* 187 N.Y.L.J., Jan. 14, 1982, at 1, col. 2.

16. P. Gulliver, *supra* note 3, at xv–xvi, 82–89 (1979).

primary goal. Only the negotiation can give him the information necessary to decide these issues.

In most cases, the lawyer learns much about the problem being negotiated from the other lawyer. Often the negotiation itself is a primary source of information about the underlying subject matter of the negotiation. The discovery process is available only in litigation matters; even there, neither discovery nor independent investigation may be feasible because of the expense they require and the time necessary to complete them. In addition, the negotiation process usually is the lawyer's best source of information regarding the other party's view of the dispute or transaction. Finally, the negotiation is the lawyer's only means of learning what the other party is willing to offer her client.

The client's expectations and the emphasis he places on a particular issue, when compared with other issues, are not fixed and static, but are continuously subject to change during the negotiation. As he learns more about the facts of the situation and how the other party views the issues, his own evaluation of the case often changes. In some cases, the client actually changes his "bottom line"—the least advantageous settlement he is willing to accept—rather than to terminate the negotiation. In some cases, of course, the "bottom line" is fixed and unchangeable. A parent may be unwilling to change his position on the custody of his minor children regardless of what new information he learns during the course of the negotiation; the criminal defendant is unwilling to accept any plea bargain that includes a jail sentence. Even when the client's "bottom line" does not change, however, his expectations about the other party's posture in the negotiation, or about what will happen if agreement is not reached, often do change.

Thus, negotiation is an *information-gathering* process. Much of the new information gained during negotiation—particularly how the other party views the matter being negotiated—usually cannot be obtained any other way. The nature of the negotiation process confirms the importance of the communication requirements contained in Model Rule 1.4. The client reacts to the new information gained during negotiation, often changes his expectations and preferences, and decides, with his lawyer, how together they will respond in the next round of bargaining. The negotiation cycle described by Gulliver begins again.

D. THE ROLE OF NEGOTIATION STRATEGY

The negotiator's goal can be defined as an attempt to reach a joint decision with the other party that provides the greatest possible benefit to her client. This book describes how to maximize the opportunities to achieve that result: how can the other party and his negotiator be convinced, persuaded, enticed or threatened into agreeing to a negotiated settlement which is desirable for the negotiator's client?

One idea is critical to understanding the approach taken in this text. At each point in the negotiation, the attorney has three basic choices in deciding how to respond to the most recent proposal or communication from the other party. She consciously may respond with either *competitive, cooperative,* or *problem-solving* behaviors. *Competitive* tactics, such as high demands, threats or arguments, are those negotiating behaviors designed to undermine the other negotiator's confidence in his bargaining position, and to induce him to enter into an agreement less advantageous to his client than he would have agreed to prior to the negotiation. The other choices involve more *collaborative* bargaining behaviors. *Cooperative* tactics include reasonable opening offers, arguments based on what is fair and just, and making concessions to encourage the other negotiator to reciprocate. The use of *cooperative* tactics is premised on the notion that when one party displays behavior which is fair, reasonable and accommodative, the other party is likely to respond in kind. Finally, *problem-solving* techniques are those negotiating behaviors designed to identify and exploit opportunities for joint gain in negotiations.

The effective negotiator is the one who knows when to cooperate, when to compete and when to offer problem-solving solutions. Within a single negotiation, a lawyer usually uses tactics from more than one strategy. Each *strategy* prescribes different tactics to be used at various points in a negotiation. For example, a *competitive* initial proposal in a negotiation might be a very high demand; a *cooperative* demand would be more moderate and reasonable; and a *problem-solving* approach would avoid establishing initial positions and, instead, seek to address the parties' underlying interests.

E. THE COMPONENTS OF THE NEGOTIATION PROCESS

Most negotiations are characterized by a series of components or "sub-processes" of the larger negotiation whole. In other words, although every negotiation is unique, lawyers face certain inherent elements of the bargaining interaction in most negotiations. As analyzed in this text, negotiation is divided into six component parts:

(1) negotiation planning and preparation;

(2) establishing a beginning orientation in the negotiation and an initial relationship with the other negotiator;

(3) initial proposals;

(4) information exchange;

(5) narrowing of differences; and

(6) closure.

These negotiation sub-processes do not constitute a rigid sequential model of the negotiation process, although some scholars identify specific negotiation stages or phases.[17] Sometimes the sequence varies; for example, in many business negotiations, the parties frequently exchange information for a substantial period of time before either negotiator makes a bargaining proposal. Information exchange and narrowing of the differences between the parties almost always overlap, and occur simultaneously. In other negotiations, threatened stalement leads the negotiators to revert to an "earlier" sub-process in the bargaining process. This frequently occurs when negotiators who begin with predominantly competitive tactics find they are deadlocked; in such a situation, the negotiators may begin to use problem-solving approaches typically identified with the initial proposal or information exchange aspects of negotiation.

Further, most negotiations are multiple issue negotiations. Negotiators often consider distinct issues simultaneously. The negotiators may be nearing resolution of some issues at the same time that they are exchanging initial proposals on other issues. Consider the sale of a business. The parties achieve closure on the form that the transaction will take—for example, whether it is to be a purchase of corporate assets or a purchase of the corporate stock. At the same time, consideration of the issue of how much is to be paid by the purchaser is characterized by arguments and threats—tactics typically occurring during the narrowing of differences process. Finally, the negotiators have not begun to discuss initial proposals, or even to exchange information on which key employees will continue with the firm following the purchase.

In short, the sequence of these six negotiation "sub-processes" vary from one negotiation to another and even may occur simultaneously on different issues within a single negotiation. Nevertheless, these six sub-processes are present, if only fleetingly, in most legal negotiations. Further, each of the three negotiation strategies described in the previous section suggests separate and distinct ways that the negotiator should approach these negotiation sub-processes. Accordingly, the core of this book is organized into chapters reflecting the components of the negotiation process: negotiation planning, the initial orientation toward the other party, initial proposals, information bargaining, narrowing of differences and closure. Each chapter describes how the *competitive, cooperative* and *problem-solving* strategies address that aspect of the negotiation process.

17. *See e.g.,* D. Pruitt, *supra* note 14, at 131–33; P. Gulliver, *supra* note 3, at 121–175.

TABLE 1–1

HOW EACH STRATEGY ADDRESSES COMPONENTS OF THE NEGOTIATION PROCESS

STRATEGY	I. PLANNING CHAPTER FOUR	II. INITIAL ORIENTATION CHAPTER FIVE	III. INITIAL PROPOSALS CHAPTER SIX
A. COMPETITIVE	Discuss with client: 1. Minimum disposition. 2. Sources of power and leverage. 3. Advantages and disadvantages of competitive tactics. 4. Negotiator's restricted authority.	1. Agenda issues. 2. Location of negotiation. 3. Deadlines. 4. Outnumbering other party's negotiators. 5. Bargaining with credentials.	1. High initial demand. 2. Firm demand. 3. Justification of initial proposal. 4. False demand. 5. Demand as a precondition to bargaining. 6. Inflexible first offer (Boulwarism). 7. Outrage as response to other party's first offer.
B. COOPERATIVE	Discuss with client: 1. Minimum disposition. 2. Objective criteria. 3. Advantages and disadvantages of cooperative tactics. 4. Negotiator's flexible authority	1. Cooperation facilitators. 2. Answering competitive tactics. 3. Initiating trusting behaviors. 4. Discussing bargaining relationship. 5. Active listening.	1. Reasonable and moderate demand. 2. Justification with objective criteria. 3. Varied responses to other party's extreme first demand.
C. PROBLEM-SOLVING	Discuss with client: 1. Underlying interests. 2. "Best alternative to a negotiated agreement." 3. Bridging solutions. 4. Relative priorities among issues. 5. Negotiator's flexible authority.	1. Cooperation facilitators described in (B) above. 2. Identification of other party's interests. 3. Communication of client's interests.	1. Information exchange preceding initial proposals. 2. Probing for underlying interests by responding to other party's opening "positions." 3. Establishing "search model." 4. Presentation of bridging proposals conceived with client. 5. Developing solutions with other negotiator.

TABLE 1–2

HOW EACH STRATEGY ADDRESSES COMPONENTS OF THE NEGOTIATION PROCESS

STRATEGY	IV. INFORMATION-BARGAINING CHAPTER SEVEN	V. NARROWING OF DIFFERENCES CHAPTER EIGHT	VI. CLOSURE CHAPTER NINE
A. COMPETITIVE	1. Information gathering suggesting other party's minimum disposition. 2. Concealment of information suggesting client's minimum disposition or reducing bargaining leverage. 3. Revealing information increasing bargaining power.	1. Convincing other party to concede by using: (a) Arguments, (b) Threats, (c) Breaking–off negotiations. 2. Limitation of concessions. 3. Justification of concessions.	1. Use of deadlines and ultimatim. 2. Drafting agreement where possible.
B. COOPERATIVE	1. Both information gathering and revealing.	1. Initiating exchange of concessions. 2. Promises to induce concessions. 3. Arguments based upon objective criteria. 4. Limiting risks of unreciprocated concessions.	1. Making final concession and inviting reciprocation. 2. Splitting the difference. 3. Constructive ambiguities. 4. Interpreting "Final Offer" as firm, but not final. 5. Re-opening deadlocked negotiations.
C. PROBLEM–SOLVING	1. Exchanging of information about parties' respective interests.	1. Evaluation of proposed bridging solutions. 2. Refinement of bridging solutions through incorporation. 3. Heuristic trial and error.	1. Agreement on bridging solution. 2. Logrolling. 3. Cost-cutting. 4. Compensation.

An overview of the negotiation tactics described in this book is provided by Tables 1–1 and 1–2. Each of the three rows in the tables lists the tactics included within a particular negotiation strategy—the *competitive, cooperative,* or *problem-solving* strategy. The columns in the table identify the six components of the negotiation process just described. Using the table, you can determine the tactics each negotiation strategy would prescribe for each aspect of negotiations. For example, to identify the manner in which a negotiator using competitive tactics would approach initial negotiation proposals, locate the third column on Table 1–1 identified as "III. INITIAL PROPOSALS." Then move down the column to the row identified as "A. COMPETITIVE." This block in the matrix lists competitive initial proposal tactics:

(1) High initial demand;

(2) Firm demand;

(3) Justification of initial proposal;

(4) False demand;

(5) Demand as a pre-condition to bargaining;

(6) Inflexible first offer (Boulwarism);

(7) Outrage as response to other party's first offer.

Tables 1–1 and 1–2 thus serve as a road map of the tactics to be presented in Chapters Four through Nine of this text. Some of the brief references in the tables probably have little meaning to you now. As you study the remainder of this book, however, return to these tables to review how the specific negotiating tactic described fits into both the ongoing negotiation process and into one of the three basic negotiation strategies. Be aware, however, that most of the tactics listed in Tables 1–1 and 1–2 are presented only in cursory form and that some techniques discussed in the text are deleted from the table because of space limitations.

Before proceeding to consideration of specific negotiation tactics, the next two chapters examine two broader topics. First, Chapter Two discusses the goals and underlying assumptions about human behavior inherent in each of the three basic negotiation strategies: the *competitive* strategy, the *cooperative* strategy and the *problem-solving* strategy. Chapter Three then considers how the negotiator should decide, at any particular point in a negotiation, which negotiation tactics are most likely to lead to a better negotiation result for her client.

Chapter Two

NEGOTIATION STRATEGY

The lawyer as negotiator engages in representation of her client's interests. As such her professional role obligates her to attempt to achieve an agreement which will best serve her client's interests, as long as the agreement does not require or contemplate any illegal conduct.[1] Because the other party will respond in different ways depending upon the lawyer's statements and actions during the negotiation, the quality of the negotiated agreement often depends upon the tactics used by the lawyer as negotiator.

A. THE CONCEPT OF STRATEGY

The lawyer's behavior during negotiation can be broken down into discrete tactics or strategic moves. A *tactic*, as the term is used here, is a specific negotiating behavior the lawyer uses when initiating the negotiating exchange with the other attorney or in responding to the other negotiator's negotiation behavior.[2] A *negotiation strategy* is a series of tactics or specific negotiating behaviors that the lawyer uses to facilitate a resolution to the negotiation process that is favorable to her client's interests. The lawyer's negotiation strategy includes decisions

---

1. Canon 7 of the *ABA Code of Professional Responsibility* explicitly provides that "[a] lawyer should represent a client zealously within the bounds of the law." Model Code of Professional Responsibility Canon 7 (1987). The Code qualifies this statement by providing that the lawyer should not knowingly assist the client in engaging in illegal conduct. Model Code of Professional Responsibility EC 7–5 (1987). The *Model Rules of Professional Conduct* implicitly are premised upon zealous representation, *see e.g.,* Rule 1.1 ("competence"), Rule 1.2 (client's primary role in decisions affecting him) and Rule 1.3 ("diligence"). The *Model Rules* also provide, however, that "[a] lawyer shall not counsel a client to engage, or assist a client, in conduct that the lawyer knows is criminal or fraudulent * * *" Model Rules of Professional Conduct Rule 1.2(d) (1983); *see also* Model Code of Professional Responsibility DR 7–102(A)(7) (1987).

The lawyer's conduct during negotiation is also limited by ethical rules governing the negotiation process itself, such as those which prohibit lying under most circumstances. *See* Model Rules of Professional Conduct Rule 4.1 (1983); Model Code of Professional Responsibility DR 7–102(A)(5); *see also* Chapter Seven, *Information Bargaining,* at 133–35.

2. The meaning of "tactic" in this text is devoid of any military or necessarily competitive connotation.

made regarding the first proposal, or opening bid, in the negotiation and the subsequent modifications of that initial proposal.

The lawyer's negotiation strategy is a separate and distinct concept from the lawyer's negotiation *style*. This book will not alter your personal style in interacting with other negotiators or anyone else for the matter. If your basic nature is to be courteous, friendly, tactful and trustful, it probably is not possible or desirable for you to seek a metamorphosis that will turn you into a "raging tiger." On the other hand, if you are naturally inclined to be forceful and aggressive in your relationships with other people, that also will probably not change. To a limited extent, it is possible for negotiators to feign or mimic personal styles. For the most part, however, it is negotiation tactics or techniques that can be consciously analyzed and learned. Specific examples illustrating the distinction between strategy and style will be provided below, but first it is necessary to outline the three basic negotiation strategies.

B. A BASIC TYPOLOGY OF NEGOTIATION STRATEGIES

It is useful when studying negotiation to identify three separate and distinct negotiation strategies or classifications of specific negotiation tactics: *competitive, cooperative* and *problem-solving*. It is important to recognize that no consistent nomenclature of negotiation strategies exists in either the legal or social scientific literature.[3] In this text, "competitive," "cooperative," and "integrative" are terms of art used as organizing concepts designed to help you better understand negotiation behavior.

Negotiation tactics can be classified into one of these three "pure" negotiation strategies using the following two criteria:

(1) Does the negotiation tactic attempt to garner the largest possible share of a fixed quantity of resources for the lawyer's client or does it seek to benefit the client by increasing the joint level of satisfaction of both parties? and

(2) Does the tactic facilitate a *collaborative* working relationship with the other party or is it designed to foster an *adversarial* relationship?

3. For example, as compared with the three basic negotiation strategies described here, Harnett, Cummings, and Hamner identify four separate strategies. *See* Harnett, Cummings & Hamner, *Personality, Bargaining Style and Payoff in Bilateral Monopoly Bargaining Among European Managers,* 36 Sociometry 325, 328 (1973). Similarly, Horowitz and Willging identify five distinct strategies, *see* I. Horowitz & T. Willging, The Psychology of Law: Integrations and Applications 284 (1984), as does Pruitt. *See* Pruitt, *Strategic Choice in Negotiation,* 27 Am. Behavioral Scientist 167, 167 (1983).

1. DISTRIBUTIVE AND INTEGRATIVE NEGOTIATION CONTEXTS

A tactic which seeks to increase the joint level of satisfaction for both parties works only if the bargaining situation allows for such joint gains. Negotiation theorists refer to situations in which such gains are possible as *integrative* bargaining contexts and to those in which they are not feasible as *distributive* bargaining situations.

A surprising number of negotiations include opportunities for problem-solving bargaining on at least some issues. An *integrative* bargaining situation exists when the parties' interests are not directly in conflict, and agreements are possible in which the level of satisfaction of one party is not necessarily inversely related to that of the other. Instead of dividing a fixed quantity of resources between them, an integrative bargaining context allows the parties to "problem-solve," *i.e.*, devise mutually satisfying solutions. An obvious example of an integrative context is a profit-sharing agreement between management and labor which will both increase the workers' satisfaction with the negotiated agreement by providing higher compensation and heighten management's enthusiasm by augmenting worker productivity.

Distributive bargaining situations, on the other hand, are those in which there is a pure conflict of interest between the parties; most often, the parties are deciding how to divide a fixed quantity of resources between them. In this context, the one party's gain is necessarily the other's loss. This type of bargaining problem has been referred to by various bargaining theorists as a "fixed pie," [4] a zero-sum game,[5] or share bargaining.[6] Examples of zero-sum negotiations include the bargaining between the buyer and the seller about the cash price to be paid immediately for anything—a used car, a sophisticated piece of manufacturing equipment or a block of capital stock in a corporation—or the negotiation between the prosecutor and a defense attorney about the length of a recommended criminal sentence.

2. THE RELATIONSHIP WITH THE OTHER NEGOTIATOR

The other factor applied here in classifying negotiation tactics is whether the tactic results in an adversarial or a collaborative relationship with the other negotiator. The *competitive* strategy produces an adversarial relationship, while both the *problem-solving* and *cooperative* strategies foster a *collaborative* or accommodative working relationship.

The *competitive strategy* consists of tactics intended to undermine the other negotiator's confidence in his bargaining position. These tactics are designed to induce the other negotiator to enter into an agreement with terms less advantageous to his client than those he

4. Schwartz, *The Professionalism and Accountability of Lawyers,* 66 Cal.L.Rev. 669, 675–76 (1978).

5. E. McGinnies, Social Behavior: A Functional Analysis 414 (1970).

6. C. Karass, The Negotiating Game 127 (1970).

would have accepted prior to the negotiation. The competitive negotiator focuses on the *distributive* aspects of the problem being negotiated and tends to see little advantage to her client that does not come at the expense of the other party. Therefore, the other party to a negotiation is perceived as "the opponent." Competitive tactics include extreme initial demands, hiding information from the other party, threats, arguments and conceding reluctantly.

It is possible to use competitive negotiation tactics in an *integrative* bargaining context, but when this approach is taken, the inherent opportunities for problem-solving are ignored. The competitive negotiator focuses on those aspects of the negotiation which are "win-lose" situations, and seeks to induce the other negotiator to give up as much as possible. In other words, competitive negotiation tactics can be used in both *distributive* and *integrative* contexts, but when used on *integrative* issues, they ignore opportunities to devise solutions to benefit both parties.

The remaining two groupings of negotiation tactics, the *cooperative* and problem-solving strategies, stress a more accommodative approach with the other negotiator. The factor which distinguishes the two separate strategies is the context in which they operate: the *cooperative* strategy includes *collaborative* negotiation tactics used in *distributive* situations, while the *problem-solving* strategy functions in an *integrative* bargaining context. *Cooperative* negotiation behaviors are those tactics which the negotiator uses when she believes that her client's best interests will be served by seeking an agreement which is fair and just to both parties, and by developing a relationship with the other party that is based upon trust and good will. Although *cooperative* negotiation tactics are intended to facilitate a collaborative working relationship with the other bargainer, they remain premised on the belief that the negotiators are dividing a fixed quantity of resources between them.

What negotiation tactics are included within the *cooperative* strategy? A *cooperative* opening bid in a negotiation is a proposal which is favorable to the lawyer's client, but moderate. The cooperative negotiator often initiates the concession-granting process, assuming that the other negotiator will feel bound to reciprocate. Cooperative strategy arguments address what is "fair and just," and do not disparage the other negotiator's alternatives to a negotiated agreement. Thus, cooperative arguments frequently suggest objective criteria as a standard for resolving a disagreement.

Among the three principal negotiation strategies, the use of the *cooperative* strategy in the actual practice of law is perhaps most difficult to visualize. Why—in a *distributive* bargaining situation where every widget gained by a party comes at the expense of a widget lost by the other side—would an attorney strive for an agreement which is "fair and just" to both parties?

The reasons why *cooperative* negotiation tactics might be preferred over *competitive* ones will be considered in Chapter Three, *Choosing*

Effective Negotiation Tactics. In fact, however, the questions raised in the previous paragraph are more troubling in the abstract than they are in the "real world." In contexts other than legal practice, when most individuals interact with friends, acquaintances or family members, *cooperative* tactics are used frequently. When a neighbor seeks to borrow a cup of sugar, most individuals yield to the request because they recognize that at some indeterminate point in the future, they may be asking for an unspecified return favor (or they may be motivated by altruism). It is unheard of for the borrowing neighbor to couple his request with a competitive tactic, such as a threat—"If you do not let me borrow the sugar, I will play 'heavy metal' rock music until the wee hours of the morning and disrupt your family's sleep."

But neighbors are not lawyers with clients who have adverse interests, a skeptic would respond. A survey of the negotiating tactics of practicing lawyers has shown the prevalence of *cooperative* tactics, however.[7] Attorneys who plan a variety of business deals with each other over a period of decades do not use exclusively competitve tactics when bargaining with each other, even on *distributive* issues. Even in personal injury negotiations, among the most typically *competitive* of all negotiations, there often comes a time when two wizened veteran trial lawyers, after days of depositions and motion hearings, sit down together to determine a "just value" for the claim. Prosecutors and public defenders in plea bargaining discuss what constitutes a "fair" deal.[8] At a more theoretical level, Professor Robert Axelrod, in his notable book, *The Evolution of Cooperation,* concludes that "cooperation can indeed emerge in a world of egoists without central authority."[9]

The third negotiation strategy, the *problem-solving strategy,* consists of negotiation tactics designed to identify and exploit opportunities for problem-solving and joint gain. Returning to the two criteria used to define the negotiation strategies or classifications of negotiation tactics, the *problem-solving* strategy obviously operates in the *integrative* bargaining context, and the approach to the other party in the negotiation is a positive, *collaborative* one, in which the parties try to work together to create joint gains.[10]

7. *See* G. Williams, Legal Negotiation and Settlement 15–24 (1983); *see also infra* Chapter Three, *Choosing Effective Negotiation Tactics,* at 29.

8. *See* M. Heumann, Plea Bargaining: The Experience of Prosecutors, Judges and Defense Attorneys 103–10 (1978); D. Newman, Conviction: The Determination of Guilt or Innocence Without Trial 114–30 (1966); P. Utz, Settling the Facts: Discretion and Negotiation in Criminal Court 134–36 (1978).

9. R. Axelrod, The Evolution of Cooperation 20 (1984). According to Axelrod, the main results of cooperation theory "show that cooperation can get started by even a small cluster of individuals who are prepared to reciprocate cooperation, even in a world where no one else will cooperate." *Id.* at 173. Cooperation will be viable, Axelrod argues, when the cooperation is reciprocal and the parties involved are adequately concerned with the future as well as the immediate consequences of their actions. *Id.* Axelrod believes that "once cooperation based on reciprocity is established in a population, it can protect itself from invasion by uncooperative strategies." *Id.*

10. Fisher and Ury, leading proponents of the *problem-solving* negotiation strategy, claim their strategy does not depend on developing an accommodative working relationship with the other negotiator. *See*

An alternative system for organizing negotiation tactics would be to recognize only two strategies, *competitive* and *collaborative,* and to recognize that the *collaborative* strategy uses one set of tactics in *distributive* situations and an additional set of tactics in *integrative* bargaining situations.[11] Under this organizing scheme, *collaborative* tactics in the *distributive* context would correspond with what is referred to here as *cooperative* tactics, and *collaborative* tactics in the *integrative* context would correspond with tactics of the *problem-solving* strategy.

The negotiator should think of *cooperative* and *problem-solving* tactics as two separate categories, however, to highlight the distinction between identifying integrative potential and viewing the issue being negotiated solely as a distributive one but negotiating in a collaborative manner. One of the critical aspects of a lawyer's negotiating ability is how many of the issues she perceives to have integrative potential and how many she views solely as distributive issues. The manner in which the negotiator initially defines the problem, the possible resolutions she can identify and the facts which she regards as important, help to determine whether a bargaining context is *distributive* or *integrative.* In other words, any *integrative* bargaining situation, to some extent, is in the eyes of the beholder: the negotiator, as well as the issues being negotiated, create *integrative* bargaining possibilities. The recognition of *problem-solving* tactics as a distinct strategy encourages negotiators consciously to seek *integrative* potential and not to be relegated to dividing a fixed pie—either competitively or cooperatively—by default.

C. DISTINGUISHING STYLE FROM STRATEGY

With a basic understanding of the characteristics which define the three negotiating strategies, it is now possible to provide specific examples of the difference between a negotiator's personal style and her negotiation strategy. *Style,* it will be recalled, is the lawyer's personal characteristics in interacting with other people; *strategy,* on the other hand, is a set of specific negotiating behaviors.

Differences between *competitive style* and *cooperative style* are somewhat difficult to describe in print because style often is demonstrated most vividly by the negotiator's tone of voice, non-verbal communications and similar nuances. Consider however, a negotiation between Bev Bailey, a young newcomer to the practice of law representing Banana Computers, Inc., and Dan Darrow, a middle-aged and experienced lawyer representing the Chestnut Development Corpora-

R. Fisher & W. Ury Getting to Yes: Negotiating Agreement Without Giving In 13 (1981). Instead, they urge the negotiator to "separate the people from the problem." *Id.* at 11. Their entire approach to negotiation, however, is based upon developing a relationship with the other party during the negotiation which is conducive to *problem-solving. Id.* at 38.

11. *See e.g.,* G. Williams, Legal Negotiation and Settlement 53 (1983); Lowenthal, *A General Theory of Negotiation Process, Strategy and Behavior,* 31 U.Kan.L.Rev. 69, 73 (1982).

tion, which owns and operates the Chestnut Mall. Banana Computers recently pioneered a new generation of personal computers using a super-fast patented micro-chip enabling it to produce state-of-the-art computers at prices unheard of previously. Banana, however, lacks a national reputation and is seeking to finance tremendous nationwide expansion as quickly as possible in order to seize the competitive advantage. Although Banana wants the added visibility that only a shopping mall offers, it is finding that owners of shopping malls generally are skeptical about computer outlets. In the two excerpts from the negotiation which follow, both attorneys use *competitive* tactics such as extreme opening bids and arguments. Each lawyer tries to lessen the opponent's confidence and to induce the other party to enter into a deal on less satisfactory terms than the client originally anticipated. But how do the two segments of the same negotiation differ?

1—Bev: Dan, it is a pleasure to meet with you. I've heard so much about your reputation as a negotiator.

2—Dan: Well, it's always a privilege to show you kids straight out of law school something about how the real world works. I understand your client will be leasing space in the Chestnut Mall.

3—Bev: Well, I'm not so sure. Originally my client, Banana Computers, had some interest in your client's mall, as well as a number of other possibilities. But when you sent us the proposed lease, and listed a base rental figure of $35 per square foot, we pretty well decided to pursue other options. My client asked me to come over here today to see if we could work something out. But really, Dan, your client's way out-of-line. I'm not sure who you are trying to fool. You've got several vacant stores in your mall, the going rate for base rentals in this market is $18 per square foot and you're asking $35. My client mentioned to me something about Jack Kelly, one of Chestnut's officer's. Is the IRS still investigating him?

4—Dan: You certainly have done your homework. Now that you have projected your macho image perhaps I can bring you a little closer to reality and we can do business the way that business is done around here. What I sent your client was a copy of the standard lease for the Chestnut Mall. Quite frankly, I'm not sure that was a prudent move on our part. We both know about the huge turnover in computer firms. Our standard rate is $35 per square foot; our other clients are major department stores and high quality speciality shops and not "fly by night" computer outlets. It's an act of grace on my client's part that we are offering you this rate.

Both of these lawyers are negotiating with a *competitive style*. Each attacks and belittles both the opposing negotiator and the other party. Dan targets his insults to Bev on the potentially sensitive areas of her relative inexperience—by talking about showing "kids out of law school" how to negotiate—and her role as a woman—accusing her of needing to project a "macho image." His tone is sarcastic and condescending. He also directly belittles Bev's client by calling Banana Computers a "fly by night" operation. Bev responds in kind, calling Dan's client "out-of-line," and raising the unpleasant issue of Jack Kelly's problems with the IRS.

Compare the following opening communications in the same negotiation:

5—Dan: Bev, it is a pleasure to meet you and to be working with you for the first time. I've always found it to be terribly important to establish good working relationships with the other lawyers in this community.

6—Bev: Well thank you, I appreciate that. I have certainly heard nothing but excellent things about you. Shall we get down to business? I've looked at the proposed lease that you sent us. My client remains interested in leasing the property from you, but they have now asked me to explore a number of other options. I want to be frank with you, the $35 per square foot base rental is causing some hard feelings and is scaring my client off. We know that the going rate for mall space is $18 per square foot, that you have plenty of space available to lease and that you're having trouble filling it because of that new mall on the other side of town.

7—Dan: I have to be realistic with you, Bev. We both know that there is a huge turnover in the computer retail market. The stores that are getting a somewhat better rate are the large department stores which will draw customers to the mall and that will be around for years to come. I think you understand that your client has not yet established that kind of track record—perhaps you can convince us differently. We think your retail outlet will benefit enormously by being a part of this well-established mall. I'm afraid though that I really do not have much room to negotiate over rates—if I agreed to a lesser rental, your next negotiation with Chestnut would be with a different lawyer. They simply won't put up with it.

The *substance* or *strategy* communicated by the two lawyers in this second example is identical to that in the first negotiation—the initial demand, that is, the price that Chestnut is asking for the rental space, is exactly the same, as are the substance of the arguments and each party's unwillingness to concede. What *is* different, however, is the *style* of the negotiators. Both of the negotiators here flatter each other and expressly articulate the importance of a good working relationship.

Dan blames his unwillingness to concede on his client, thus removing any personal animosity that Bev may have as a result of his initially high demands. Arguments that are designed to lessen the other's confidence in her position, and which are therefore competitive negotiation behaviors—such as Dan's suggestion that a retail computer outlet is not as stable an enterprise and is not as valuable to his client as a major department store—are presented almost apologetically. Bev's response to the initial demand of $35 per square foot is presented not as a hostile threat—"if you can't do better than that, we can't negotiate—but instead as a warning, or a matter of fact reporting of her client's reaction to the initial figure—"the $35 per square foot figure is causing some hard feelings and is scaring my client off." The strategy remains the same, but the style of interaction is much different.

It is important for the lawyer to distinguish style from strategy in a real negotiation for two reasons. First, many of the disadvantages of *competitive tactics*—the possibilities of deadlock and a premature breakdown of negotiation, and of generating ill-will and distrust with the other party—can be mitigated if the *style* of the negotiator is cooperative. Even when the substance being communicated to the other negotiator is very demanding and competitive, friendliness, courtesy and politeness help to preserve a positive working relationship.

Conversely, the beginning lawyer needs to be able to identify *competitive tactics* even when the style of the negotiator is *cooperative*. Often, lawyers will be misled by the polite and friendly style of the other lawyer and assume that he is using *cooperative tactics, i.e.,* that his goals include a fair and just agreement and a positive, trusting working relationship between the parties. To the extent that the negotiator confuses cooperative style for cooperative substance, she may be inclined to reciprocate, and the resulting agreement will disadvantage her client.

Admittedly, the personal *style* of the negotiator often is intertwined with the negotiation strategy she is using in a specific negotiation or that she prefers to use. A negotiator who has an aggressive and forceful personal style frequently will succeed in causing the other negotiator to lose confidence in himself or his case, thereby inducing him to settle for less than he initially expected, a goal of the competitive strategy. In another instance, however, a negotiator who is courteous, personable and friendly may, through competitive strategic moves such as extreme opening demands and infrequent concessions, be even more successful in destroying the other party's confidence in his case and inducing unilateral concessions from him. Although a negotiator's personal style of interaction positively correlates with her preferred negotiating strategy, separating personal style from negotiation strategies and techniques yields new flexibility for the negotiator. It is possible for the negotiator with a *cooperative* personal *style* to adopt *competitive tactics* when it is advantageous, and naturally *competitive* individuals can adopt *cooperative tactics*.

D. THE STRATEGIC CHOICE MODEL

Lawyers are not born as *competitive* negotiators, *cooperative* negotiators or *problem-solving* negotiators. Specific negotiation behaviors are learned, and as such, they may be selectively employed. The same lawyer who uses *competitive* tactics in one bargaining session will find her client's interests better served by employing *problem-solving* methods on another occasion.

Claims that any particular negotiation strategy is superior to the others all of the time, or even most of the time, promise too much. It is the thesis of this book that the answer to which negotiation *tactic* is most effective is: *it depends.*[12] Chapter Three will explore how the negotiator should proceed with deciding which negotiation *tactic* is likely to succeed at a given point in a negotiation.

The effective negotiating attorney is not only able to use different negotiation strategies in different negotiations, she is also able to use tactics or negotiation behaviors from more than one negotiation strategy during the course of a single negotiation. Most negotiations, for instance, include both *integrative* and *distributive* aspects. In collective bargaining, there are predominantly *distributive* issues, such as the hourly rate of wages, as well as issues with significant *integrative* potential, such as the possibility of a job security agreement that yields both security for the worker and reduced re-training costs for the employer. Even in the largely *distributive* context of personal injury negotiations, the insurance company frequently is interested in the timing, as well as the amount, of payments to the claimant, and the possibility of a structured settlement thus yields *integrative* potential. Under these circumstances, the effective negotiator may elect to use *problem-solving* tactics on the issues with integrative potential at the same time that she uses either *competitive* or *cooperative* tactics on *distributive* issues.

The negotiator's preferred approach to a single issue also may change as the negotiation proceeds. Frequently, as will be discussed below, negotiation proceeds from an early phase where both negotiators use predominantly competitive techniques through subsequent stages

---

12. Other scholars of legal negotiation are more confident that a single approach to legal negotiation is superior to other possibilities. In their seminal book *Getting to Yes: Negotiating Agreement Without Giving In,* Fisher and Ury outline a predominantly *problem-solving* approach to negotiation, and claim that they have found "an all purpose strategy" that can be used in any negotiation. *See supra* note 10, at xiii. Fisher and Ury's *principled negotiation* theory, however, although based predominantly on *problem-solving* tactics, is not a "pure" strategy and also includes both *cooperative* tactics and com- *petitive* tactics. For example, Fisher and Ury recognize that the negotiator "will almost always face the harsh reality of interests that conflict," that is, a *distributive bargaining context,* on at least some issues and that when this occurs, the negotiators should resolve the dispute through the use of "objective criteria," *Id.* at xiii, a *cooperative* tactic. Finally, if the other party continues to use competitive tactics, Fisher and Ury recognize that the negotiator may be forced to present the other party with a "take it or leave it" choice, or even walk away from the negotiation. *Id.* at 84. These are *competitive* tactics.

where *problem-solving* or *cooperative* tactics, or both, predominate. It is to be anticipated, therefore, that a negotiator may begin with competitive tactics such as an extreme opening bid and communication of an unwillingness to concede. Later the negotiator may employ *cooperative* tactics such as expressing a willingness to make concessions if the other negotiator reciprocates, or *problem-solving* techniques such as proposing that the parties together try to find a solution that will satisfy both of the parties' underlying interests.

The effective negotiator does not decide in advance that she will use only *competitive* or *problem-solving* tactics. Instead, the negotiator realizes that at each point in the negotiation, when she has the opportunity to respond to the latest message from the other party, she has three choices. First, she can use a *competitive tactic* such as a high demand, a refusal to concede, a threat or an argument. Second, she can respond with a *cooperative* tactic such as making a concession with the expectation that the other side will reciprocate, or referring to objective criteria suggesting how the case should be resolved. Finally, the lawyer can use a *problem-solving* approach and propose a solution to the parties' problems, suggest an exchange of concessions on different issues or in some other manner initiate a problem-solving process by the parties. Once she has made her strategic negotiation move, the lawyer awaits a response from the other negotiator. When it comes, the lawyer evaluates the other party's response and once again decides whether to continue with the same type of negotiation behavior or to switch to another method.

For example, assume Dan Darrow, the attorney for the Chestnut Development Corporation, used a *cooperative* negotiation tactic by suggesting that he might be able to reduce the base price per square foot for the rental from $35 per square foot to $28 per square foot for the first twelve months if Bev's client would accept a fifteen year lease. If Bev summarily rejects the possibility of a longer lease and makes no other compensating gesture of goodwill, it probably would be unwise and counterproductive for Dan to follow with another *cooperative* tactic; instead, his best response would be either a *problem-solving* tactic, or more likely, a *competitive* tactic. A lawyer's negotiation strategy can shift frequently within a single negotiation; she is not stuck with the strategy she began with if she is not getting the desired responses.

The idea that the negotiator has the freedom to switch and choose between three very different kinds of behaviors at different points in the negotiation was first advanced by social psychologist Dean Pruitt as the *strategic choice model*.[13] There are, however, practical limits to the lawyer's ability to change strategies during the course of a single negotiation. Assume Bev uses *competitive negotiation tactics,* such as an extremely low offer and threats, at the beginning of her negotiation with Dan. These tactics may jeopardize the positive working relation-

---

13. D. Pruitt, Negotiation Behavior 15–16 (1981).

ship between the two attorneys which is necessary for *cooperative* and *problem-solving* tactics to succeed.

Two factors assist Bev's attempt to shift successfully from the *competitive tactics* she initially uses to *cooperative* or *problem-solving* tactics. First, if she maintains a *cooperative style* in her interactions with Dan, even while using *competitive* tactics, it is easier to switch to *cooperative* or *problem-solving* tactics at a later point. She does not generate the same mistrust and ill-will that results from a combination of *competitive* tactics coupled with a *competitive* personal style. Second, the length of time that it takes to complete most legal negotiations, and the frequent breaks and interruptions in the negotiations, allow tempers and emotions to cool, and facilitate changes from competitive to more cooperative or problem-solving tactics.

Chapter Three

CHOOSING EFFECTIVE
NEGOTIATION TACTICS

———————

A. AN OVERVIEW

To a great extent the negotiator's final success depends upon her ability at each point in the negotiation to choose the most effective among the competitive, cooperative or problem-solving tactics. The answer to that question usually changes continuously throughout a negotiation. It is a rare negotiation when either of the parties employs solely a pure competitive, cooperative or problem-solving strategy throughout. Indeed, it frequently is the case that negotiation on various separate and distinct issues progresses at uneven rates, and that the most effective negotiation strategy may consist of employing differing tactics on distinct issues at the same time. For example, an attorney representing a commercial tenant in lease negotiations might use competitive tactics in negotiating over the amount of monthly rental to be charged, at roughly the same time that she is conceding a separate issue relating to who will pay increased utility costs (a cooperative tactic) or engaging in problem-solving bargaining on the location of the store.

The choice of whether the negotiation tactic most likely to be effective on a particular issue and at a specific time in the negotiation is a *competitive, cooperative* or *problem-solving* one requires a balancing of the factors to be considered in this chapter. Most of the factors discussed influence the negotiator's decision to use a tactic from one of the collaborative strategies—either the problem-solving or the cooperative—or a competitive tactic. In this discussion, the two negotiation strategies which foster a positive and accommodative working relationship between the parties, the cooperative and problem-solving strategies, are referred to as "collaborative strategies." The other factor analyzed, of course, is whether the negotiation presents sufficient integrative bargaining opportunities to allow effective use of problem-solving bargaining tactics.

The first factor discussed is the other negotiator's probable negotiating strategy. It is the single most important factor to be considered by the negotiator when she chooses her own negotiating tactics. The second factor to be discussed is the question of whether the bargaining context has integrative potential. The chapter then describes the other significant factors to be considered in choosing between competitive tactics and collaborative tactics:

(1) the stage of the negotiation;

(2) the relative bargaining power of the parties;

(3) prospects for an ongoing relationship with the other party and concerns about honoring negotiation norms within the bargaining community;

(4) the attitude of the negotiator's client; and

(5) the negotiator's own personality.

B. THE OTHER PARTY'S NEGOTIATION STRATEGY

The purpose of any negotiating tactic is to affect the other negotiator's bargaining behavior in a way that will facilitate an agreement which is advantageous to the negotiator's client. The collaborative strategies attempt to accomplish this by encouraging the other party to reciprocate the negotiator's own cooperative or problem-solving tactics. To be successful, the cooperative and integrative strategies require that both negotiators adopt similar strategies.

The whole basis of the cooperative strategy is to concede and adopt other cooperative tactics with the expectation that the other party will reciprocate. The major weakness of the cooperative strategy is its vulnerability to exploitation by a negotiator who does not reciprocate by matching the cooperative negotiator's concessions. Instead of reciprocating, the competitive opponent will interpret the concessions as a sign of weakness and will grant fewer concessions. Thus, the cooperative strategy succeeds only if the opponent reciprocates and makes concessions. Although the problem-solving strategy is somewhat less vulnerable to exploitation by a competitive negotiator than the cooperative strategy, it also requires an exchange of information and a responsiveness to the other negotiator's interests and needs. These tactics may be exploited by the competitive negotiator who refuses to exchange information or to acknowledge the other party's needs.[1]

The harm that is inflicted on the cooperative negotiator when negotiating with a competitive counterpart is demonstrated by the results in the Prisoner's Dilemma Game, an experimental tool used by game theorists to study negotiation.[2] Game theory is a mathematical

1. See Pruitt, *Strategic Choice in Negotiation,* 27 Am. Behavioral Scientist 167, 168 (1983).

2. See E. McGinnies, Social Behavior: A Functional Analysis 417–18, 423–24 (1970); D. Pruitt, Negotiation Behavior

discipline used to study joint decision making in conflict situations.[3] The participants in game theory experiments, while attempting to maximize their own outcomes, must take into account the actions of other participants who aspire to different goals and whose actions affect, in part, the participants' joint outcomes.

In its original form, the Prisoner's Dilemma Game is based upon a hypothetical incident in which two suspects, Smith and Jones, have been taken into custody by the police.[4] They are interviewed separately by the district attorney who attempts to encourage each to confess and turn state's witness against the other suspect in exchange for a lighter sentence. Each prisoner's decision whether or not to confess, like negotiation behavior, must take into account his own actions as well as those of the other suspect (party). Both prisoners know that if neither confesses, the district attorney does not have enough evidence to convict them on a serious offense and that both will receive only relatively light sentences for lesser offenses such as vagrancy. If one confesses and the other does not, the one who confesses will be shown leniency and given perhaps an even lighter sentence, while the other party will be severely punished for the more serious crime. Finally, if both sides confess, each will be punished with a moderate rather than a severe sentence.

Each prisoner thus has two possible "tactics" to choose between—to confess or not to confess—and a variety of possible outcomes depending not only upon his decision, but also upon the other suspect's decision to confess or not to confess. A matrix illustrating the respective parties' pay-offs therefore looks like this:

FIGURE 3–1

		Prisoner Jones	
		Does not confess	**Confesses**
Prisoner Smith	**Does not confess**	1 year for Smith; 1 year for Jones	15 years for Smith 6 months for Jones
	Confesses	6 months for Smith 15 years for Jones	7 years for Smith 7 years for Jones

The prisoner's decision matrix is analogous to the negotiator's. If Prisoner Smith *cooperates* with Prisoner Jones by *not confessing,* he is banking on his trust that Jones will reciprocate the cooperation and also not confess. The risk, however, is that Jones will view Smith's cooperation as an opportunity to exploit Smith by engaging in the competitive tactic of confessing and realizing a short prison term at Smith's expense.

102–10 (1981); H. Raiffa, The Art and Science of Negotiation 123–26 (1982).

3. *See generally* A. Rapoport, Two–Person Game Theory: The Essential Ideas (1966).

4. E. McGinnies, *supra* note 2, at 417–18.

In short, the best possible result for a negotiator in a single negotiation exists when she makes competitive moves and the other party engages in cooperative behavior. When both parties cooperate, a reasonable, but unspectacular, result is likely for both parties. If both suspects in the Prisoner's Dilemma compete by confessing, then both prisoners receive a substantial prison sentence of seven years. Analogously, if both negotiators engage in competitive tactics, a fairly undesirable result—usually a negotiation stalemate or deadlock—is likely to occur. Finally, however, the worst possible single negotiation pay-off for the negotiator occurs when she trusts the other negotiator and engages in cooperative tactics and the other party does not reciprocate, but instead pursues competitive tactics. She receives the negotiator's version of a 15 year prison sentence.

The Prisoner's Dilemma Game thus suggests that use of cooperative or problem-solving tactics is dangerous if the other negotiator is pursuing competitive tactics and cannot be induced to switch to cooperative or problem-solving negotiation approaches. The game also suggests that the negotiator may be able to use the competitive strategy to take advantage of the other negotiator when he is using cooperative or problem-solving tactics.

This lesson should not be overlearned, however. Unlike the negotiating lawyer, the research subject in the Prisoner's Dilemma Game need not be concerned about the prospect of future negotiations or what other lawyers in the bargaining community think about her negotiating behavior. Other factors considered below, particularly the importance of ongoing relationships with the other party, often suggest that the negotiator use cooperative or problem-solving tactics even when a more competitive approach might achieve better quantifiable results in a single negotiation. Too often, new lawyers have the false impression that their clients' interests are best served by competitive tactics and that cooperative tactics are hopelessly naive and vulnerable to exploitation by opposing negotiators. It takes months or years of prematurely terminated negotiations at their clients' expense before they realize that relationships between negotiators and parties "in the real world" are more important determinants of ideal bargaining behavior than outcomes achieved in research settings.

The Prisoner's Dilemma illustrates the importance of the other negotiator's behavior in the negotiator's choice of effective tactics. A key issue, therefore, is to predict the other negotiator's tactics. Recognizing that the negotiator is not a prophet, and may even be a poor poker player, how can she intelligently speculate about the other negotiator's choice of competitive or collaborative responses to her tactics?

First, it is helpful to know something about the negotiation behavior of lawyers generally. Are negotiating lawyers *always* raging, sneering, sarcastic antagonists ready to devour the recently graduated lawyer? Although there is considerable variation from one geographical area to another, and among the various substantive law specialties, the available data suggests that negotiating attorneys are considerably more cooperative than might be expected.

Professor Gerald Williams has surveyed the actual negotiating behavior of a representative sampling of lawyers in Denver, Colorado and Phoenix, Arizona.[5] Each attorney surveyed was asked to complete a questionnaire describing the characteristics of the attorney with whom she had most recently negotiated and to rate his effectiveness. Williams found that 65 percent of the attorneys exhibited a pattern of negotiating traits that he described as the *cooperative approach,* and that 24 percent of the negotiating attorneys displayed a set of characteristics which he designated the *competitive approach.* The criteria used to divide the sample into these two groups included both characteristics of what has been referred to previously as *style,* and specific *negotiating behaviors* which are categorized in this text as *tactics.*[6] What is illuminating from the Williams study, however, is the pervasiveness of both the *cooperative style* and *cooperative tactics* among the lawyers surveyed.

The extent of the use of cooperative tactics varies dramatically from one geographical area to another, and among various legal specialties. It is widely perceived that negotiators in large urban areas are far more competitive than those in rural areas. The novice negotiator who expects to find a prevalence of cooperative tactics in the big city probably will be disillusioned quickly. Similarly, negotiation norms vary dramatically depending upon the substance of what is being negotiated. Williams' survey of Phoenix lawyers suggests that the mere threat of filing a lawsuit in a commercial or real property dispute is regarded as a "heavy-handed tactic, likely to incur the wrath of the opponent and be counterproductive."[7] On the other hand, according to Williams, personal injury specialists typically regard a desire to settle a case either prior to filing a lawsuit, or perhaps even more than a few months before trial, as a dangerously naive tactic likely to lead to exploitation by the predominantly competitive negotiators in that environment.

A description of the negotiating behavior of lawyers generally is the crudest possible tool to use to predict how a specific negotiator will

---

5. G. Williams, Legal Negotiation and Settlement 15–24 (1983).

6. For example, the traits Williams uses to describe his "effective/cooperative" negotiator include both attributes of *style,* such as "courteous," "personable," "friendly," "tactful," and "sincere," and descriptions of *negotiation behaviors or tactics,* such as "willing to share information," "willing to move from original position," "objective," and "reasonable." *Id.* at 21–22, 31, 34–35. Conversely, Williams' description of the *competitive approach* also includes *style* elements, such as "tough,"

"dominant," "forceful," "aggressive," "attacking," "ambitious," "egoist," and "arrogant," and terms roughly describing *negotiation tactics,* including "made a high opening demand," "used take-it-or-leave-it approach," "rigid," "revealed information gradually," and "used threats." *Id.* at 23–24, 32, 33, 37–39. Obviously, Williams' survey did not identify the dichotomy between negotiating *style* and negotiation *tactics* previously described in Chapter Two.

7. *Id.* at 81–2.

react in a specific negotiation to a specific negotiating tactic. What more refined data may be available to assist the negotiator in predicting what negotiating tactics the other party will use?

1. THE OTHER NEGOTIATOR'S BEGINNING TACTICS

The other negotiator's early moves in a negotiation, such as his initial proposals and subsequent modifications of these proposals, often indicate whether he is using predominantly competitive, cooperative or problem-solving tactics. Determining which tactics the other party is using often is more difficult than it sounds. It is possible that the negotiator will misinterpret an extreme demand cloaked in a cooperative style as being a reasonable demand, a cooperative tactic. If this happens, she may enter into an agreement unnecessarily disadvantageous to her client. The negotiator's ability to detect the tactics being used depends heavily upon her level of preparation and her understanding of the substance of the negotiation. If she knows what constitutes a fair and reasonable agreement in advance of the negotiation, she will not mistake a competitive initial proposal, camouflaged with cooperative style, as a fair and reasonable proposal.

The other negotiator's early collaborative tactics which expose him to actual risks or costs are more likely to be true indicators of his intention to continue to pursue collaborative approaches than are less risky opening moves. For example, by openly sharing information with the negotiator, the other party risks use of this information to his detriment by the negotiator. This approach, therefore, is a strong signal that the other negotiator is prepared to risk a genuinely cooperative strategy. Conversely, if there are alternative explanations for the other negotiator's initial moves in a negotiation, or if the other party's initial cooperative tactics are dictated by his weak bargaining position, this early cooperation is a less reliable indicator of continued cooperative tactics.

2. THE OTHER NEGOTIATOR'S STRATEGY IN PRIOR NEGOTIATIONS

The other negotiator's past negotiation history, bargaining with either the negotiator personally or with others, may indicate which tactics he is likely to employ in the present negotiation. Insurance defense attorneys who practice regularly with a plaintiff's personal injury attorney soon come to appreciate whether an initial opening demand of $200,000 from him means that the probable value of the case is $120,000 or only $30,000. If the negotiator has not negotiated with the other attorney previously, she should talk with those who have.

Knowledge of the other negotiator's personality, for example whether he is argumentative or amiable, may also tell the negotiator something about his negotiating tactics. When American presidents negotiate with important foreign leaders they are provided with complete psychological profiles of the other heads of state. Unfortunately, such information is seldom, if ever, available to the practicing attorney. When considering the other negotiator's personality traits, however, it also is important to remember the distinction between *style* and *tactics*. Although there is often a correlation between personality traits and negotiation tactics, dominant personality traits more closely mirror negotiating *style* than tactics. Thus, an amiable personality usually correlates with a *cooperative style,* but it might mask *competitive tactics* which the negotiator consciously has developed and learned to use.

3. THE STRATEGY OF SIMILARLY SITUATED NEGOTIATORS

If the negotiator has no information about the past negotiating behavior of her counterpart, less reliable information must be used to make educated guesses about the other negotiator's likely tactics. She may, for example, have information about the past performance of similarly situated negotiators. All claims adjusters for a particular insurance company may tend to use competitive tactics; all labor lawyers representing a specific union may be competitive in the opening rounds of negotiation; most prosecutors working in a congested urban office may be cooperative. In any of these instances, the socialization of the specific negotiator on the other side of the table probably has been influenced by these patterns.

4. DETERMINING STRATEGY THROUGH ROLE REVERSAL

Perhaps no form of analysis is more useful in determining how the other negotiator will behave in a negotiation than engaging in role reversal. A negotiator may be able to anticipate the other party's negotiating tactics by placing herself in the other's position and determining what tactics she would use if confronted with the pressures and the incentives facing him. The negotiator must be aware however, that although she probably can understand the external factors influencing the other negotiator's behavior, it is more difficult to predict his motivations and internal personality needs as they influence the negotiation. It is dangerous, for example, to assume that the other party necessarily has the same degree of risk tolerance as the negotiator.

C. INTEGRATIVE OPPORTUNITIES

From the perspective of a negotiator trying to decide between *problem-solving* tactics and other approaches, no single issue is more important than deciding whether the matter to be negotiated is a *distributive* or an *integrative* one, or more likely, a mixture of both. Problem-solving negotiation techniques work only in those situations in which at least some integrative potential exists. In a purely distributive bargaining context, the negotiator who wishes to use collaborative tactics is limited to cooperative ones. These cooperative tactics require the negotiator to accept a proposal less satisfying to her client with the hope that the other party will reciprocate.

The most important development in legal negotiation theory in recent years has been the recognition that most negotiable problems contain integrative elements; if the negotiators are sufficiently skilled and motivated to explore opportunities for joint gains, they usually will find them.[8] Advocates of *problem-solving* bargaining suggest that most negotiators err when they assume that in order to obtain greater satisfaction for their clients, other parties must suffer lower satisfaction with the agreement. However, even proponents of problem-solving bargaining admit that some negotiations pose purely distributive problems (one time deals where the only significant issue is price, for example) and that many more negotiations have at least some issues which are predominantly distributive.[9]

Locating integrative potential is an important aspect of preparing for negotiation. The process of indentifying these opportunities for joint gain is considered fully in the next chapter, *Negotiation Planning.* For now, it is sufficient to recognize that the two most important types of problem-solving solutions are:

(1) "bridging proposals" which satisfy both parties' underlying interests; and

(2) "logrolling agreements" in which the parties trade concessions on different issues on which they place differing priorities, so that both parties are more satisfied than if they merely conceded equivalent amounts on each issue.

The number of disputed issues in a negotiation therefore is a factor to be considered when choosing negotiation tactics. The more issues that the parties must negotiate, the greater the opportunity for problem-solving tactics. Other types of problem-solving solutions which create joint gains also are described in the next chapter.

D. STAGES OF A NEGOTIATION

Many social scientists [10] and legal scholars [11] studying negotiation have noted that the negotiation process appears to progress through a

8. *See generally* R. Fisher & W. Ury, Getting to Yes: Negotiating Agreement Without Giving In (1981); Menkel–Meadow, *Toward Another View of Legal Negotiation: The Structure of Problem Solving,* 31 UCLA L.Rev. 754 (1984).

9. *See* Fisher, *The Pros and Cons of Getting to Yes,* 34 J. Legal Educ. 120, 123 (1984) (printed as epilogue to White, Book Review, 34 J. Legal Educ. 115 (1984) (Reviewing R. Fisher & W. Ury, Getting to Yes; Negotiating Agreement Without Giving In (1981))).

10. *See, e.g.* D. Pruitt, *supra* note 2, at 131–33; P. Gulliver, Disputes and Negotiations: A Cross–Cultural Perspective 121–175 (1975).

11. *See, e.g.* G. Williams, *supra* note 5, at 70–91. Williams identifies four stages of legal negotiation: (1) orientation and positioning, (2) argumentation, (3) emergence and crisis and (4) agreement or final breakdown. *Id.* at 70–85. Menkel–Meadow summarizes the stages of negotiation which she finds in the "adversarial" literature as follows:

(1) Prenegotiation strategizing or planning to determine target and resistance points, location and timing of negotiations;

(2) offers and responses (expressions of differences and issue definitions);

(3) information-gathering (positions, arguments and objectives presented);

series of developmental stages. Although it probably is impossible to impose a rigid structural model of negotiation, the beginning lawyer should be careful that her negotiating behavior is appropriate for the specific phase of the negotiation. In particular, it is important to acknowledge that negotiation often progresses from phases dominated by competitive tactics to stages dominated by cooperative and problem-solving tactics.

In some negotiations, a lawyer's attempts to use *problem-solving* or *cooperative* tactics early in a negotiation, and to encourage the other negotiator to reciprocate, will be successful. In other cases, however, the use of *cooperative* or *problem-solving* tactics is effective only after the negotiators become frustrated with their lack of success using *competitive* tactics. An amusing example of the premature use of *cooperative* tactics is recounted in the folklore of labor relations.[12] During a strike, union leaders reportedly had demanded a wage increase of 8 cents per hour. Management, interested in returning immediately to production, magnanimously offered 10 cents per hour. The union leaders refused to settle and made additional demands, whereupon a costly and lengthy strike followed. How can such seemingly irrational behavior on the part of the union be explained? The early *cooperative* bargaining behavior of management apparently communicated to the union that if the company was willing to accede and indeed surpass its wage demands, then the union was entitled to receive more than it had originally demanded. If the union had received 8 cents an hour after tiring negotiations, it presumably would have been satisfied. A quick victory, however, would have left the union negotiators with the difficult task of explaining to their constituents their apparent lack of vigor in representing the workers.

Although some commentators claim that an identifiable pattern of progression through the negotiation process exists, it is important to recognize that every single negotiation is unique and that a rigid model cannot be imposed on the negotiation process. Sometimes a negotiation stage will occur very quickly; on other occasions it will take years. The phases of a negotiation often overlap, and the negotiators may return to an earlier phase, either intentionally or not. Most negotiations are multiple issue negotiations, and the various issues are often in different phases of development at any given time. Nevertheless, the lawyer's recognition of the negotiation phase assists her in determining what negotiation techniques are likely to be effective at that time.

The social scientists and legal scholars who claim to have defined negotiation stages use different labels, but a significant amount of consistency is apparent in their descriptions of the negotiation process.

(4) bargaining, where concessions are made and analyzed; and

(5) closure or agreement where agreements are made and parties allocate final responsibilities for negotiated relations.

Menkel–Meadow, *supra* note 8, at 777.

12. *See* Douglas, *The Peaceful Settlement of Industrial and Inter–Group Disputes,* 1 J.Con.Resol. 69–81 (1957).

According to those who study the negotiation process, bargaining typically begins with an *orientation and positioning* phase during which the negotiators usually set the "tone" for the negotiations. Initial encounters between the negotiators are likely to be indicative of both the negotiators' *styles* and the *tactics* that will follow. For example, if the attorneys share *competitive* styles at this stage, the negotiation is likely to be a nasty one. As a part of this orientation and positioning process, the negotiators also make initial presentations to each other about how they view the merits of the transaction or case being negotiated. This often is followed by initial proposals for resolving the disputes between the parties; these early proposals usually are not to be taken as serious attempts to resolve the issues in dispute.

Negotiation then progresses through a phase which many negotiation theorists refer to as *exploration of the issues.* Both lawyers present arguments and selectively disclose information supporting their proposals. At the same time, each negotiator engages in an important information-gathering process concerning the other side's interests and attitudes towards the issues being negotiated. She also learns about facts previously known only by the other side. This stage of the negotiation also includes the initial narrowing of differences between the parties as the two negotiators begin to make concessions from their initially extreme positions and drop their arguments on behalf of issues or positions in which their clients are not genuinely interested.

These two phases, *orientation and initial proposals* and *exploration of the issues,* often are contentious and time-consuming. It is typical in personal injury negotiations, for example, for these stages to go on for many months—and frequently for several years—and then to have the remaining stages of the negotiation take place in weeks, days or even hours. In these cases, it is important for the beginning negotiator not to mistake anything that happens until this point in the negotiations as a serious effort to resolve the case. These two early phases are also typically more competitive, particularly in negotiations involving fields such as personal injury cases and labor negotiations, than are the later stages.

It is not until a subsequent stage, variously referred to as "*bargaining*" or "*convergence*" [13] that most serious attempts to resolve the differences between the parties occur. Realizing that deadlock is near, one of the parties typically makes a realistic proposal on one or more of the issues—an offer that is intended to be the basis for a final agreement as opposed to a strategic move. Realistic proposals, involving considerable modifications of earlier unrealistic proposals, flow back and forth. Both sides typically make concessions or suggest problem-solving alternatives. This is not to say that all is sweetness and light. Threats and arguments continue; each negotiator still hides her mini-

---

13. Gulliver recognizes three separate phases in what is described here as the single stage of *convergence. See* P. Gulliver, *supra* note 10, at 141–168. These stages are Gulliver's "Phase 4: Narrowing the Differences," "Phase 5: Preliminaries to Final Bargaining," and "Phase 6: Final Bargaining."

mal or "bottom line" settlement requirements. The issues which are
genuinely disputed separate out from issues on which compromise or
other agreement can be more easily achieved. Then the negotiators
move on to trading concessions on issues that the clients would rather
not concede, or to deciding that they would rather give up something
than have the negotiation stalemate.

Eventually, the negotiation reaches a final stage in which the
parties either reach agreement or terminate the negotiation. If the
parties successfully negotiate an agreement, the final stage often includes resolving a number of details that have been ignored pending
closure on the major issues in dispute.

For someone approaching legal negotiation as a practitioner, and
not predominantly as a scholarly observer, two points are critical.
First, many—but certainly not all—negotiations follow a pattern of
proceeding from *competitive* phases to more *cooperative* or *problem-
solving* stages.[14] Second, legal negotiations are often lengthy, and
cooperative and *problem-solving* techniques sometimes can be risky
early in the negotiation unless the negotiator can be sure that such
techniques will not lead to exploitation by a *competitive* negotiator.

Competitive tactics early in the negotiation, perhaps ironically,
sometimes increase the prospects for successful use of cooperative or
problem-solving tactics later in the negotiation. Pruitt, a social psychologist who has studied conditions that foster problem-solving bargaining, concludes that "successful problem solving is made possible, in
part, by some of the activities in the competitive stage." [15] According to
Pruitt, as the negotiation progresses, deadlock is likely because neither
party can make unilateral concessions. If agreement is to be reached,
therefore, *cooperative* or *problem-solving* moves are necessary. At the
same time the negotiator herself is becoming more realistic, she understands that her counterpart's goals are being moderated as well. As a
result, trust increases and *cooperative* and *problem-solving* bargaining
become possible. To put it another way, a negotiator sometimes will
not seriously attempt *cooperative* or *problem-solving* techniques until
she realizes that her efforts to use *competitive* tactics, and to exploit the
other side's weaknesses, have failed.

In summary, the negotiator should consider *timing* as an essential
factor in deciding whether to use competitive tactics or the more
collaborative tactics of the cooperative and problem-solving methods.
In the earliest stages of the negotiation, cooperative and problem-
solving tactics are less likely to be reciprocated than later in the
negotiation. Early in the process, cooperative moves may be regarded
by some negotiators as signs of weakness or inexperience. This is not
to assert that meaningful collaborative negotiation is necessarily impossible before extended haggling occurs, but rather to suggest that the

14. *See* D. Pruitt, *supra* note 2, at 131–
32; R. Walton & R. McKersie, A Behavioral Theory of Labor Negotiations: An Analysis of a Social Interaction System 141–68
(1981).

15. D. Pruitt, *supra* note 2, at 135.

negotiator must be realistically confident that the other party is also willing to use cooperative or problem-solving tactics.

E. RELATIVE BARGAINING POWER

In choosing negotiation tactics, the negotiator also should consider the relative bargaining power of her client and the other party. Power can be defined as the capacity to influence the other party's negotiation behavior.[16]

The extent of a negotiator's power over the other party depends largely on the alternatives available to the other party if an agreement is not reached.[17] If the other party perceives that a negotiation breakdown produces severe detrimental consequences for him, then the negotiator has great leverage to dictate the terms of an agreement. Conversely, if the negotiator's counterpart has other viable options if negotiation fails, the negotiator has relatively little power. In the litigation context, for example, a negotiator's power is dependent on both the likely outcome at trial and the other party's costs of proceeding through trial.

The value of a negotiated settlement to a client and the value to the other party include factors other than the obvious quantifiable results of the negotiation. The value of the agreement is also subjective—strictly in the eye of the beholder. For example, delay in reaching agreement may be extremely important to one party or the other; such concerns substantially reduce bargaining power. Thus, concessions and other cooperative tactics become more attractive, because they may lead to a quick agreement. Clients often desire an early conclusion to negotiations for a number of reasons: they may need settlement proceeds immediately, they may desire to minimize legal fees and other expenses resulting from prolonged negotiation, and they may want to minimize the psychological strain associated with continued conflict.

Unfortunately, pressures on counsel herself, such as the heavy caseload of an urban prosecutor or a public defender, often lessen bargaining power and cause her to accept expeditious settlement. If the pressures on counsel result in her encouraging her client to accept a settlement offer not in the best interests of the client, the lawyer violates her ethical obligations to her client: the Model Rules of Professional Conduct require the "thoroughness and preparation rea-

---

16. *See id.* at 87; *see also* S. Bacharach & E. Lawler, Bargaining Power, Tactics, and Outcomes 37–40 (1981); Tjosvold & Okun, *Effects of Unequal Power on Cooperation in Conflict,* 44 Psychological Rep. 239, 239–42 (1979).

17. *See* S. Bacharach & E. Lawler, *supra* note 16, at 60–62; R. Fisher & W. Ury,

supra note 8, at 106–08. Fisher and Ury use the phrase "Best Alternative To a Negotiated Agreement" or "BATNA" to identify the standard against which any proposed agreement should be measured. *Id.* at 104; *see also* Fisher, *Negotiating Power: Getting and Using Influence,* 27 Am. Behavioral Scientist 149, 156–57 (1983).

sonably necessary" [18] for representation of the client, and the Code of Professional Responsibility includes a similar provision.[19]

When a negotiator's power is greater than that of the other party, she may choose tactics from any one of the three strategies without considering the impact of relative bargaining power. A negotiator with a viable alternative to a negotiated agreement is exposed to minimal risk if she chooses competitive tactics, despite the increased risk of settlement impasse. In addition, the use of threats, a competitive tactic, by a powerful negotiator will be perceived as more credible by the other negotiator—and therefore will more likely be effective—than would similar threats by a less powerful negotiator.

The less powerful negotiator has two options available: (1) she can attempt to change the perceived balance of negotiating power between the two parties, or (2) she can use either cooperative or problem-solving negotiation tactics. The parties' perceptions of their own and their counterparts' bargaining power are not static; instead, they change throughout the negotiation. The negotiator can attempt to alter the relative distribution of power between the parties by convincing her counterpart that his initial perceptions of both parties' alternatives to a negotiated agreement were inaccurate. For example, in a personal injury settlement negotiation, the plaintiff's attorney can shift power by convincing her counterpart that her expert medical witnesses will convince the jury of higher damages than the other negotiator previously anticipated. If the negotiator succeeds in altering the power balance by changing the other negotiator's assessments of the alternatives to agreement, she increases her ability at a later point to employ effective competitive tactics, thus increasing her negotiation flexibility. This factor helps to explain the frequent use of competitive negotiation tactics in the early phases of negotiation.

For negotiators with less bargaining power, the collaborative tactics of the cooperative and problem-solving strategies are more effective than competitive tactics. The competitive tactics of the low-power negotiator, for example, threats and a reluctance to concede, generally fail because they are not viewed as credible. The negotiator with greater power does not respond to such tactics, because he senses he can extract further concessions. Therefore, the greater the other party's power over the negotiator, the greater the negotiator's incentive to engage in cooperative or problem-solving tactics. Competitive tactics simply do not work well.

18. Model Rules of Professional Conduct Rule 1.1 (1983). An action for legal malpractice also is available as a remedy for the client who suffers from his attorney's lack of thoroughness and preparation. *See generally e.g.,* Woodruff v. Tomlin, 616 F.2d 924 (6th Cir.1980) (en banc) cert. denied 449 U.S. 888, 101 S.Ct. 246, 66 L.Ed.2d 114 (1980); Smith v. Lewis, 13 Cal. 3d 349, 360, 118 Cal.Rptr. 621, 628, 530 P.2d 589 (1975).

19. DR 6–101(A)(2) provides that "[a] lawyer shall not handle a legal matter without preparation adequate for the circumstances." Model Code of Professional Responsibility DR 6–101(A)(2) (1983). *See also* Model Rules of Professional Conduct EC 6–4 (1983).

Fortunately for less powerful negotiators, research suggests that powerful and high-status negotiators are likely to respond favorably to cooperative and problem-solving tactics.[20] This is true in part because normative concerns constrain the use of power—powerful negotiators are inclined to be generous toward less powerful negotiators.

Cooperative or problem-solving tactics, therefore, appear more likely than competitive ones to yield favorable results for a negotiator who faces a more powerful counterpart. Some social scientists have reached the somewhat different conclusion that "[p]erhaps the only way to offset the disadvantage of low power is to be tough initially and then become more yielding over time."[21]

F. ONGOING RELATIONSHIPS

The terms of the negotiated agreement are only one part of the results of negotiation. The other product of the negotiation is the status of the relationships between the parties, and between their attorneys, when the negotiation is completed. Most negotiations do not occur in a vacuum, but rather as a part of bargaining networks or communities. Leaving aside, for a minute, the relationship between the negotiating attorneys, the attitudes that the parties themselves have as a result of the negotiation process affect their own ongoing relationships and their reputations among other individuals and organizations with whom they will be negotiating in the future. An agreement which achieves a two percent cost savings for a client but which also results in a rupturing of future business dealings with both the other party and the business community is not an agreement which satisfies the client's interests.

When a relationship between the parties is likely to continue beyond the negotiation, use of either cooperative or problem-solving tactics is recommended.[22] Competitive tactics often generate distrust and ill will, negative feelings that may impair future dealings with the other party. Competitive tactics also often result in social disapproval within the bargaining community and invite retaliation in the future for violating bargaining norms.

The negative consequences of using competitive tactics are most pronounced when such tactics are used late in a negotiation. Social research suggests that negotiators concerned about enhancing prospects

20. *See* Cook & Emerson, *Power, Equity and Commitment in Exchange/Networks,* 43 Am.Soc.Rev. 721, 737 (1978); Donohue, *Analyzing Negotiation Tactics: Development of a Negotiation Interact System,* 7 Hum.Com.Research 273, 285 (1981); Tjosvold, *Commitment to Justice in Conflict Between Unequal Status Persons,* 7 J.Applied Soc.Psychology 149, 160 (1977).

21. Hamner & Baird, *The Effect of Strategy, Pressure to Reach Agreement and Relative Power on Bargaining Behavior,* in Bargaining Behavior 247, 265 (H. Sauermann ed. 1978).

22. *See* D. Pruitt, *supra* note 2 at 39–40, 109–12 & 184; Roering, Slusher & Schooler, *Commitment to Future Interaction in Marketing Transactions,* 60 J. Applied Psychology 386, 386–87 (1975).

for a good future working relationship with the other party should avoid entering the negotiation with a cooperative orientation while planning to switch to a competitive strategy at a later stage.[23] Goodwill between the negotiating parties is more likely to result when the negotiator changes from an early competitive strategy to a collaborative approach.

Other research demonstrates that parties, in fact, are likely to reciprocate cooperative or problem-solving tactics when continued contact in the future is anticipated and when the negotiator displays cooperative tactics early in the negotiation.[24] This important finding shows that a negotiator's early cooperative moves are less likely to be exploited when the other party anticipates an ongoing relationship.

In many but not all instances, the issue of whether the parties will have an ongoing relationship depends upon whether it is a *transactional* or a *dispute resolution* negotiation. In *dispute resolution* negotiation, each party has the opportunity to litigate or have the case submitted to a third-party decision-maker failing agreement. Typical examples include settlement talks in any kind of lawsuit—personal injury negotiations, plea bargaining or settlement discussions after an antitrust suit has been filed—or the negotiation of an employee's grievance against the employer when the employee has a contractual right to arbitration. *Dispute resolution* negotiation generally is characterized by the parties attempting to agree upon the historical facts which led to the dispute and the invocation of *norms* to resolve the dispute. These norms include the applicable substantive law contained in prior judicial decisions—for example, precedents which establish when a plaintiff may recover for intentional infliction of emotional distress—or prior settlement negotiations which suggest a pecuniary value for the plaintiff's permanent psychiatric disturbance.

In contrast, *transactional* negotiations are those in which agreement depends entirely on the consent of the parties and neither party can compel the other to submit the dispute to a third-party for resolution. In most instances, such negotiations are not premised on the "rights" or "entitlements" of the parties; they involve neither restoring the situation to the way that it was (tort liability) nor enforcing an expectancy that never occurred (*e.g.* contract liability). Instead, *transactional* negotiations are opportunities for the parties to agree voluntarily on the rules that will govern their affairs in the future. Examples include any purchase and sale agreement—whether the object of the transaction is a used car or a large corporation—as well as collective bargaining or international treaty making. To be sure, the distinction between *dispute resolution* and *transactional* negotiation may not be as clear as it first appears. When the attorneys for the government negotiate a consent decree in a prisoners' rights case or a consent

23. Slusher, *Counterpart Strategy, Prior Relations, and Constituent Pressure in a Bargaining Simulation,* 23 Behavior Sci. 470, 476 (1978).

24. Gruder, *Relationships with Opponent and Partner in Mixed–Motive Bargaining,* 15 J. Conflict Resolution 403, 413–15 (1971).

decree in a complex antitrust suit, such negotiations have elements of both *dispute resolution* and *transactional* negotiation. Either party may compel adjudication and claims certain rights and entitlements, but the agreement between the parties is designed to govern their future conduct.

For the lawyer as a negotiator, the distinction between *dispute resolution* and *transactional* negotiations often—but not inevitably— has two consequences. First, the parties in *dispute resolution* negotiations frequently are engaged in "one-shot" negotiations; they do not have a continuing relationship. In *transactional* negotiations, this is somewhat less likely to be true. On one hand, many *transactional* negotiations—such as the sale of a parcel of real estate—are also isolated transactions without any continuing relationship between the parties. On the other hand, in many *transactional* negotiations, the essence of the issues to be negotiated is generally how the parties will conduct themselves in their future relationship. Accordingly, not only the substance of the agreement reached in *transactional* negotiations is important, but so is the negotiating process itself.

Threats and blustering that might be appropriate or effective negotiating techniques in some *dispute resolution* negotiations will be counterproductive in most transactional negotiations for two reasons. First, the other negotiator probably responds by terminating the negotiation and seeking other business partners or other persons to whom to sell his real estate. A lawyer negotiating in a *dispute resolution* context does not have the same freedom to change with whom she is negotiating. Second, in the large number of *transactional* negotiations that are not "one-shot" deals, extremely competitive tactics jeopardize the continuing partnership or relationship between the parties.

Often transactional negotiations also present more opportunities for problem-solving bargaining. Frequently, there are multiple issues, thus presenting integrative potential for logrolling, the mutually advantageous exchange of concessions on issues upon which the parties place differing priorities. Further, because transactional negotiations involve ongoing relationships between the parties, the positive working relationships established by problem-solving tactics are attractive.

Whether the likelihood of a continuing relationship between the parties occurs in a transactional negotiation, or in a dispute resolution negotiation, the use of cooperative or problem-solving tactics, particularly in later stages of the negotiation, makes sense. If, on the other hand, the negotiating party knows that the negotiation is a one-shot situation, then his interests will not necessarily be adversely affected by the use of competitive tactics.

A potential ethical concern arises when the attorneys focus on their own ongoing relationship in choosing negotiation tactics. Many negotiations which are "one-shot" transactions from the standpoint of the parties—such as plea bargaining or personal injury negotiations— involve attorneys who deal with each other on a continuing basis. The risk is that the public defender, in an effort to maintain a credible and cooperative working relationship with the prosecutor, will not negotiate as competitively as she would if she did not need the prosecutor's continued good will. Similar conflicts may exist in civil cases. An attorney who vigorously represents her client's interests and refuses to accede to the pressures for accommodative working relationships between attorneys may be dismissed as a lightweight who "can't control" her client.

This ethical concern is not as simple as it may first appear. On one hand, the Comment to *Model Rule of Professional Conduct* 1.7 states that the loyalty required to the lawyer's client is impaired when she "cannot carry out an appropriate course of action for the client because of the lawyer's other responsibilities or interests," [25] including responsibilities to other clients or her own interests. If the lawyer believes her client's particular interests would be best served by competitive negotiation tactics, is she committing an ethical violation if she does not pursue such tactics because she fears repercussions in subsequent negotiations? [26] What is involved is not only a trade-off between the client's interest and the attorney's desire for comfortable working relationships with other attorneys with whom she will have contact in the future, but also potentially her effectiveness in representing future clients. To some extent, the conflict can be minimized by packaging competitive negotiation tactics, when justified, in a cooperative style. This may facilitate continued contact with the other negotiator, even when the client's best interests dictate competitive tactics.

The reality is that lawyers often do respond to pressures from their negotiating counterparts and pursue settlements that are fair and just to both parties. The pressure on the lawyer to use cooperative and problem-solving tactics results not only from the expectation of future contact with the other lawyers, but also from the traditions of courtesy and fair play among lawyers. As Professor Shaffer describes it, "on most matters, the two lawyers implicitly agree to cooperate." [27] Shaffer believes that each lawyer "probably is committed to the idea that what [s]he seeks is a fair settlement of the matter at issue, and each attempts

25. Model Rules of Professional Conduct Rule 1.7 Comment (1983). Rule 1.7(a) itself arguably addresses this concern by limiting conflict of interest obligations to those instances where the representation of one client is "*directly* adverse" to the interests of another client. *See also* Model Code of Professional Responsibility EC 5–14 (conflict with interests of another client) and EC 5–2 (conflict with lawyer's own interests) (1987).

26. When the client's best interests suggest that the lawyer use very competitive negotiation tactics, there exists a potential ethical conflict between the interests of the client and the professional interests of the attorney. Arguably, Model Rule of Professional Conduct 1.7(b), or the parallel provision of the Code of Professional Responsibility, Disciplinary Rule 5–101(A), applies in this case. Model Rules of Professional Conduct Rule 1.7(b) (1983); Model Code of Professional Responsibility DR 5–101(A) (1987). The application of this provision to the conflict would require the attorney to obtain the client's consent in a case where the client's best interests would be served by competitive tactics but the lawyer prefers to use cooperative or problem-solving tactics because of the implications of competitive tactics on her working relationships with other attorneys.

27. T. Shaffer, Legal Interviewing and Counseling 300 (1976).

to decide exactly where the sense of fairness will lead, in [her]self and in the other lawyer." [28]

In addition to being concerned about her future relationship with the other attorney, the negotiator also inevitably considers the norms of the bargaining community. As previously described, negotiation behavior varies greatly from one specialized area of practice to another, and among geographical districts. The lawyer who uses competitive tactics, such as the threat of filing a lawsuit, in a commercial or real estate dispute where bargaining tends to be accommodative, invites ill will from her colleagues in the bargaining community, and possible retaliation. A novice public defender in a rural area who plea bargains aggressively likely will be told by both the judge and the prosecutor "That's not the way things are done here."

The negotiator's tactics should not be dictated solely by standard operating practice within the community in which she bargains. However, she must be aware of negotiating behavior norms, and consider them along with other factors in choosing effective negotiation tactics.

G. ATTITUDE OF THE LAWYER'S CLIENT

Legal negotiation is negotiation on behalf of a client. As previously discussed, the American Bar Association's Model Rule of Professional Conduct 1.2 provides that decisions as to whether to accept a settlement proposal are to be made by the client.[29] Although lawyers generally decide what "means" or methods and tactics they use in the representation of clients, Model Rule of Professional Conduct 1.2 further requires the attorney to consult her client regarding the "means" of representation.[30] Arguably, this provision requires the attorney to consult with the client regarding negotiation tactics she intends to use.

If not required as a matter of professional obligation, then certainly as a matter of client relations and good business practices, the lawyer should consider the client's input regarding negotiation tactics. Sometimes the client's concern is with one of the factors described previously, for example, the impact of the choice of negotiation tactics on continuing relationships with the other party. In other instances, the attorney's desire to maintain rapport with an adversarial or angry client may necessitate that she adopt competitive tactics in bargaining on behalf of the client.[31] A client not inclined to trust his attorney may be convinced by visibly competitive tactics that she is representing his interests, and is not "selling out" to the other party. In simulated negotiations, social scientists have found that representatives who are

---

28. *Id.*

29. Model Rules of Professional Conduct Rule 1.2 (1983).

30. *Id.,* Rule 1.2(a) (1983).

31. *See* D. Pruitt, *supra* note 2, at 41–45; R. Walton & R. McKersie, *supra* note 14, 417–19; Lamm, *Group–Related Influences on Negotiation Behavior: Two–Person Negotiation as a Function of Representation and Election,* in Bargaining Behavior 284, 297–302 (H. Sauermann ed. 1978).

accountable to constituents are more likely to be tough and to use competitive tactics.[32]

H. THE NEGOTIATOR'S PERSONALITY

A fundamental thesis of this book is that the negotiator's personality does not necessarily dictate her choice of negotiation tactics. Personal traits, however, inevitably affect the ability of the negotiator to carry out certain tactics. The negotiator who instantly dominates the room when she walks in is going to have an easier time using competitive negotiation tactics effectively than will a more reserved peer. On the other hand, the more assertive and aggressive negotiator may find it difficult to employ collaborative strategies which may seem to her needlessly "touchy-feely" or even convoluted.

As you initially study negotiation tactics, it is recommended that you try a variety of negotiation techniques and, in effect, engage in role-playing behavior in order to use those tactics that may not come naturally to you. Ultimately you probably will find yourself comfortable with certain tactics that you would not use if you were negotiating "naturally." These tactics can become a part of your negotiation *repertoire,* to be used at appropriate times. On the other hand, your preferred negotiation tactics, even after studying negotiation and trying out other approaches, probably will reflect, to some extent, your basic personality and the negotiating style you have used, more or less habitually, in the hundreds of negotiations that ordinary, non-legal life demands from us all.

I. BUT HOW DO YOU CHOOSE THE BEST TACTIC?

This chapter discusses various factors to consider in choosing effective negotiation tactics at each and every point during the negotiation. Table 3–1 presents a summary of how the issues considered in this chapter influence the choice of effective negotiation tactics.

The factors influencing the choice of negotiation tactics often point in contradictory directions regarding which tactics will be effective. Unfortunately, there is no method for either ranking the importance of the factors or for weighing the effects of various factors.[33] As with all strategic decisions made quickly by lawyers—whether during appellate argument, trial or interviewing and counseling—tactical negotiation choices are matters of individual judgment. Nevertheless, the lawyer who systematically considers the full array of factors involved in making such choices is more likely to make an informed and effective decision.

---

32. *See* D. Pruitt, *supra* note 2, at 42, 120–21, 196; Lamm, *supra* note 31, at 297.

33. Similarly, the United States Supreme Court, and other courts for that matter, frequently prescribe a balancing test for deciding constitutional and other legal issues but do not suggest how the balancing of factors is to be accomplished.

TABLE 3–1
CHOOSING EFFECTIVE NEGOTIATION TACTICS: A SUMMARY

ISSUE INFLUENCING CHOICE OF TACTICS	TYPE OF TACTIC SUGGESTED BY "YES" ANSWER	TYPE OF TACTIC SUGGESTED BY "NO" ANSWER
Will *other negotiator* continue *competitive tactics?*	Competitive	Any
Does negotiator offer *integrative potential?*	Problem-solving	Competitive or Cooperative
Is Negotiation in *early phases?*	Often Competitive	Increasing Possibility of Problem-solving or Cooperative
Does Negotiator possess *superior bargaining power?*	Any	Cooperative, or Competitive Followed by Cooperative or Problem-solving
Is there an *ongoing relationship* between the parties?	Cooperative or Problem-solving	Any, including Competitive
Do competitive tactics violate *bargaining norms?*	Cooperative or Problem-solving	Any
Does *client's input* favor competitive display?	Competitive	Any
Does *negotiator's own personality* make her more comfortable with collaborative tactics?	Cooperative or Problem-solving	Competitive

In summary, negotiation theory—like theory in any discipline involving human behavior, and unlike mathematics or physics—is not everything. But neither is it nothing. "Judgment"—not algorithmic, cook book procedures—guides us through most of life's demanding situations.

Chapter Four

NEGOTIATION PLANNING

A. AN OVERVIEW OF STRATEGIC PLANNING

Planning for legal negotiation consists of two discrete tasks: subject matter preparation and negotiation strategy preparation. The more important of these, subject matter preparation, will be mentioned only briefly here. The lawyer must understand thoroughly the subject matter of the case or transaction being negotiated. Otherwise the prosecutor who has not yet examined the case is not in the strongest possible negotiating position when confronted in the courthouse halls by a well prepared defense attorney. Effective negotiation is also difficult for the inexperienced plaintiff's personal injury attorney unaware of the local norms in personal injury settlements when she bargains with a wizened veteran. Insofar as the other party's *competitive* tactics are designed to induce the negotiator to lose confidence in her case, nothing assures his success as the negotiator's sense that she does not understand the case and is inadequately prepared. The lawyer's legal and factual preparation provides the substance of her arguments and her questions during negotiation, and helps her evaluate the case. This chapter, however, discusses the other kind of negotiation planning: strategy preparation.

The lawyer cannot script the negotiation process in the same way that a trial lawyer can prepare an opening statement or questions for direct examination. The lawyer's second and third communications in a negotiation depend upon the other negotiator's initial responses. Although negotiation is somewhat unstructured and spontaneous, the lawyer who has not considered her strategy in interacting with the other party is at a severe disadvantage. What then can be done to prepare for the strategic aspects of negotiation?

For several reasons negotiation planning should be a joint process between lawyer and client. First, ultimately the client will need to approve any agreement reached by the negotiating lawyers, and therefore it is sometimes desirable to have the client approve any proposals or concessions made by his lawyer in advance.[1] Second, as suggested in the previous chapter, the choice of tactics often affects the client in ways other than success in achieving a desirable agreement, and therefore he should have a role in formulating them. Third, the client is usually more knowledgeable about both the dispute or transaction being negotiated and his own interests in it; this familiarity allows him to assist his lawyer in developing negotiation proposals, arguments and other tactics.

In some instances, it may be more feasible or advantageous for the lawyer to do the negotiation planning without significant assistance from the client. If the attorney and client have had a long-standing relationship and the lawyer understands the transaction thoroughly, a client may decide to delegate all responsibility for negotiation planning to the attorney. For example, a business client and his lawyer may decide in the interest of time and money that it is not desirable or realistic for them to consult extensively about the negotiation for a collection of a modest overdue debt.

The lawyer and client should discuss the following topics prior to beginning bargaining:

(1) What are the client's interests that will be affected by the results of the negotiation and by the negotiation process itself?

(2) What alternatives to a negotiated agreement are available to the client, and what is the least advantageous outcome of the negotiation that the client would prefer to these alternatives?

(3) What alternatives to a negotiated agreement are available to the other party, and what is the least advantageous negotiated outcome that he probably would prefer to these alternatives?

(4) What implications, other than the result of the negotiation, does the lawyer's negotiating behavior have for her client?

The remaining topics of the planning conference between lawyer and client depend upon whether the lawyer anticipates using predominantly *competitive, cooperative,* or *problem-solving* negotiation tactics, or a mixture of tactics. If the lawyer plans on using *competitive* tactics, she should also discuss the sources of leverage and power that the client has over the other party. If *cooperative* tactics are to be used, the lawyer should investigate with her client the potential sources of objective criteria that she could use to resolve a dispute. The *problem-solving* approach to negotiation suggests that the lawyer and client formulate solutions that will satisfy the parties' underlying interests. Also, in anticipation that the lawyers may "horse-trade" on the various issues, this approach requires the client to determine her relative order of preferences among these issues.

1. On other occasions, there are tactical reasons to avoid giving the attorney authority to settle the case. *See infra,* at 70–1.

B. DETERMINING THE CLIENT'S INTERESTS

The quality of a negotiated agreement is determined by the extent to which it serves the client's interests. Accordingly, the lawyer must accurately understand the client's interests before beginning to bargain. This often is not as simple as it initially seems. When questioned about what he expects from a negotiation, the client often responds with a "bottom line" or negotiating *position*. For example, consider again the commercial lease negotiation between Chestnut Development Corporation and Banana Computers. Assume Maria Mortimer, the manager of Chestnut, tells Chestnut's attorney, Dan Darrow, that its "bottom line" is to lease the available retail store space in the mall at the standard rate which consists of a "base rental" figure of $35 per square foot, six percent of all gross sales in excess of $500,000 and additional fees for common maintenance, insurance and taxes totaling $8 per square foot. Neither Dan nor Maria realizes that Banana Computer's initial year's sale projections preclude paying a base rental this high because Banana's product is a new one on the market. Deadlock will result because no agreement appears possible.

If the lawyer probes beneath the client's stated *position* to determine its *underlying interests,* however, agreement may be possible.[2] Focusing on the underlying *interests* of the parties instead of *positions* is an important part of *problem-solving* negotiation. Consider how Dan might explore the underlying interests of his client with Maria:

1—Dan: As I understand it, $35 per square foot is your "bottom line" in my negotiation with Banana. How do you arrive at that figure?

2—Maria: It's our standard rate; the amount we must charge to cover our actual and anticipated expenses and get a decent return on our stockholder's investment.

3—Dan: I assume then that you leave some margin in that rate for increases in expenses?

4—Maria: You're darn right we do. If it's not one thing, it's the other. Last year we were faced with an incredible rise in our insurance rates and now our employees are threatening to unionize.

5—Dan: So one of your main concerns is to protect yourself against rising labor and insurance costs. Is there any other reason that you think you must have $35 per square foot?

2. In some instances, the client's "bottom line" might be determined more by market prices or "what the market will bear" than by the client's underlying interests. In all but the simplest and most routine legal negotiations, however, market price is not a sole determinant of the client's "bottom line" because potential partners to a transaction and what they have to offer are not fungible. This lack of fungibility suggests the limitations of price alone as a proxy for client satisfaction.

6—Maria: Yes. It's true that we do have vacant space, but if we offered Banana a lower rate, it would set a pattern for future tenants and would demoralize those tenants who are already paying $35 per square foot.

Dan has learned that behind Chestnut's stated *position* of $35 per square foot are Chestnut's *interests* in being protected against rising expenses and in setting a precedent for other leases. A variety of negotiation proposals now can be devised which adequately will protect these interests at the same time that they meet Banana's needs. For example, Banana Computer might agree to a contingency clause increasing its rent in the event that Chestnut's labor and insurance costs rise at a rate in excess of eight percent per year, in exchange for a base rent lower than $35 per square foot. Banana might also agree to keep the rate confidential so that it does not set a trend among future tenants or create morale problems with existing tenants.

One of the classic examples of agreements that are possible when the negotiators focus on the underlying interests of the parties and not on their stated positions is the peace treaty negotiated by Egypt and Israel in 1978 at Camp David.[3] Egypt's stated demand was the return of the entire Sinai peninsula captured by Israel in the 1967 War. Israel's seemingly irreconcilable position was its continued possession for security purposes of at least a portion of the Sinai. The underlying interests of the parties, however, were not inherently incompatible. Israel's interest was security: to prevent Egyptian forces from being poised in the Sinai to launch an invasion of Israel. As a matter of principle and national pride, Egypt's *interest* was the Sinai's return to its sovereignty. At Camp David, the two sides agreed to return the Sinai to Egyptian sovereignty, but to demilitarize major portions of the peninsula so as not to pose a military threat to Israel. In this case, stated *positions* obscured the fact that the interests of the parties were not inherently in conflict.

These two examples, one from a commercial lease negotiation and the other from the world of international diplomacy, show the importance of determining the client's underlying *interests*. How can the lawyer do this? As demonstrated by Dan, the basic approach is to delve behind the client's stated position and ask *why* the client articulates his position as he does. Negotiating positions are inherently conclusory statements that hide the specifics of the client's needs.

---

3. *See* R. Fisher & W. Ury, Getting to Yes: Negotiating Agreement Without Giving In 42–3 (1983); H. Raiffa, The Art and Science of Negotiation 205–07 (1982). Pruitt provides another simple but vivid example of a case in which identifying underlying interests led to an agreement. D. Pruitt, Negotiation Behavior 137–138 (1981). A wife and a husband are deciding where to spend their vacation. The respective *positions* of the parties are that the husband would prefer to go to the mountains and the wife would prefer to spend her vacation at the seashore. When questioned about their preferences, the wife's real interests are in swimming, sunbathing and eating seafood. The husband's underlying interests are to hike in the mountains and to fish in streams. It is possible, therefore, for the parties to meet most of their preferences if they agree to a resort located on a large lake near the mountains.

It is important not to construe the client's interests too narrowly. Too often, when lawyers consult with clients about negotiation, they focus exclusively on monetary and other easily quantifiable factors. The client's interests in the negotiation are not only economic, but also psychological and social. For instance, reaching agreement reduces anxiety for the client, whether the client's alternative to a particular negotiated agreement is to seek another tenant for vacant space in the Chestnut Mall or is to proceed to trial. The client's interests are also social: how will the existing tenants at the Chestnut Mall respond if the "new kid on the block" gets a break in the rental rate? Thus, to produce a negotiated agreement which is satisfying to the client, the lawyer should be aware of all of the client's interests in the matter, including economic, psychological and social ones.

C. CONSULTATION CONCERNING NEGOTIATION STRATEGY

The client's interests affect not only the substance of negotiation proposals and positions; they also should influence the choice of negotiation tactics. One consequence of the choice of negotiation strategy warrants reiteration at this time because of its considerable impact on the client's interests. The lawyer and client should explore, during a pre-negotiation conference, the implications of negotiation tactics on the future relationship between the client and the other party. If the parties anticipate a continuing relationship, either *cooperative* or *problem-solving* bargaining tactics usually will be preferred,[4] because *competitive* tactics often generate distrust and ill-will. Further, the client's best interests may not be served by *competitive* tactics because they often result in social disapproval within the bargaining community and invite later retaliation for violating fairness norms. On the other hand, a particular client might prefer the use of *competitive* tactics in a negotiation with a party with whom it has a continuing relationship because the client believes such tactics establish a strong bargaining image and discourage future attempts at exploitation by the other party. The client's input into the lawyer's choice of negotiation tactics is critical precisely because of the different concerns clients may have about how their lawyers' negotiating behaviors affect their own relationships with other parties.

4. *See* R. Axelrod, The Evolution of Co-operation 129 (1984); D. Pruitt, *supra* note 3, at 39–40, 109–12; Roering, Slusher & Shooler, *Commitment to Future Interaction in Marketing Transactions,* 60 J. Applied Psychology 386, 386–87 (1975); Rubin, *Negotiation: An Introduction to Some Issues and Themes,* 27 Am. Behavioral Scientist 135, 137 (1983).

D. THE CLIENT'S "BEST ALTERNATIVE TO A NEGOTIATED AGREEMENT" AND MINIMUM DISPOSITION

The most important aspect of determining the client's interests in the negotiation is to ascertain what alternatives the client has to a negotiated agreement and, perhaps, what negotiated agreement is least advantageous, yet acceptable, from his viewpoint. The least advantageous settlement acceptable to the client, or the "bottom line," is referred to as the client's *minimum disposition*.[5] The advantage of determining a *minimum disposition* in advance of the negotiation is that a quantified "bottom line" prevents both the client and the negotiator from being "swept away" during the negotiation process. Without an explicit *minimum disposition,* a lawyer occasionally accepts a bad deal for her client because she becomes anxious or is persuaded by the other party's assertions during bargaining.

Determining the client's *minimum disposition* in advance of the negotiation, however, may be both unrealistic and undesirable. Any consideration of a "bottom line" prior to the negotiation requires an understanding of both the alternatives to settlement and the likely settlement outcome. At this early stage, though, the information available to lawyer and client usually is incomplete: lawyers typically begin negotiating prior to completing their own investigation of facts, legal research and discovery. In addition, the lawyer is unaware at this stage of how the other side views the case and of additional facts and information that will be gleaned from the other party during the negotiation process. The lawyer, therefore, should make disclaimers about the adequacy of her information during her counseling sessions with the client concerning alternatives. These same factors suggest that any *minimum disposition* determined by the client at this time be regarded as flexible and subject to change as the negotiation continues.

Fisher and Ury, leading proponents of problem-solving bargaining, suggest two additional reasons why a client should not set a "bottom line" prior to bargaining.[6] First, the bottom line is likely to be set too high. Before hearing from the other party, and at a time when uncertainty prevails, it is very easy for the client and the attorney to assess the client's situation through "rose-colored glasses." There is a natural tendency among most people, including lawyers, to defer bad news as long as possible; one reason is that lawyers may believe that good news assists client relations. After all, the other party's unwillingness to fulfill the client's expectations always can be blamed on "unreasonableness." If a rigid *minimum disposition* is set too high,

5. *See* G. Bellow & B. Moulton, The Lawyering Process: Materials for Clinical Instruction in Advocacy 487 (1978).

6. R. Fisher & W. Ury, *supra* note 3, at 103.

according to Fisher and Ury, the client may subsequently decide to reject a negotiated settlement that meets his interests.

In addition, as with the adoption of a fixed negotiation position, a specific *minimum disposition* inhibits *problem-solving* bargaining. If Chestnut Development Corporation establishes a *minimum disposition* of $35 per square foot as a base rental, it will reject any proposed lease calling for a base rent of $28 per square foot. Even with a base rental of $28 per square foot, such an agreement could be in Chestnut's best interests if it includes clauses obligating the retail tenant, Banana Computer, to pay a proportionate share of increases in labor and insurance expenses and to keep the rental rate confidential from the other tenants.

Regardless of whether a lawyer believes that on balance it is good negotiation practice to establish a *minimum disposition,* she should review with the client his alternatives to the negotiated agreement and determine his "Best Alternative to a Negotiated Agreement" or "BATNA." [7] Fisher and Ury use this term to represent the option available to the client that best satisfies his interests if the negotiation is unsuccessful; they suggest that the client's BATNA be the standard against which any negotiated agreement be measured. In many cases, the client's explicit awareness of his BATNA prevents him from being too optimistic about his prospects if negotiation deadlock occurs. In other cases, it prevents the client from being overly pessimistic and thus entering into an agreement that is not as satisfactory to him as an available alternative.

One of the most valuable types of expertise that the experienced lawyer brings to her professional relationship with her client is knowledge and inventiveness about possible alternatives to the negotiated agreement. For example, Banana Computers will want to investigate comparable retail space at other locations. In another negotiation, if a client is interested in purchasing a small chain of nursing homes, he will be interested in knowing the purchase price of comparable businesses which have sold recently, and what other investment opportunities may be available to him. In many instances, the client will know more about the alternatives than anyone else, and sometimes he will have his own professional investment counselors or accountants to rely upon. In other situations, however, depending upon the nature of the relationship agreed upon by the lawyer and the client, the lawyer also might be expected to provide advice of this kind. If the lawyer is not aware of the necessary information from her own professional experience and background, she needs to research her client's alternatives by consulting with other appropriate professionals.

In personal injury negotiations, plea bargaining or other litigation settlement talks, the expected trial outcome usually is the client's alternative to a negotiated agreement. The lawyer takes the lead in describing for the client both the expected trial outcome and the

7. *Id.* at 104.

probable range of any negotiated settlement.[8] Lawyers use a variety of methods to predict jury verdicts in litigation. Sometimes in a routine case the experienced lawyer can predict confidently for the client the likely legal consequences of the trial alternative. For example, assume a defendant who has been charged with driving under the influence of alcohol and who:

(a) has recorded a blood alcohol breath test result of .15% alcohol in the blood by weight;

(b) was observed by a police officer for a distance of one-half mile weaving left of center;

(c) has three prior convictions for DUI; and

(d) could not touch his finger to his nose.

An experienced lawyer who routinely handles DUI cases (driving under the influence of alcohol) in a particular jurisdiction and locale can predict both the expected trial outcome and the prosecutor's plea bargaining position with some accuracy.

Suppose, however, that the lawyer has never handled a similar case before, even though the case is not extraordinary. As an example, consider the case of a chemical engineer who leaves his employer and sets up a competing business, even though his contract with his original employer included agreements precluding him from using either trade secrets or customer lists after his employment ended. Even if the legal issues are clear, the lawyer probably does not have sufficient information from her practice experience to predict how the jury would react to the liability and damage issues. Under these circumstances, the inexperienced lawyer should seek the advice of more experienced attorneys who have handled similar cases. Indeed, ready sharing of this kind of information among lawyers is one of the benefits of practicing with a large firm or maintaining good relations with other attorneys in the community.

Finally, consider the "big case" for which there are no precedents in a particular locale. How is it ever possible to predict trial outcomes so that the client knows whether she is better off to settle or to go to trial? First, it is important to acknowledge that valuing cases and predicting trial outcomes is far from an exact science. Rosenthal, in his seminal work on client counseling, *Lawyer and Client: Who's In Charge?*[9] reports on a survey in which he asked three experienced personal injury lawyers and two insurance company representatives to place a settlement value on sixty-one personal injury claims after looking at the actual case files. In one of the cases, the highest

8. *See* D. Binder & S. Price, Legal Interviewing and Counseling: A Client–Centered Approach 149–153 (1977). The process of decision analysis in choosing between settlement and litigation alternatives is analyzed in Bodily, *When Should You Go To Court?* Harv.Bus.Rev. 103 (May–June 1981) and in Johnson, *Lawyer's Choice: A Theoretical Appraisal of Litigation Investment Decisions*, 15 L. & Soc'y Rev. 567 (1981).

9. D. Rosenthal, Lawyer and Client: Who's in Charge? 200–08 (1974).

valuation by an expert was $30,000; the lowest was $2,000. Differentials of 600% in the other cases were not unusual.

Assume however that the injured plaintiff is Patrick Finney, a 28 year old married truck driver who was struck by a speeding locomotive at a railroad crossing that was obscured and invisible to him and other drivers because of bushes, trees and other vegetation. Patrick is rendered a paraplegic by the accident. How much are his claims worth? Neither the lawyer handling the case nor any other attorney practicing in that area is likely to have represented a plaintiff with similar injuries or with similar facts on liability. Yet she must advise her client of the alternatives he has to acceptance of the latest settlement offer from the railroad company. In this context, the lawyer must predict:

(1) how the trial court judge will resolve all legal issues;

(2) the credibility of her witnesses;

(3) what version of historical facts the jury will accept;

(4) if the jury will find that these facts constitute liability;

(5) what damages the jury will award; and

(6) if the judgment of the trial court will be upheld on appeal.

Presumably both law school and practice both teach lawyers something about predicting the legal decisions of trial courts and the appellate courts. Common sense, educated by trial practice and evidence courses, make lawyers more capable of predicting the factual findings of the jury. How, then, can the lawyer predict damages?

Once again, in fairly routine cases, the lawyer can rely upon her experience or that of her colleagues. In the more unusual case, there are several tools that may be of assistance. For example, various formulas have been devised to predict personal injury verdicts. "The three times specials" or other multiples of the plaintiff's "out of pocket" expenses that are sometimes used as a rough approximation of a claim are clearly inadequate in many instances—such as when a child's eye is damaged and vision is totally lost but medical expenses are modest. Other personal injury attorneys suggest a more sophisticated formula approach allocating "points" for liability, damages, credibility of the parties and similar issues.[10] Most of the time, even these more sophisticated calculations are risky. Of more use are services such as the *Personal Injury Valuation Handbook*[11] or the *ATLA Law Reporter*[12] which report the amount of settlements and jury verdicts for various types of injuries and also frequently provide some description of the characteristics of the jurisdiction in which the award was granted— that is, whether juries are likely to be liberal or conservative in

10. *See, e.g.,* Werchick, *Settling the Case—Plaintiff,* 4 Am.Jur.Trials, 289–378 (1966).

11. Jury Verdict Research, Inc., Personal Injury Valuation Handbooks.

12. Association of Trial Lawyers of America, ATLA L.Rep.

estimating damages. Finally, experts can be retained who value personal injury claims by looking at cases with comparable liability and damage issues in similar jurisdictions.

The methods used for valuing personal injury claims are only examples of the wide array of approaches that lawyers use to predict the legal consequences of the trial alternative in a litigation context. It is important to reiterate that the psychological, economic and social consequences for the plaintiff of proceeding to trial are also important factors in describing and evaluating the alternative to a negotiated settlement. These factors often are highly personal to the client, and weighing these factors is a uniquely individual decision. Patrick Finney's lawyer might conclude that he has an eighty percent chance of a favorable verdict and the likely amount of that verdict would be $1.2 million dollars. Nevertheless, the client may legitimately decide to accept any settlement offer in excess of $400,000. From a strictly economic standpoint, has the client behaved irrationally? Perhaps, but it is the client who will live with the consequences of his decision while the lawyer goes on to her next case.

Regardless of whether the lawyer and client decide upon a rigid *minimum disposition* figure prior to negotiation, or only evaluate the client's Best Alternative to a Negotiated Agreement, each serves as a check on the negotiator. Many lawyers also establish a negotiation *target*. The *target* is set at some level above the *minimum disposition* acceptable to the client, and provides a higher level of satisfaction to the client than an agreement that achieves only the client's *minimum disposition*. Interestingly, the empirical work of Karass suggests that negotiators who have "higher targets" or greater aspirations achieve more for their clients in negotiations than others.[13] In addition, a negotiation *target* can serve as a "tripwire" in a negotiation; when the negotiator makes a proposal on an issue that is less advantageous than the negotiation target, she knows the bargaining is approaching her client's minimum requirements.

The lawyer should also evaluate the other party's alternatives to the negotiated agreement. It is useful to the lawyer to understand the other party's probable BATNA for prediction of eventual agreement and detection of bluffing. Understanding the other party's interests also assists the lawyer in her efforts to use *problem-solving* methods.

In summary, prior to the negotiation the lawyer and client dyad should discuss the client's interests, the chosen negotiation strategy's implications for the client, and alternatives to a negotiated agreement for both the client and the other party. The balance of the pre-negotiation planning conference depends upon whether the issues to be negotiated have *integrative* potential or are predominantly *distributive* ones, and upon whether the lawyer intends to use *competitive, cooperative,* or *problem-solving* tactics, or a mixture of strategies.

13. *See* C. Karass, The Negotiating Game 12–26 (1970).

E. IDENTIFYING INTEGRATIVE POTENTIAL

In preparing for negotiation, the lawyer should explore if there are any integrative opportunities in the bargaining situation, that is, whether the parties could resolve their differences in ways that provide a high degree of satisfaction for both parties. This result can be achieved in one of two possible ways, as described in Chapter Three. First, is there a potential solution to the parties' respective problems that will satisfy both their underlying interests? Second, are there multiple issues involved in the negotiation for which the parties have differing levels of priorities so that both parties may be more satisfied if they engage in *logrolling* and exchange concessions on different issues?

The appropriate time for the lawyer to begin to identify any integrative potential is prior to the negotiation. The mere presence of integrative potential, which would allow the lawyer to use *problem-solving* tactics, however, does not necessarily dictate that the lawyer use such a strategy. In some circumstances, the lawyer may decide that it is in her client's best interests to use *competitive* tactics, even if a *problem-solving* approach also could be used.

How can the lawyer decide what *integrative* potential exists in a bargaining situation? The analysis begins when the lawyer and client discuss the underlying interests of the client and those of the other party. The process continues with possible identification of potential solutions to problems facing both parties that would satisfy their underlying interests.

1. "BRAINSTORMING"

One of the techniques to be used in developing proposals which satisfy both parties' interests is "brainstorming." [14] The purpose of brainstorming is to produce as many potential solutions to the parties' problems as possible. The participants in brainstorming, in this case the client and his attorney, are encouraged to articulate whatever possible solutions come to mind, regardless of how ridiculous or non-viable they initially appear. The lawyer and client suspend critical evaluation and judgment until all possible proposals have been listed, and only at that point do they consciously and systematically consider the viability of each option and its advantages and disadvantages. This technique mitigates the possibility that a viable option will not be carefully considered because the participants have excluded it as a result of intuitive or subconscious prejudices that, upon further reflection, are not valid. Brainstorming also serves to counteract the tendency of many lawyers to be too critical and, as a result of either their personalities or their legal training, to seek only the "best answer".

To illustrate the use of brainstorming as part of a client counseling session prior to the negotiation, consider the pre-negotiation counseling

---

14. *See* R. Fisher & W. Ury, *supra* note 3, at 62–71.

session between Banana Computer's lawyer, Bev Bailey, and Jeff Walton, the Banana employee responsible for finding a location for the retail outlet. Bev is aware that the going rate for space is a $35 per square foot base rental, plus six percent of gross sales in excess of $500,000 and additional charges for common maintenance, insurance and tax costs. Jeff informs Bev, however, that $35 per square foot coupled with the additional charges is more than Banana can afford at this time. In the following example, observe as Bev actually educates her client about the use of brainstorming techniques. This is not unique, however, as a lawyer frequently teaches her client about other aspects of the legal process such as cross-examination or depositions:

1—Bev: Jeff, I'm scheduled to meet with Dan Darrow, the attorney representing the Chestnut Mall, tomorrow to see whether we can work out a rental agreement for the new store. What most concerns me is whether we can reach an agreement on the amount of the monthly rent. As I recall, you told me before that I was not authorized to pay anything more than $20 per square foot. Is that still the case?

2—Jeff: I'm afraid that it is. Anything more than that and we would not be able to make it through the first two years.

3—Bev: Well, our problem, as I told you on the phone, is that Chestnut has a standard policy of charging $35 per square foot. They justify that figure on the basis of the uncertainties in the cost of labor and insurance. They also want a uniform rate so that they don't create tensions among their tenants.

What I'd like to do today, Jeff, is to try to see if we could come up with any ideas that could produce an agreement with a rent low enough for Banana, but that would still satisfy Chestnut's concerns. If we do, I'll propose it tomorrow and try to sell it to Dan. I really wanted you involved in this process, because you have so much more experience in renting store space than I do, and I suspect you'll have more ideas because of that background.

What I have found usually works best is for you and me simply to throw out ideas that might work, regardless of how crazy they might sound. We'll just list the ideas and come back later to evaluate each of the options. That way we won't subconsciously discard what might be a good idea. Do you have the idea?

4—Jeff: I think so. You mean just to talk about whatever crazy ideas come to mind? They teach you that in law school?

5—Bev: (laughs) I think you've got the idea. And yes, they're starting to teach such things in law school.

Here the lawyer has educated the client about the technique of brainstorming.

Brainstorming often initially seems uncomfortable and unconventional to some clients. Sometimes the lawyer can ease this threatened loss of rapport by reporting how well it has worked with other clients. Brainstorming seldom will be appropriate in the first encounter between lawyer and client, but hopefully by this time in his relationship with his attorney, Jeff has enough trust in Bev that he will go along with what initially appears to be a strange and crazy idea. After this introductory phase, the actual brainstorming begins:

6—Bev: Let's begin, then. Any ideas on how we could work something out with Chestnut?

7—Jeff: You said that they were most concerned about rising labor and insurance costs and taxes. We could agree to pay those portions of the increased costs that were attributable to the space we leased.

8—Bev: Good, we'll write that down and examine it in a minute. What else?

9—Jeff: How about just starting with a low rent and having it increase each quarter as the store's revenues increase?

10—Bev: Good. Another possibility along the same lines would be to eliminate the base rental and have the rent tied entirely to the amount of the store's monthly sales.

11—Jeff: Or perhaps just a lease on a quarter to quarter basis so that we would know something more about what sales to predict and they would know something about their costs. But that wouldn't work, because we need assurance of having store space. They'd be able to demand about any price they wanted.

12—Bev: Let's wait till we've listed all the options that we can think of before we start evaluating and criticizing the various possibilities. I don't want you to get cautious in suggesting options because you are thinking about the problems with them.

13—Jeff: O.K., we'll buy the mall.

14—Bev: I'll write that down.

In this sequence, both lawyer and client contribute options through a joint brainstorming process. Bev writes each one down, but does not pause for evaluation or either favorable or critical comments. Her responses of "good" to Jeff's various suggestions are *recognition* comments on how well he is doing in the brainstorming process itself, not evaluations of his substantive suggestions. In segment number 11 of the exchange, Jeff begins to evaluate one of the options he has mentioned and suggests that it is not viable. Bev points out that this contribution is evaluative and discourages it.

Together, Bev and Jeff now have identified those options that might come readily to mind because they relate directly to the structure of the rent payments. Observe as Beth tries to keep the brainstorming process flowing by broadening the scope of the inquiry:

15—Bev: What else?

16—Jeff: That's about it.

17—Bev: So far we've mostly talked about re-structuring the rent. In what other ways can we change the situation?

18—Jeff: We could try to convince Chestnut to rent us some of that less desirable space down at the end of the mall where all the vacant space is at a lower rate.

19—Bev: Good. What else?

20—Jeff: We could try to convince the higher-ups that we would sell just as many computers at the shopping center across the street.

21—Bev: Is there any chance that the store could be redesigned to fit in a smaller space? We should consider that.

22—Jeff: O.K. We could ask Chestnut to pay the costs of furnishing our store to lower our start-up costs, in exchange for its standard rent. Or perhaps they could run a promotional campaign at their expense for our grand opening.

23—Bev: Those are interesting possibilities. Anything else?

23—Jeff: I'm out of ideas.

24—Bev: What about proposing to the mall that Banana will trade computers or computer services at cost for a lower rate?

Other than that, I can't think of anything else either. Now let's go back and decide which of these ideas are serious possibilities.

Bev's extra prodding produced a number of different options. Some of these options, such as "buying the mall" are clearly "off-the-wall" and can be quickly discarded. Others, such as trading Chestnut computer services and equipment for a reduced rent, are unconventional ideas which might not have surfaced except for the free-flowing brainstorming processes. A conscious and systematic evaluation of their viability may reveal that at a minimum they should be proposed to the other party during the negotiation session itself.

The biggest advantage of brainstorming techniques is that they tend to prevent the lawyer and client from prematurely excluding possibilities on the basis that they either "sound crazy" or are not the usual way things are done. During the second stage of brainstorming, the lawyer and client consciously and systematically evaluate the feasibility and the advantages and disadvantages of each option. Later, during the negotiation itself, the two lawyers also evaluate the proposals.

Pre-negotiation brainstorming often includes not only the client and the attorney, but also appropriate experts. Accountants or investment bankers, for example, often are capable of devising creative ways of structuring financial transactions that are not readily apparent to even the sophisticated client and his experienced counsel. Similarly, annuity experts may be able to suggest a structured settlement approach for the injured personal injury claimant.

Fisher and Ury emphasize brainstorming as an important ingredient in their approach of "principled negotiation." [15] They suggest a number of ways in which bargaining situations with possibly little or no integrative potential still can benefit from a problem-solving approach. For one thing, they argue that greater problem-solving opportunities exist if the participants in brainstorming *expand the agenda,* that is, consider enlarging the issues to be included within the proposed agreement. The brainstorming session previously described between Bev and Jeff illustrated at least one such *agenda expansion.* Near the end of the counseling session, at segment number 24, Bev suggests the possibility that Banana provide the Chestnut Mall with computers or computer services in exchange for a reduced rental. The issue of providing computers to the mall was not previously present in the negotiation, but this suggestion provides a way that both parties can benefit. The value of the computers or services to Banana is their cost to Banana, which probably is considerably less than their retail value to Chestnut. Both parties benefit, and the advantage to Chestnut may be significant enough to trade for a reduced rental. By *expanding the agenda* as a result of the brainstorming process, the lawyer and client have discovered integrative potential that was not readily apparent.

As a further means of using brainstorming to create problem-solving opportunities where they are not obvious, Fisher and Ury suggest agreements of "different strengths." [16] For example, during their brainstorming session, Bev and Jeff could consider a procedure for adjusting rents periodically if a single rate can not be agreed upon for the entire lease term. Both sides legitimately are concerned with uncertainties. Chestnut believes it needs a higher initial rent to cover the possibilities of higher labor and insurance costs; Banana is worried that a beginning store's revenues are not sufficient to pay the higher rent. As a result of their brainstorming session, Bev and Jeff might propose to Chestnut that the initial rent be set at a figure lower than the market rate, but that every six months the rent would be revised by an arbitrator, who would consider trends in expenditures for labor and

---

15. *Id.* at 72–3.

16. Fisher and Ury's complete list of agreements of different strengths is as follows:

Stronger	Weaker
Substantive	Procedural
Permanent	Provisional
Comprehensive	Partial
Final	In principle
Unconditional	Contingent
Binding	Non–Binding
First–order	Second–order

Id. at 72.

insurance, as well as other expenses. This agreement would be a "procedural" agreement, as contrasted with a "substantive" one.

2. PREPARATION FOR OTHER PROBLEM-SOLVING TACTICS

The lawyer and client, during the pre-negotiation counseling session, should discuss the possible use of other problem-solving techniques. First, the lawyer should determine the relative importance of the issues to the client. Most negotiations involve multiple issues. For example, the lease negotiation between Banana and Chestnut involves not only the base rental rate, but also the percentage of gross sales and the amount of other charges, the length of the term of the lease, the exact location of the store, and how escalating insurance and labor costs should be apportioned between the parties. One problem-solving technique, "logrolling," [17] consists of conceding on some issues while the other party concedes on other issues. To the extent that the parties place differing emphasis on the various issues, logrolling increases the parties' joint benefit beyond what it would be if each party conceded an equivalent amount on each individual issue. In other words, in logrolling each party concedes more on the issue about which it cares less. To be effective, logrolling requires the lawyers to clearly understand their clients' relative priorities among the multiple issues.

Do not underestimate the importance of either the logrolling technique or the accompanying need to counsel continually with the client regarding his relative preferences among the various issues. In actual negotiation, the fact that parties place differing priorities on various issues is a significant reason why agreements are reached in most cases. Therefore, discussing the logrolling process and ascertaining the client's priorities prior to the negotiation are important aspects of negotiation planning.

The lawyer also should anticipate, during the client conference, the possibility of using two other problem-solving negotiation techniques, *cost-cutting* and *compensation*.[18] If one party to a negotiation is to achieve its goals, this often imposes significant *costs* on the other party. *Cost-cutting* and *compensation* are two methods of making such an agreement less painful to the other party while allowing the first party to achieve its goals. In *cost-cutting,* the parties find ways of making the concessions less onerous. For example, in the Banana retail outlet example, Chestnut was concerned that a lower rental rate would impose costs on it by causing a morale crisis among other tenants who were paying the higher rate. The cost imposed upon Chestnut, therefore, was damage to its relationships with the other tenants. This cost could be "cut", however, by a confidentiality clause which provides that Banana will not disclose to anyone else the rate it is paying.

---

17. *See* D. Pruitt, *supra* note 3, at 153–55.

18. *Id.* at 142–53.

Compensation is a *problem-solving tactic* in which the negotiator provides substitute satisfaction in exchange for the other party conceding on an issue. Obviously, logrolling is one form of compensation: the negotiating party is compensated for making a concession on one issue by receiving a concession on the other issue. Both *cost-cutting* and *compensation* will be discussed more fully in Chapter Nine, *Closure.*

F. DISTRIBUTIVE ISSUES

Not all issues in negotiation have significant integrative potential; some issues remain predominantly distributive ones. When the insurance company's lawyer and the paraplegic plaintiff's lawyer negotiate a settlement in a personal injury action, they are somewhat concerned with structured settlements or with having both parties avoid the costs of litigation. Neither party, however, would suggest that its primary interest is anything other than the dollar amount to be paid on the claim, a *distributive* situation. In the negotiation between the criminal defense attorney and the prosecutor over the length of a sentence recommendation, the lawyers perceive that their interests directly conflict. Even in the negotiation situation between Chestnut and Banana, used to illustrate brainstorming techniques, the single most important issue to both parties probably is the amount of the monthly rental payment.

How does the lawyer plan for negotiation on distributive issues? This chapter previously described the idea of a *minimum disposition,* that is, the least advantageous settlement acceptable to the client. The client, of course, prefers an agreement more advantageous to her than her minimum disposition. For example, even if Banana Computer were able and willing to pay $35 per square foot as a monthly rental, Banana's executives would be even more pleased to pay only $25 per square foot. There may be limits, of course; if the agreement is excessively favorable to Banana, it may justifiably fear that its future relationship with Chestnut will not be an entirely positive and comfortable one.

Theoretically, at least, a *range* of solutions to the matter being negotiated will always be present. Even if these solutions do not fit into readily quantifiable variables, such as dollars, it still is possible to rank-order the various negotiated settlements according to the client's relative order of preference. For example, Banana may list the options previously developed during the brainstorming session into the following sequence with the least desirable option listed first and the most desirable option listed last:

1. Buy the mall;
2. Quarter-to-quarter lease;
3. Locate in shopping center across street;
4. Rent a smaller spaced store;
5. Rent space at vacant end of the mall;

6. Amount of rent to be determined periodically by a third party;

7. Rent to increase periodically in accordance with pre-determined schedule;

8. Banana to pay specified share of increased labor and insurance costs;

9. Chestnut to subsidize start-up costs by paying construction costs for furnishing store and initial promotional expenses;

10. Amount of rent to be based solely upon gross sales (no base rent); or

11. Banana to trade computers or services at cost for lower rent.

It would be possible to place each of these options sequentially on a horizontal line graph with the distance from the beginning point of the line graph at the left end representing Banana's level of satisfaction with the agreement:

FIGURE 4–1

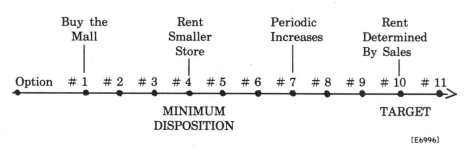

[E6996]

Banana's Level of Satisfaction

If it is assumed that option number 4, renting space at the vacant end of the mall, is the least attractive option which would be acceptable to Banana, then this option is Banana's *minimum disposition.* On the other hand, Banana realistically hopes that Chestnut will agree to option number 10, the amount of rent determined solely by gross sales. Accordingly, option number 10 would be Banana's *target point.* The negotiator's goal or *target point* often reflects her prediction of what terms constitute the other side's minimum disposition.

The analysis of *minimum dispositions* and *target points* is much easier in a truly *distributive* bargaining situation where the parties are confronted with a single issue consisting of a fixed quantity which must be divided between the parties. Consider a personal injury case. Patrick Finney, a truck-driver, is rendered a paraplegic as a result of a collision between the truck he is driving and a railroad locomotive. His lawyer, Gary Gerstein, brings an action against the railroad alleging negligence on its part. The evidence obtained during discovery shows that the railroad arguably was negligent in a variety of ways, including operating its train at an excessive rate of speed, allowing brush and shrubbery to grow near the tracks that make it impossible to see down the tracks from the highway, and failing to use statutorily required "crossbuck" warning signs. The attorney for the railroad, Roberta Martinez, asserts that liability should be precluded, or at least damages reduced substantially (in a comparative fault jurisdiction in which the defendant's liability is reduced, but not eliminated by the plaintiff's own negligence), because of Patrick's contributory negligence in not looking more carefully for an oncoming locomotive and in driving across the railroad tracks when visibility was obscured.

In analyzing Patrick's case after extensive discovery, Patrick's attorney, Gary Gerstein, reaches the conclusion that Patrick has approximately an eighty percent (80%) chance of proving the railroad's negligence. Gary also determines that on the comparative negligence issue there is about a sixty percent chance the jury will find Patrick negligent and that if it does, the jury probably will assess his comparative degree of fault in the twenty to thirty-five percent range. In other words, the best prediction is the jury will hold the railroad liable for somewhere between sixty-five and eighty percent of the damages. Gary also believes the most likely result is that the jury will assess Patrick's total damages at roughly $1.8 million dollars. Based upon his counsel's predictions and his moderate adverseness to risk, Patrick reasonably establishes his *minimum disposition* as being $950,000. He hopes for a better result, however, and establishes a *target point* of $1.2 million based upon his counsel's most optimistic predictions about the trial results and the additional costs to the railroad of trying the case. These *minimum disposition* and *target* points are illustrated as follows: [19]

FIGURE 4–2

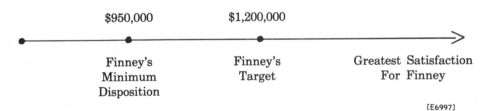

$950,000 $1,200,000

Finney's   Finney's   Greatest Satisfaction
Minimum   Target   For Finney
Disposition

[E6997]

Patrick would reject any offer from the railroad or its insurer of less than $950,000, his *minimum disposition.* Patrick would accept any settlement in excess of $950,000 and his level of satisfaction, theoretically at least, would increase proportionately with the increase in the dollar amount. Patrick would have achieved his *target* or goal if the settlement exceeded $1.2 million.

What possible significance does the client's subjective *goal* or *target* have for the negotiation? Karass, in his research on negotiation, established that those negotiators with high aspiration levels, or target

19. This graph of the bargaining range, and those on the next several pages, follow the format used by G. Bellow & B. Moulton, *supra* note 5 at 459–62.

points, did better in negotiations than negotiators with lower aspirations.[20] In other words, negotiators who expected more, in fact received more.

Most often, but not inevitably, the other party also will have some idea as to what constitutes its minimum disposition. Of course either party's minimum disposition may change, and often does change, during the course of the negotiation itself. The most typical bargaining situation, therefore, is one in which at the beginning of the negotiation, each party knows its own *minimum disposition,* but has only probabilistic information, based upon its own knowledge of the bargaining problem and prior communications with the other party, about the other's *minimum disposition.*[21]

Looking at the bargaining situation from an omniscient perspective, instead of the actual perspective of one party with only limited information, the interval between the two parties' disposition points defines the *bargaining range.* If the two negotiating parties behave rationally, an agreement will be reached at some point within the *bargaining range,* because by definition both parties prefer a negotiated agreement within this range to the other available alternatives. For example, if the railroad determines that it is in its best interests to offer Patrick Finney $1.1 million rather than to face the risks of a larger judgment after trial, then its *minimum disposition* is the payment of $1.1 million to Patrick. Its level of satisfaction increases to the extent it can settle the claim for *less* than its *minimum disposition.* If Patrick is willing to accept any amount in excess of $950,000 and the railroad is willing to pay up to $1.1 million dollars, then it is in the interests of both parties to settle for an amount somewhere between $950,000 and $1.1 million. Graphically, it looks like this:

FIGURE 4–3

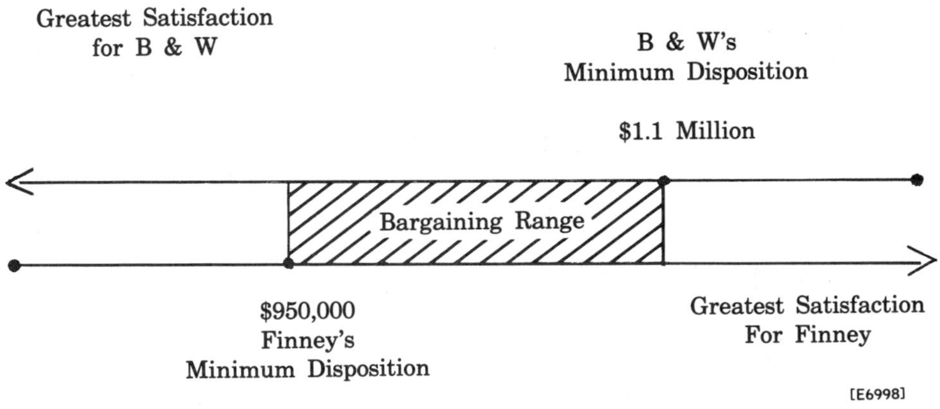

Greatest Satisfaction
for B & W

B & W's
Minimum Disposition

$1.1 Million

Bargaining Range

$950,000
Finney's
Minimum Disposition

Greatest Satisfaction
For Finney

[E6998]

---

20. C. Karass, *supra* note 13, at 42.

21. *See* H. Raiffa, *supra* note 3, 56–8 (1982).

As the negotiated agreement approaches a party's *minimum disposition,* its level of satisfaction decreases. In other words, the more that the railroad pays and the closer it comes to paying $1.1 million, the less satisfied it is. Conversely, as the amount of the settlement increases, and the amount by which it exceeds Patrick's *minimum disposition* increases, Patrick's level of satisfaction increases.

It is possible that there is no *bargaining range* in which the parties both prefer agreement instead of pursuing the alternatives. In a litigation situation such as this one, if Roberta valued Patrick's chances for recovery and the probable amount of his recovery far more conservatively than Gary, then both parties would believe that it was in their interests to proceed to trial rather than to accept the most favorable proposal of the other party. Similarly, in the lease negotiation between Banana and Chestnut, a transactional negotiation, Banana might decide that it was better off opening a store in another location, or not opening a store at all, rather than accepting Chestnut's best offer of $35 per square foot. In these two situations, the only *bargaining range* is a *"negative"* one,[22] and if the parties behave rationally, they will forgo settlement and pursue other options.

Frequently, parties fail to reach a negotiated agreement even when their *minimum dispositions* overlap, and there is in reality a *bargaining range* where both parties prefer an agreement to the available alternatives. This is one of the risks of bluffing during negotiation. If Gary continues to assert vigorously throughout the negotiation that Patrick would not accept any amount less than $1.5 million, then Roberta may decide either that Gary is not negotiating in good faith or that the parties have an honest disagreement as to the settlement value which makes continued negotiation futile. She may break off negotiation, even though in reality her client would be willing to pay more than Patrick's *minimum disposition* of $950,000.

1. THEORETICAL OVERVIEW OF COMPETITIVE GOALS

In a distributive bargaining situation, the negotiator using *competitive* tactics views her goal as the acquisition of the largest possible share of the bargaining range for her client. The competitive negotiator considers the other negotiator as an "opponent" or "opposing party"; her function is to convince the other negotiator to settle on terms extremely favorable to her client. The way to accomplish this, according to the competitive negotiator, is to demonstrate to the opposing negotiator that he could not obtain a better deal for his client either through further negotiation or by pursuing his alternatives to a negotiated settlement. Roberta, the lawyer for the railroad, may try to show Patrick's lawyer Gary that if Patrick does not accept the railroad's offer of $500,000, no further offers will be forthcoming, and that at trial the jury will return a defendant's verdict. If the Chestnut Mall's lawyer

---

22. *See* R. Walton & R. McKersie, A Behavioral Theory of Labor Negotiations 17, 43 (1965).

uses competitive tactics, he may assert that the mall has several other prospective tenants for the vacant retail space who are willing to pay the $35 per square foot and that no other location would be a viable alternative for a computer outlet.

Returning to the concept of bargaining range, the competitive negotiator attempts to do several things. First, she hides her *minimum disposition* from the other negotiator and tries to convince him that her *minimum disposition* is higher than it is. The lower limit on the bargaining range thus becomes the other side's *perception* of the party's *minimum disposition* and *not* the party's *actual minimum disposition.* For example, Gary wants to convince Roberta that his client, Patrick, will not settle for less than $1.0 million. Graphically, the bargaining situation looks like this:

FIGURE 4–4

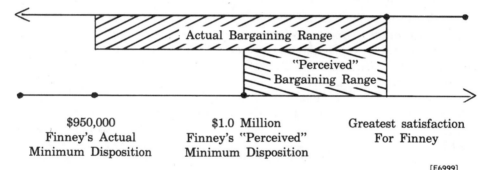

Greatest Satisfaction for B & W   B & W's Minimum Disposition
                                    $1.1 Million

Actual Bargaining Range

"Perceived"
Bargaining Range

$950,000 $1.0 Million   Greatest satisfaction
Finney's Actual   Finney's "Perceived"   For Finney
Minimum Disposition Minimum Disposition

[E6999]

Subsequent chapters describe the various specific competitive tactics that can be used to conceal a negotiator's *minimum disposition* and to establish a bargaining range containing a range of more desirable solutions than the *minimum disposition.*

The second objective of the competitive negotiator is to determine the agreement most advantageous to her client that also is acceptable to the opposing party. In a true distributive context where the utility of the agreement for one party is inversely proportional to the utility of the agreement to the other party, determining the agreement most advantageous to the client that also is acceptable to the other party is the same as determining the other party's *minimum disposition.* It is important to remember, however, that the situation in which the agreement most favorable to one's client and acceptable to the other party constitutes the other party's *minimum disposition* ignores the integrative potential in most bargaining situations and is probably the exception and not the rule. Finding out what agreements are acceptable to the other side is a critical function in negotiation. This goal permeates many different types of techniques used by the negotiator, but is most directly connected with the information gathering tactics discussed in Chapter Seven.

Finally, competitive tactics can be used to change both the other party's *minimum disposition* and his *target*. In many cases, the specific techniques used to convince the other party that the negotiator's minimum disposition is less flexible than it is in reality are the same techniques used to induce the other party to change his *minimum disposition* or *target*. Once again, the basic approach is "If you don't settle on these terms and conditions favorable to my client, your client will be disadvantaged." Discussed in Chapter Eight, *Narrowing of Differences,* arguments and threats are among the primary *competitive* tactics to be used in this manner.

2. ANALYZING SOURCES OF LEVERAGE AND POWER

The negotiator with a competitive orientation views the process as one in which she is trying to influence the other party to do what is in the best interests of her own client. As part of the preparation for negotiation, therefore, lawyer and client together should consider what sources of influence, leverage and power they hold over the other party. The kinds of leverage and power available to the negotiator form the substance of *competitive* arguments and threats. Later in this section, the potential sources of influence that form the basis for the different kind of argument employed as a *cooperative* tactic will be examined.

The most important determinant of the negotiator's power over the other party is the nature of the alternatives to a negotiated agreement available to both the client and the other party. To the extent that the competitive negotiator is able to argue successfully that her own alternatives are more desirable than previously perceived by the other party, her ability to influence the terms of the agreement increases. Similarly, her bargaining leverage increases when she convincingly argues that the other party's alternatives to an agreement are less palatable than they first appeared.

While the comparative disadvantages of the parties' alternatives to a negotiated agreement are the most important determinants of bargaining power, other factors influence power as well. These other factors often are more easily controlled by the skillful negotiator than the alternatives to a negotiated agreement. For example, the party's level of *commitment* to the matter being negotiated affects its bargaining power. Consider the criminal defendant charged in a case that both the prosecutor and the defense attorney agree is almost certain to result in conviction, but one that will require substantial resources to try. Even though the defendant's alternative to a plea bargaining agreement initially seems bleak, by refusing to "cop a plea" he imposes considerable costs on the government. Accordingly, his level of *commitment* to not pleading guilty gives him bargaining power he would otherwise not have. Similarly, the legal services attorney who is prepared to contest her client's eviction all the way to the United States Supreme Court has considerable bargaining power with the landlord's attorney, even if the letter of the law clearly suggests the eviction was lawful.

The lawyer also may increase her client's bargaining position through her *expertise* and *preparation*. As mentioned previously, the lawyer who knows everything about the case or the transaction being negotiated often is able, during the course of the negotiation, to undermine the confidence of the other party in his original negotiation *target* and even in his *minimum disposition*. If a negotiator has superior knowledge of the situation, there is a natural human reaction to credit her evaluations and proposals. Accordingly, the well prepared negotiator with expertise is in a more powerful negotiating position than the less capable one in the same situation.

In the planning process, the lawyer and client also should consider whether bargaining power can be augmented by *external rewards* that a negotiator can grant the other party or *external punishments* that she can inflict upon him. These *rewards* and *punishments* result from something other than the consequences of the breakdown of the negotiation. For example, it is possible that Banana Computers is interested in locating more than one retail outlet in a locale and that Chestnut Development Corporation owns and manages locations that would be suitable for additional retail outlets. Banana Computers then would have additional power in its negotiation concerning the Chestnut Mall location because favorable treatment by Chestnut Development Corporation in this negotiation might lead Banana Computers to further negotiations with Chestnut regarding other locations. Further, most negotiations involve continuing relationships, not "one-shot" deals. A party possesses additional bargaining power if it has the capacity to bestow benefits or inflict punishments on the other party in future negotiations, or in other interactions.

The lawyer also must consider how past relationships between the two negotiators affect the lawyer's ability to influence the other negotiator. If past dealings suggest to the other negotiator that a plaintiff's personal injury attorney fairly and accurately values her cases, and that she has the capability to represent her client effectively in the courtroom if the negotiation breaks down, then her prior reputation substantially increases her bargaining power.

The parties' alternatives to a negotiated settlement and their relative needs for an agreement remain the most important factors in determining their bargaining power. One aspect of the other party's need for an agreement warrants separate mention because the negotiator frequently can manipulate it. This factor is *time*. If Banana Computers and the Chestnut Development Corporation are negotiating in August rather than in February, Chestnut possesses additional leverage because Banana wants to reach an agreement quickly so that its retail outlet will be ready for the Holiday sales season, the busiest time of the year for retail computer outlets. If a criminal defendant is incarcerated pending trial because he cannot post bail, the passage of time creates an additional hardship on him. His attorney's bargaining power is comparatively weaker because the defendant is interested in *any deal* that would end his incarceration. Negotiators often seek to exploit time pressures on the other party, and even to create time pressures.

3. PREPARATION FOR COOPERATIVE TACTICS: OBJECTIVE STANDARDS

As previously discussed, the orientation of the negotiator using cooperative tactics is to reach a solution which is fair and just to both parties. Proponents of the cooperative strategy believe that negotiators are motivated not only to gain as much as possible for their clients, but also to reach a fair solution.[23] Arguments in the cooperative strategy are addressed to what is "fair and just," not to disparaging the other negotiator's alternatives to a negotiated agreement; accordingly, the cooperative negotiator frequently refers to objective criteria.

To prepare for making such arguments, the negotiator and her client should discuss which normal practices or other objective standards would be useful in resolving the dispute with the other party. For example, in the commercial lease negotiation between Chestnut and Banana, the rental rate being paid by comparable retail outlets in the shopping mall certainly is one measure of what is a fair and just rental figure. In the settlement discussions between Patrick Finney and the railroad, either side may try to locate similar cases that have settled or have been tried and argue that those cases establish an objective value for Patrick Finney's claims. Such criteria then form the basis for arguments on Patrick's behalf that a "fair and just" value of his claims is $1.1 million or whatever other figure is suggested by the outcomes of comparable cases.

These arguments are different than competitive ones; they do not try to persuade the other party that it would be better off settling for $1.1 million; rather, they assert that this is the fair and just, or objective, value for the claim. The use of objective criteria is one of the techniques recommended by Fisher and Ury as a part of their approach of principled negotiation.[24] They suggest, among others, objective criteria based upon market value, precedents, professional standards, established moral standards, tradition, equal treatment, principles of reciprocity, scientific judgment, and efficiency.

The ability to argue effectively using objective criteria depends upon prior preparation by the lawyer and the client. Most often the client knows more about market values, professional standards, scien-

23. *See* Bartos, *Simple Model of Negotiation: A Sociological Point of View* in The Negotiation Process; Theories and Applications 13 (I. Zartman Ed.1978); *see also* O. Bartos, Process and Outcome of Negotiations 44–47 (1974); D. Pruitt, *supra* note 3, at 91–135.

24. *See* R. Fisher & W. Ury, *supra* note 3, at 88–91.

tific judgments and costs than does the lawyer. In some instances, the lawyer and client may decide to use experts or other professionals in establishing criteria such as fair rental values or professional standards. Further, a professional economist could project the lifetime earnings of Patrick Finney and determine the present discounted value of this income stream. The argument constructed from this data is not "Look what we can prove to the court," but rather "This is a fair value for Patrick's lost income."

4. THE LAWYER'S AUTHORITY TO NEGOTIATE

During the pre-negotiation counseling session, the lawyer and client also should consider the lawyer's authority to enter into an agreement binding on the client. The type of authority a client delegates to his lawyer ranges from unlimited authority, which gives the lawyer *carte blanche* to enter into an agreement on behalf of a client, to "open authority," which authorizes the lawyer to negotiate, but does not give her any authority to enter into a binding agreement.

The type of the authority granted by the client affects both the negotiation process itself and the prospects for a client-centered counseling process. In simulated negotiations, social scientists have found that attorneys held strictly accountable to their clients, and given only *limited* authority, are likely to be vigorous and "tough" in their use of competitive tactics.[25] Attorneys given *unlimited* authority are less competitive. Surprisingly, attorneys with *unlimited* authority behave more competitively than those whose authority is *nominally* limited by the client.[26] In these cases, the clients authorize settlement within an extremely broad range that is readily obtainable, and the attorneys accordingly behave even less competitively than if the clients have given them unlimited authority. Apparently the broad authority explicitly granted by the clients relieves the attorneys, to some extent, of their sense of obligation to obtain the best deals possible for their clients. When the lawyer intends to engage in *problem-solving* bargaining, a grant of unlimited authority however, gives her greater flexibility to consider proposals from the other party and to invent solutions for the parties' problems.

Even though granting the lawyer broad authority facilitates *problem-solving* and *cooperative* negotiation tactics, a more restricted grant of authority also has distinct advantages both as a *competitive* negotiation tactic and as a means of facilitating client-centered advocacy. If the client grants his attorney only limited authority to enter into an agreement, the lawyer can tell the other lawyer that she does not have authority from her client to accept his proposal, without facing the

25. *See* D. Pruitt, *supra* note 3, at 42, 120–21, 196; Lamm, *Group–Related Influences on Negotiation Behavior: Two–Person Negotiation as a Function of Represen-* *tation and Election in Bargaining Behavior* 284, 297–302 (H. Sauermann ed. 1978).

26. *See* H. Raiffa, *supra* note 3, at 146.

question of whether a false denial of authority is ethical.[27] Denying that she has authority is an excellent means of justifying why a concession cannot be made or why a concession must be limited in amount.[28] Claim adjusters or attorneys representing insurance companies in personal injury negotiations sometimes use this technique. If insurance companies set their "reserves"[29] on cases sufficiently low, plaintiffs' demands can be met with statements such as "our reserve is only $45,000, I don't have authority to pay more."

Restricting the lawyer's authority to enter into an agreement binding on the client also aids client-centered advocacy because the client retains greater control over his attorney's conduct during the negotiation. A series of incrementally increasing grants of authority during the course of the negotiation guarantees regular attorney consultation with her client. Presumably, lawyers precede such requests for additional authority with reports on the current status of the negotiation, and thus keep the client better informed about the negotiations and more directly involved in them.

G. CONCLUSIONS

Nothing in this chapter should suggest to the beginning lawyer that a negotiation can be scripted in advance. The negotiator will not be able to plan intricately the exact content, timing and sequence of her concessions or other negotiating proposals, or the precise words to be used in her arguments. Negotiations are interactive events between at least two individuals, both of whom are trying to control the process and outcome. Any attempt to execute a detailed plan prepared in advance imposes a counterproductive straitjacket on the negotiator. This is not direct or cross-examination in the courtroom where the trial attorney controls the stage and frequently prepares his questions in advance. Nor is it client interviewing and counseling where the

27. Model Rule of Professional Conduct 4.1 prohibits a lawyer from knowingly making a false statement of material law or fact to a third party, including opposing counsel. Model Rules of Professional Conduct Rule 4.1 (1983). How should Gary Gerstein, representing Patrick Finney, respond when asked by counsel for the railroad whether $975,000 will settle the case when in fact he knows that his client's *minimum disposition* is only $950,000? If Gary answers "no," he violates the literal language of Rule 4.1. On the other hand, if he answers "yes," the negotiation concludes immediately and his client loses the chance to obtain an even larger settlement. Finally, if Gary avoids answering or even hesitates in answering, perceptive opposing counsel realizes that he has authority to accept the $975,000 offer. *See* White, *Machiavelli and the Bar: Ethical Limitations on Lying in Negotiation,* 1980 Am B.

Found. Research J. 926, 932–35 (1980); Guernsey, *Truthfulness in Negotiation,* 17 U.Rich.L.R. 99 (1982). Addressing this dilemma, the Comment to Rule 4.1 provides that "[u]nder generally accepted conventions in negotiation, certain types of statements ordinarily are not taken as statements of material fact." Model Rules of Professional Conduct Rule 4.1 comment (1983).

28. Recognizing this, many judges now require that attorneys come to pre-trials either with full authority to settle, or accompanied by the client or a client representative with settlement authority.

29. A reserve is the amount an insurance company sets aside, after receiving notice of an actual or potential claim, to pay the eventual settlement or judgment. 4 J. Kelner, Personal Injury: Successful Litigation Techniques 1453, 1469 (1978).

effective lawyer generally guides the interview through an established structure,[30] even if she does not control the content.

General approaches to negotiation, potential proposals, opening demands or offers, concessions and other negotiating tactics, however, should be thought about in advance. Whether the negotiator actually uses a specific tactic, and the timing of its use, are dependent upon the other negotiator's behavior and the flow of the negotiation process. This is not a new idea for a law student. Preparing for negotiation is like preparing for law school examinations. Students do not prepare the exact answers to exam questions in advance. Instead, they learn about rules, doctrines and policies and a process for analyzing legal problems. When they confront the first exam question they are better "prepared" than they would have been without preparation. No one familiar with law school examinations would suggest that preparation is unimportant merely because answers to exam questions cannot be written and memorized in advance. So it is with negotiation planning.

30. *See* D. Binder & S. Price, *supra* note 8, at 53–59.

Chapter Five

THE RELATIONSHIP BETWEEN THE NEGOTIATORS: INITIAL ORIENTATION

A. BEGINNING NEGOTIATION: AN OVERVIEW

The primary goal of negotiation is to have the other party agree to a resolution that satisfies the client's interests; therefore, the attorney's relationship with the other negotiator is crucial. Chapter Two uses the attorney's goals in establishing relationships with the other negotiator as a criterion for classifying negotiation strategies and tactics. To review briefly, the *competitive* strategy is defined as a group of negotiating behaviors designed to undermine the other negotiator's confidence in his bargaining position and to induce him to enter into an agreement less advantageous to his client than he would have prior to the negotiation. The negotiator using the *cooperative* strategy seeks an agreement which is fair and just to both parties and hopes to develop a relationship with the other party that is characterized by good will and trust. Finally, the negotiator using the *problem-solving* strategy develops a relationship with the other bargainer that permits them to search together for solutions to their clients' mutual "problems."

First impressions are as important in negotiation as they are elsewhere in life. Negotiations vary widely, making a specific description of the "first phase" impossible. What is clear, however, is that the "first phase" sets the initial tone, or relational ambience, between the parties.

The early phases of negotiation typically include one or more of the following activities:

(1) exchange of initial proposals;

(2) information gathering and disclosure; and

(3) tactics explicitly designed to affect the relationship between the parties instead of the substance of the negotiation.

For example, in personal injury negotiations such as Patrick Finney's claims against the Baltimore and Western Railroad, the bargaining often begins with an initial proposal, in the form of a demand letter from the plaintiff's lawyer to the insurance company adjuster or the defendant. This letter includes a specific demand figure calculated to establish both the bargaining range and the initial tone of the relationship between the parties. In addition, the demand letter is accompanied by documentation and arguments—sometimes even a "settlement brochure" presenting the plaintiff's liability and damage claims in a perspective most appealing to a jury.

In other negotiations, such as Banana Computer's lease negotiation with the Chestnut Mall, the bargaining begins only with an extremely broad initial proposal: "We want to lease retail space from you." In all probability, neither party presents an initial proposal as to the price and other terms of the lease until after the parties have shared information and bargained for some period of time. Prior to these initial proposals, both parties disclose certain information about their client's needs and expectations and attempt to gather information about the other party's situation. In other words, information disclosure and gathering precede the exchange of opening proposals.

Regardless of the order in which they occur, *initial proposals* and *information exchange* are important interactions in all negotiations. Both processes occur in a wide variety of forms and contexts, and each activity is the subject of a chapter of this book. It is important to remember, however, that in any particular negotiation, the sequence of these activities may differ from the sequence in which these behaviors are analyzed in this book.

From the beginning of the negotiation, particularly when important issues are at stake, skilled negotiators also focus specifically on the relationship between the negotiators. This chapter considers the tactics employed for this purpose. These tactics are loosely grouped in this chapter according to whether they are a subset of negotiation tactics from the competitive strategy, the cooperative strategy or the problem-solving strategy. Many of the same orientation issues arise, however, regardless of what strategy is used. Therefore, even though the issues of "Agenda" and "Physical Arrangements at the Negotiation Site" are discussed under the heading of "Competitive Orientation Tactics," the manner in which these issues are handled by negotiators using the cooperative or the problem-solving strategies are considered in these initial discussions. Similarly, the discussion of "Cooperation Inhibitors" and "Cooperation Facilitators" describes tactics which play important roles in the problem-solving strategy as well as in the cooperative strategy.

B. COMPETITIVE ORIENTATION TACTICS

Every contact between two negotiating attorneys is part of the negotiation process, because each passing comment, letter or telephone call—no matter how seemingly innocuous—affects the relationship between them and the ultimate resolution of the dispute. Indeed, the current negotiation must be considered in light of the prior professional and social contacts between the two negotiators that obviously affect their present relationship.

Because the underlying psychological relationship between the negotiators is a critical variable in negotiation, the effective negotiator must be aware of psychological factors and seek to influence them to achieve her client's objectives. For example, the negotiator planning a problem-solving or cooperative negotiation strategy works from the beginning to build the rapport that will facilitate a collaborative negotiation process.

For the negotiator employing the competitive strategy, the goal, simply stated, is the pervasive projection of power [1] through means that are as subtle as possible. How can the other party be made to feel uncomfortable about the prospects of disagreeing with the negotiator? How can the negotiator seize a psychologically dominant position? Subsequent chapters discuss competitive negotiation tactics such as extreme opening demands, threats and arguments. A dominating personality, enabling the negotiator to be the focus of attention whenever she enters a room, is certainly a big advantage, but unfortunately, one that cannot be learned through reading this text. This section describes a variety of competitive tactics designed to achieve a "psychological edge" in negotiation that can be learned.

1. AGENDA CONTROL

Because every interaction between negotiating parties is a part of the ongoing negotiation process affecting subsequent phases of the negotiation, the *agenda* for the negotiation session, or the order in which the issues are considered, often has important implications. In most instances, parties do not explicitly bargain over the negotiation agenda. Nevertheless, when Roberta Martinez, the railroad's attorney, asks Gary Gerstein, Patrick Finney's attorney, "How much is it going to take to settle this case?," she begins to define the negotiation agenda by indicating her desire to negotiate the amount of the claim before considering such peripheral issues as whether or not the payment is to be made in a lump sum or through a structured settlement. In more complex negotiations, such as those involving international diplomacy, labor relations or corporate mergers and acquisitions, the negotiation agenda sometimes is explicitly negotiated.

The order of issues to be negotiated, whether decided through explicit bargaining or more subtle suggestions, often affects the negotiation. The negotiator employing a competitive strategy sees the ability to control the agenda as an initial indication of the bargaining power of

---

1. In her attempts to dominate her opponent, and wrest from him a more favorable outcome for her client, the competitive negotiator has goals similar to those of a nation at war. *See generally* C. Clausewitz, On War (Princton University Press ed. 1976).

each negotiator. Both the selection of issues chosen by the negotiator for initial consideration and the other negotiator's reactions to a proposed agenda for proceeding indicate much about their respective priorities and values. For example, suppose Bev Bailey, representing Banana Computers, begins her bargaining with Dan Darrow by discussing which vacant store space Banana wants to lease. By stressing location, she sends a strong message to Dan that this issue is an important one for Banana.

A negotiator can achieve far greater control of an agenda by presenting the other party with an initial draft agreement or written offer. The natural tendency is for negotiators to work from the draft and to consider the issues in the order they are presented. Any party who wishes to depart from this sequence assumes a subtle psychological burden to justify a different sequence.

Agendas frequently change or are modified during the course of a negotiation. Three basic agenda strategies, however, are possible in multiple issue negotiations: (1) considering the least contentious issues first; (2) considering the most important issues first; or (3) simultaneously considering multiple issues.

a. Considering the Least Contentious Issues First

Why does a negotiator sometimes want to negotiate first on the least contentious issues? Dealing with the easiest issues first helps to build rapport between the negotiating parties because they jointly experience bargaining success.[2] This cooperative working relationship can then facilitate resolution of more difficult issues. Addressing the least contentious issues first also prevents a premature breakdown of the negotiation during the earliest phases when the parties might engage in substantial competitive posturing.

How can a negotiator identify in advance which issues are likely to be least contentious? Such issues are ones where the differences between the parties as revealed through prior communications are relatively small, where the issues are relatively unimportant, or where the issues do not include substantial emotional or symbolic implications. Often, however, it is not possible to identify which issues can be easily resolved before some initial bargaining on the entire range of issues.

b. Considering the Most Important Issues First

The second approach to agenda control is to address the one or two most important issues first. The expectation here is that once the negotiators reach agreement on the major issues in dispute, they will resolve the minor issues quickly. Presumably the parties will have established an accommodative working arrangement and will not want

2. *See* P. Gulliver, Disputes and Negotiations: A Cross–Cultural Perspective 145–47 (1979); J. Rubin & B. Brown, The Social   Psychology of Bargaining and Negotiation 148 (1975).

to jeopardize the agreement on the major issues. The risk, of course, is a greater possibility of a deadlock if major contentious issues are considered first. Also, animosity resulting from contentious bargaining over the major issue may overflow into negotiation on less important issues.

Addressing the most important issues first probably is good practice in transactional negotiations in which the parties are trying to create a relationship where none existed before. In these cases, the parties perceive that it may not be worth-while negotiating over the details if agreement cannot be achieved on the major points. Further, it is often easier for parties to reach agreement initially on the major point in a transactional negotiation than it is in a litigation context where resolution of the major issue typically requires a party to admit "fault."

c. *Simultaneous Consideration of Multiple Issues*

The third option is to consider multiple issues simultaneously. In the abstract, such a suggestion may seem unwieldy. Yet, many agreements are reached because the parties engage in "logrolling" or trade concessions on different issues on which they have differing priorities. Chestnut Development Corporation may be most interested in protecting itself against dramatically increased labor and insurance costs if Banana locks in a low base rent; Banana may be most concerned with the location of its store. If Banana agrees to a clause obligating it to pay a portion of increased labor and insurance costs in excess of a specified threshold, Chestnut will agree to give Banana a location near the center court of the mall with high visibility and customer traffic. Logrolling on these issues thus requires simultaneous consideration of increased expenses and the location of the store.

Considering multiple issues together exponentially expands the number of combinations of proposals which may be available to address the issues. As such, this sequence facilitates the problem-solving approach to negotiation. If issues are considered together, a party may propose a "package deal" designed to resolve a number of issues. The other party may respond either by modifying some elements of the package or by proposing his own package deal.

Even when negotiators consider a single issue at a time, they often agree that final agreement on that issue is contingent upon agreement on all issues. Unless this is made explicit, issue reconsideration may be seen as a breach of an often-observed negotiation norm of not reopening an issue once it is decided. "Tying-in" resolution of the issue being considered with agreement on other issues can be used as both a competitive tactic and a problem-solving tactic. As a competitive tactic, it serves notice that everything remains up for grabs until final agreement, thus creating additional pressure on the other side to concede on other issues. As a problem-solving technique, it preserves the maximum flexibility of the parties to go back and engage in logrolling later in the negotiation.

2. NEGOTIATION SITE

Negotiation folklore uniformly holds that the negotiator who operates on "her own turf" is at an advantage in the negotiation. Indeed, empirical research confirms that the negotiator who bargains on her own territory is likely to increase both her assertiveness and the chances of a favorable negotiation outcome.[3] Diplomats appear to respect this claim and frequently negotiate at a site in a neutral third country, such as Geneva, Vienna or Helsinki. In sports competition, few doubt the existence of a "home-field advantage."

The presence of an advantage for the negotiator who bargains on her own turf makes sense, especially if viewed from the perspective of competitive negotiation tactics. Because the competitive negotiator seeks to undermine the other party's confidence in his judgments about the bargaining situation, anything which produces doubt or psychological discomfort in the other negotiator is an advantage. Most people are more comfortable and less likely to lose confidence in themselves in familiar surroundings; they are more naturally assertive as host than as visitor. The attorney from a small firm in a rural area may be more comfortable and assertive negotiating the sale of a small company to a larger national corporation if the talks are held in her office than she would be on the ninety-fourth floor of the World Trade Center, particularly if her equilibrium has been upset substantially by New York City hotel prices. Similarly, in the late 1960's and 1970's, legal services attorneys sometimes attempted to arrange negotiations with attorneys from large firms and banks at offices in low income neighborhoods, expecting that these unfamiliar surroundings would make the other lawyer uneasy.

Scheduling negotiations at one's own office also has a variety of tangible advantages. Secretarial and other support personnel are available to assist if needed. More control may be asserted over factors such as interruptions and seating arrangements.

On the other hand, there are definite tangible benefits to negotiating at the other attorney's office. Most importantly, at his own office the other negotiator has greater access to his complete files, including such things as witness statements. Thus, it is difficult for him to refuse access to such files. Conversely, the visiting attorney does not have immediate access to information or statements. Further, on rare occasion, a negotiating attorney may want to terminate a negotiation abruptly by walking out; it is difficult for her to walk out of her own office.

3. J. Rubin & B. Brown, *supra* note 2, at 82–88; Martindale, *Territorial Dominance Behavior in Dyadic Verbal Interac-* *tions,* 6 Proceedings of The 79th Annual Convention of The American Psychological Association 305–306 (1971).

Ultimately, the "home-turf" advantage means only as much in a negotiation as the visiting attorney allows it to mean. The important thing is for the visiting attorney not to let unfamiliar surroundings create discomfort which then affects her negotiating behavior. Awareness of this possibility, and the concomitant ability to guard against it, usually is all that is required to neutralize any advantage. The disadvantage of negotiating at someone else's office is probably greater for the novice attorney who feels somewhat insecure about the negotiation process, the prospect of facing more experienced counsel, her new professional persona as an attorney, or the novelty of the type of case. Experienced attorneys who are more professionally secure generally are less affected when negotiating at the other attorney's office.

Awareness of the advantages of negotiating on one's own territory should not lead the lawyer to overemphasize the issue of negotiation location. It is difficult to imagine, for example, a situation in which a routine legal negotiation should break down over the site of the negotiation. If the negotiators feel strongly about this issue, the bargaining can be conducted in a neutral location such as a restaurant or courthouse conference room which gives neither side a psychological advantage.

If the lawyer negotiates at the other attorney's office and senses psychological disadvantage, what can she do about it? A simple rule of thumb would be that the negotiator should not concede anything to the other party when extraneous factors are making her uncomfortable. Also, "gimmicks," silly on their face, are not silly if they help a negotiator regain a sense of self-confidence and control over the client's case. Visitors might regain a sense of control in an alien environment by asking the host not to smoke, by asking his secretary to copy some documents, or by making some telephone calls on other "urgent cases." Analogously, trial practice manuals have suggested that key witnesses become familiar with the courtroom prior to their testimony so that they are not as uncomfortable. However, these psychological artifices backfire if they are apparent to the other party. The novice attorney viewed by the host attorney as a rookie compensating for a self-recognized insecurity or engaging in a crude power-ploy will not find herself in a stronger, more confident position.

Many negotiations, of course, do not occur in a single session scheduled in advance. Negotiation proposals are often traded during telephone calls or in courthouse halls following a deposition on an entirely different case. It is as important for the negotiator to feel comfortable operating under these often hurried and chaotic conditions, as it is for her to feel comfortable negotiating in someone else's office.

3. PHYSICAL ARRANGEMENTS AT THE NEGOTIATION SITE

Physical arrangements at the negotiation site may have subtle psychological effects on the negotiators, but the extent of these effects should not be overestimated. During the Vietnam peace negotiations, the shape of the table around which the negotiators were to sit was debated at length. In the barbershop scenes of Charlie Chaplin's classic film, *The Great Dictator,* Hitler and Mussolini each consecutively raise his barber's chair to a level higher than the other's in order to gain a perceived power advantage. Physical arrangements can prove discomforting when, for example, during a job interview with a prestigious law firm, a prospective new attorney is asked to sit in a soft, low chair facing a senior partner who is seated behind an immense walnut desk in an eight foot, high-backed, leather chair.

Research does suggest some helpful conclusions about physical arrangements and their effects on negotiations.[4] Accommodative interpersonal relationships, such as those needed for *cooperative* and *problem-solving* bargaining, are facilitated if the negotiators sit at adjoining sides of a rectangular or square table or on the same side of a circular table. This configuration allows them sufficient physical proximity to maintain verbal communication, while engaging in as little or as much eye contact as is comfortable. Conversely, the preferred configuration for competitive relationships, according to social scientists, is face-to-face, such as on opposite sides of a desk or table.

4. TIMING OF NEGOTIATIONS

Patience is power in negotiation. The competitive negotiator is aware that most serious bargaining is accomplished as deadlines approach. Personal injury cases frequently settle, figuratively and even literally, on the courthouse steps. Labor contracts sometimes are reached either immediately before or right after a strike begins. In bargaining in which competitive tactics predominate, the most serious concessions occur at or near a deadline, because each side expects that if it waits as long as possible, the other party will say "chicken."

These realities have implications both for those who intend to use competitive tactics and for those who negotiate against someone using these tactics. Let's first consider the defensive implications. In many contexts, serious negotiation will not occur until the last possible moment; all offers and proposals prior to that time probably do not represent the best possible deal for the lawyer's client. In one personal injury case in which the author was involved, for the first two years after the filing of the case, the defendant's attorney offered only to settle "for court costs" despite a settlement conference in which the trial judge strongly encouraged both parties to settle. Then, within one week of the scheduled trial date, the defendant's attorney started to ask questions such as "What would it take to settle this case?" and offered $200,000. The case ultimately settled. Patience pays.

In addition to time deadlines set by others, negotiators should be aware of their own abilities to set time deadlines within a case in order

4. J. Rubin & B. Brown, *supra* Note 2, at 88–91.

to induce settlement. For example, Banana Computers might schedule a meeting with the owner of another potential site for its store, and let Chestnut Development Corporation know the date of the scheduled meeting. As that date approaches, Chestnut will probably feel pressure to make a realistic proposal so that Banana will not sign a lease with the other potential landlord or become emotionally committed to an agreement with the competitor.

Even deadlines that are internal to the negotiation or that affect only the attorney and not his client may produce pressure to concede. If an attorney from Memphis is visiting New York and is leaving on an evening flight, she probably feels pressure to concede and reach an agreement—or at least to achieve progress—before she leaves the city. Certain days of the year, such as the day before a two week vacation starts, or December 31, may create a sense in some negotiators that matters should be settled. Awareness of the capacity of time deadlines to create psychological pressure to make concessions may mitigate the effect of such pressure, because a negotiator can guard against an unwarranted rush to reach agreement.

A lawyer need not be a true believer in the science of biorhythms to acknowledge that most people have times when they are psychologically and physically at their best and times when they are not. If a negotiator is a "morning person" and frequently is sluggish after lunch, it probably makes sense for her to schedule important negotiations at a time when she feels confident, poised, gregarious and in control of the world. If a lawyer begins work reluctantly at nine o'clock every morning, she probably is ill-advised to schedule an important meeting on Monday morning with an attorney who she knows begins work each morning at seven a.m. Such factors are subtle, and many times, imperceptible, but why allow them to influence the outcome of the negotiation?

5. NUMBER OF NEGOTIATORS

Because the psychology of bargaining power is sometimes primitive in nature, multiple negotiators for one party may sense a psychological advantage if they "outnumber" the other side. When a lone attorney finds herself negotiating with six representatives of a corporation, her psychological sense of being overwhelmed numerically may be very real.

Aside from pure intimidation value, multiple negotiators often dominate a discussion by participating more as a unit than as lone negotiators. Dividing negotiation responsibility among associates may prevent them from tiring, thus reducing the risk of ill-advised concessions influenced by fatigue. Further, additional negotiators can carefully observe the verbal and nonverbal cues of the other side's lawyer while their partner is actively interacting. On the other hand, often there are advantages to being outnumbered by the other side. A skilled negotiator may be able to read the non-verbal reactions of one of the several less experienced negotiators representing the other party.[5] One of the other side's "negotiating committee" sometimes reveals information or makes a concession that the principal negotiator would not have if she was negotiating alone.

6. PRESENCE OF THE CLIENT

Most negotiations occur between two lawyers without the presence of the client. The theory behind the competitive negotiation strategy offers several justifications for the client's absence in most cases. Unless the client is a skilled and experienced negotiator in his own right, and the client and attorney have discussed their negotiation strategy extensively, a lawyer's plan to negotiate competitively in the presence of her client is likely to be a risky venture. The client's verbal and non-verbal reactions to the other party's proposals and questions will probably be unguarded and may allow the other side to accurately gauge the client's minimum disposition. Many clients are unlikely to recognize when the other negotiator is "bluffing" and will lose confidence in their own case evaluations too quickly. Furthermore, many clients are obstreperous and are unable to participate personally in the process of identifying potential solutions and compromises. The "give and take" that lawyers typically engage in as a part of negotiation sometimes appears to the client to be acts of disloyalty. In short, one of the advantages of negotiation by representatives is that attorneys are less likely to be emotionally involved with the issues and less susceptible to being influenced by the fears, anxieties and angers that clients typically experience as part of the negotiation process.

There are exceptions to the general rule that clients should not participate directly in the negotiation process. The presence of the client during all or part of the bargaining can serve either competitive or problem-solving goals. For example, in a sex discrimination action or in a housing code violation class action, a committed plaintiff—more than an attorney—can sometimes convince the defendant's counsel that litigation will be pursued unless justice is done. Direct client involvement in negotiation often is an important aspect of problem-solving negotiation techniques because clients are more readily able to identify their respective underlying interests.

7. BARGAINING WITH CREDENTIALS

Within a bargaining relationship, the perception of power depends not only upon the merits of the matter being negotiated, but also upon the aura of power generated by the negotiator. The novice attorney often feels somewhat uncomfortable when negotiating with a seasoned veteran. A lawyer from a two-person practice often approaches the city's most prestigious law firm with some trepidation. Occasionally

---

5. *See infra* Chapter Seven, *Information Bargaining,* at 127–32, for discussion of interpreting non-verbal communications.

such discomfort is heightened by the other party's surroundings, office furnishings and dress which all exude professional and material success. The *coup-de-grace* is complete when the young negotiator observes the carefully framed letter from the Chief Justice of the United States thanking the other lawyer for helping him out of a dire personal crisis.

Once again, these perceptions of power and influence matter only if the negotiator allows them to matter. President Franklin D. Roosevelt's words, "The only thing we have to fear is fear itself," apply perfectly to these circumstances. As the lawyer matures, she becomes more secure with her own professional identity and realizes that her own clients are not at a disadvantage. For the novice attorney, preparation is the most important ingredient in negotiation. Preparation goes a long way toward compensating for a lack of experience and can be more important than the other negotiator's reputation or ability to intimidate.

Delaying serious negotiation until the attorney overcomes any discomfort generated by the negotiation site or the credentials of the other negotiator minimizes the potential psychological disadvantage. Sometimes preliminary small talk offers opportunities for the beginning attorney to discuss her own past relevant professional and educational experiences in ways that may help neutralize any psychological disadvantage. Any aggressive attempt to strut one's own qualifications, however, will probably be seen by the other negotiator as a sign of insecurity and have exactly the opposite effect of what was intended.

C. COOPERATIVE ORIENTATION TACTICS

Inherent in most negotiations are conflicting needs for the negotiators to cooperate and to compete. On one hand, the negotiator's need for something that the other party can provide is what brought her to the negotiation table, and cooperation is necessary in order to achieve this goal. On the other hand, in most cases the parties compete, at least to some extent, to determine how satisfied each will be with the eventual agreement.

The competitive element in most negotiations often leads to a counterproductive emotional cycle. The recognition by the negotiator that she needs or desires something from the other party, coupled with the realization that the parties' needs conflict, can be fear-producing. When the other party does not view the situation in exactly the same way, the negotiator may unintentionally display anger. The negotiator's anger often exacerbates the opponent's level of fear and produces a cycle of recurring reciprocal anger and fear. This cycle may obscure opportunities for mutual gains and for compromises which both parties otherwise would view as fair and just.

Negotiators using either the cooperative or the problem-solving negotiation strategies seek to emphasize the benefits of cooperation.

Sometimes past experiences with the other negotiator, or other factors, suggest that cooperation with him, and trust in him, are likely to be reciprocated. Many times this will not occur until a negotiation has progressed through initial competitive stages. What techniques can the negotiator use specifically to facilitate a trusting relationship between herself and the other negotiator?

Many law students analyze factors inhibiting rapport and techniques used to develop a trusting relationship when they learn to establish rapport with the client in the interviewing and counseling process.[6] Certainly the relationship between negotiating attorneys differs significantly from the relationship between attorney and client, but many of the same rapport-building techniques are useful in both situations.

1. COOPERATION INHIBITORS

The goal of the negotiator who wants to use cooperative tactics is reciprocation of cooperative negotiation behaviors by the other negotiator so that together they can reach a fair and just agreement without a contentious negotiation process. What factors, then, inhibit the other negotiator from cooperating?

a. *Opportunity Costs (Greed)*

The other negotiator may be reluctant to use a cooperative negotiation strategy, thinking he can achieve a better deal for his client by using competitive tactics, particularly if there is a possibility of exploiting his counterpart's trust. As discussed previously, if a competitive negotiator is bargaining with a negotiator who persists in cooperative behavior, the competitive negotiator may be able to exploit the cooperative negotiator's trust and achieve an agreement which is disproportionately favorable to his client. When faced with an opponent using cooperative negotiation behaviors, the competitive negotiator interprets concessions as signs of weakness and grants fewer concessions. There is no reason for the competitive negotiator to use cooperative negotiation tactics if he does not value his relationship with his opponent and if the opponent allows himself to be exploited.

b. *Case Threat*

If a negotiator decides it is to her client's advantage to use a cooperative negotiation strategy, the biggest factor inhibiting her use of cooperative tactics is the possibility her own cooperation will not be reciprocated, but will be exploited by the other party. If the negotiator concedes and her opponent does not reciprocate, the parties are no

---

6. *See* D. Binder & S. Price, Legal Interviewing and Counseling: A Client–Centered Approach 8–18 (1977). I am indebted to David Binder and Susan Price for the framework of analysis presented below. In the context of legal interviewing they categorize the client's motivations into "inhibitors" and "facilitators." Here, I present a somewhat different set of motivation factors for the other attorney in negotiation, but retain the analytical framework used by Binder and Price.

closer to an agreement, and the negotiator loses bargaining power. If the negotiator shares information with the other party, this information might be used to determine her weaknesses rather than to find an agreement that is fair and just to both parties. When the negotiator believes cooperative bargaining behavior will harm her case, this can be referred to as "case threat."

c. Ego Threat

The negotiator may be reluctant to cooperate because she fears her opponent will see her as a "weak" or ineffectual negotiator. The potential role of *ego threat* in negotiation is best illustrated by an exercise the author uses in his negotiation course.[7] After completion of the initial distributive negotiation exercise, the two students achieving the best results for their clients are told that they are to participate in a "play-off" to determine who is the "most effective" negotiator in the class. The students are asked to "bid" a sum to be paid for a single dollar bill held by the instructor. The students must alternate bids, but they may elect to "pass." The student bidding the highest amount receives the dollar bill, but both students must pay the author the amount of their last bid. Each subsequent bid must exceed the previous bid by 10 cents or a multiple of 10 cents.

Typically, the bidding begins between 10 cents and 50 cents. Sooner or later, the bidding reaches 90 cents. Faced with the reality that she is going to have to pay her last bid (usually 80 cents) anyway, the student rationally decides to pay $1.00 for a one dollar bill. The interesting part is what happens next. The bidding continues * * * $1.10, $1.20, $1.30, $1.40 and so forth. At some point, the two students realize that they should have reached an agreement between themselves to stop the bidding at 40 cents, so that both could have paid the piper and still experienced a modest profit. By now, however, in front of their classmates, the students' egos and competitive instincts have become involved. On one occasion, the ultimate bid exceeded $6.00; in another, the bidding passed $4.00. Ego involvement obscures the benefits to be achieved from cooperative behavior.

d. Professional Role Expectations

Closely related to the *ego threat* factor is the negotiator's perception of her role as a negotiating attorney, and how her negotiating behavior will be interpreted by other attorneys. Because the legal profession is in reality an adversarial one, and because the public perception of the profession exaggerates that adversarial image, role expectations sometimes inhibit cooperative behavior. Thus, an attorney considering a cooperative or problem-solving approach to a negotiation may confront the expectation that "real attorneys are tough negotiators and do not cooperate." Professional role expectations are particularly powerful inhibitors of cooperative behavior for new or

7. *See* H. Raiffa, The Art and Science of Negotiation 85–87 (1982).

insecure attorneys who fear they are not representing their clients' interests vigorously enough. Women practicing in a field traditionally dominated by men may have similar concerns about cooperative negotiation behavior.

e. Client Expectations

Lawyers as negotiators represent the interests of clients. In terms of effective professional service and good business relations, lawyers need to respect the expectations of their clients in the negotiations process. Most often, clients approach negotiation in a more adversarial manner than attorneys, and client expectations therefore may inhibit the lawyer-negotiator from negotiating cooperatively.[8] Visibly competitive tactics may convince a client who is not inclined to trust his attorney that his attorney is representing his interests and is not "selling out" to the opponent.

f. Personality Conflicts

Even though negotiation behaviors can be analyzed, negotiators are not robots. Instead, negotiations are intensely human interactions heavily influenced by the personalities of the negotiators. Personality conflicts, or other emotional reactions between the negotiating attorneys, often inhibit negotiation. It is difficult to work cooperatively with someone you consider a "jerk." Other emotional reactions of the negotiator toward her counterpart can also discourage cooperative behaviors. Research demonstates that negotiators who exhibit personality traits such as authoritarianism,[9] high self-esteem,[10] risk aversion,[11] and strong internal control are less likely to choose a cooperative negotiation approach.

Conscious and unconscious emotional reactions toward the other negotiator sometimes make cooperation more difficult. These reactions include the negotiator's responses to the other negotiator's bargaining behavior as well as the negotiator's distorted perceptions arising from subconscious association of the other negotiator with significant figures in her life. Psychiatrists refer to this collection of feelings as transference.[12] For example, if the lawyer negotiates with an older male with behavior or personality characteristics similar to her father, it is

---

8. *See* R. Walton & R. McKersie, a Behavioral Theory of Labor Negotiations 417–19 (1965).

9. *See* Berkowitz, *Alternative Measures of Authoritarianism, Response Sets, and Prediction in a Two–Person Game,* 74 J. Soc. Psychology 233 (1968); Deutsch, *Trust, Trustworthiness and the F Scale,* 61 J. Abnormal & Soc. Psychology 138 (1960); Haythorn, Couch, Haefner, Langham & Carter, *The Behavior of Authoritarian and Equalitarian Personalities in Groups,* 9 Hum.Rel 57 (1956); Wrightsman, *Personality and Attitudinal Correlates of Trusting and Trustworthy Behaviors in a Two–Person*

Game, 4 J. Personality & Soc. Psychology 328 (1966).

10. *See* C. Karass, The Negotiating Game 87–88 (1970). *But see* R. Walton & R. McKersie, *supra* note 8, 194–95.

11. Harnet, Cummings, & Hamner, *Personality, Bargaining Style and Payoff in Bilateral Monopoly Bargaining Among European Managers,* 36 Sociometry 340 (1973).

12. *E.g.,* A. Watson, The Lawyer in the Interviewing and Counseling Process 21–23, 75–92 (1976).

possible that the older male negotiator will invoke in her some of the same emotional reactions previously induced by her father. The response to a strongly competitive opponent in this case might include either an unconscious excessive desire to please him and to concede, or an urge to rebel. Either response could be counterproductive to the establishment of a trusting cooperative negotiation relationship.

g. Negotiation–Generated Emotions

Negotiations frequently are rife with conflict and strong emotions. As previously discussed, fear often is inherent in negotiation; fear leads to anger, and a cycle of fear and anger result. Perhaps a majority of all negotiations produces stages where one party does not believe that her counterpart is bargaining in good faith or seeking a fair and just agreement. Such anger and mistrust obviously inhibit cooperation.

2. COOPERATION FACILITATORS

The factors described above make it difficult for the negotiators to achieve the accommodative working relationships necessary to use successfully either the cooperative or the problem-solving approaches to negotiation. What techniques can be used by the negotiator to mitigate the effects of these cooperation inhibitors and to achieve the necessary rapport between negotiators? [13]

a. Answering Competitive Tactics

If the other lawyer begins with the goal of exploiting the negotiator's naivete by using competitive negotiation behaviors, then the negotiator who wants to use a cooperative or problem-solving approach must first demonstrate to the other lawyer that his competitive tactics will not succeed. Truly productive and fruitful cooperative and problem-solving negotiations often result only when the other negotiator believes that he cannot "win" by using competitive tactics.[14] Frequently negotiations initially progress through competitive stages before the parties turn to more productive cooperative or problem-solving approaches.

b. Initiating Trusting Behaviors

If both parties begin a negotiation mistrusting each other, the cycle of mistrust and competitive bargaining behavior needs to be broken if the parties are to engage in cooperative or problem-solving bargaining. The most significant way a negotiator can establish trust and encourage cooperative negotiation by the other negotiator is to begin with cooperative tactics, such as reasonable opening offers or demands, concessions or information-sharing. Such behavior can be a gamble. The other negotiator may be dedicated to a competitive negotiation

13. *See* D. Binder & S. Price, *supra* note 6, at 14, 18. Several of these "cooperation facilitators" are adapted from Binder and Price's analysis of "rapport facilitators" in the context of client interviewing and counseling.

14. *See* D. Pruitt, Negotiation Behavior 37, 113–114 (1981).

strategy. If so, he sees the reasonable opening offer or the concession as a sign of weakness. He does not respond in kind, instead he becomes increasingly convinced that his toughness is working. If the cooperative negotiator shares information with the other negotiator hoping that he will use it to the mutual advantage of the parties, he may instead use it to determine the negotiator's points of vulnerability.

For these reasons, the cooperative negotiator must not "give away the store" in the opening moves of the negotiation. If Gary Gerstein, the attorney representing Patrick Finney, believes that a fair and just settlement value of Patrick's claims against the railroad is $950,000, it probably is unwise to begin initially with a settlement demand of $995,000 unless he has already developed a trusting bargaining relationship with the other attorney. Trusting negotiation behaviors can be initiated on smaller issues where the risk is not so great if the other negotiator exploits reasonableness instead of reciprocating it. In some cases, a negotiator is able to phrase cooperative negotiation behavior in ways that clearly indicate that such proposals are contingent upon their being reciprocated.

The advice in this subsection is unavoidably inconsistent with that in previous paragraphs. On one hand, the negotiator is told to initiate trusting behaviors. On the other hand, it is suggested that competitive tactics be answered with competitive tactics. If the negotiator cooperates, he is vulnerable to exploitation; if the negotiator does not initiate cooperative negotiation behaviors, the cycle of mistrust and competitive behavior remains intact.

This section simply restates the central issue in all negotiations: when should the negotiator trust and cooperate and when should she act competitively? The answer to this question, like so many others, is really the product of a cost-benefit analysis in each negotiation. What does one risk for her client if the other party does not respond cooperatively to a cooperative negotiation behavior? Will a reasonable offer or concession at this point in the negotiation move the parties out of the distrust-competitive cycle into a situation where both parties are working in good faith to reach an agreement satisfactory to both parties?

The answers to these questions turn upon a wide variety of contextual factors, largely surveyed in Chapter Three, *Choosing Effective Negotiation Tactics*. What does the negotiator know about the other negotiator's negotiation behavior or personality? Are there signs in the negotiation that the parties are ready to cooperate? Are the risks of misplaced confidence in the other negotiator manageable ones that will not seriously impair the client's interests? The negotiator's judgments about these issues, albeit imprecise and often risky ones, are the best guidance available on the question of whether to cooperate or to compete.

c. *Explicit Discussion of the Benefits of Cooperation*

Because in fact, lawyers do negotiate over the kind of negotiation process they are going to use, often it is appropriate to explicitly discuss the benefits of a cooperative or problem-solving negotiation strategy. However, this may be disadvantageous because of the tendency to sound either naive or "preachy" when the lawyer talks about the benefits of negotiating in some way other than a pure competitive strategy. The discussion should be as specific and subtle as possible, and should focus on the lawyer's own negotiation preferences, not on how the other negotiator "should" negotiate.

The negotiator who wishes to discuss the process with her counterpart directly can make two kinds of appeals to him. First, she can suggest that any cooperative moves from the other party will be reciprocated by her. Gary Gerstein might suggest to Roberta Martinez that if the railroad makes a reasonable first offer, he will follow with a sizable concession designed to bring the parties quickly into a narrow bargaining range and avoid the expense of protracted negotiation or litigation. Second, the negotiator can explicitly discuss the advantages of cooperative or problem-solving bargaining. If Roberta and Gary have not previously negotiated personal injury claims, at an appropriate point he might raise the issue of their negotiating relationship:

1—Gary: You know, Roberta, I find that I negotiate with some defense counsel in a much different way than with others. Have you had that experience with plaintiff's counsel?

2—Roberta: You mean there are some who demand a million bucks on a thirty thousand dollar claim, holler and scream and shout, and others who work with you within reasonable ranges to determine the fair and just amount of a claim?

3—Gary: Exactly. I much prefer the more cooperative relationship. It makes my life more pleasant, and I think I do a better job for my clients.

The risk is that such an opening will be seen as a sign of weakness and an opportunity for exploitation by the competitive negotiator. As previously mentioned, the negotiator facing an unknown counterpart should not make concessions which, if not reciprocated, significantly impair her client's interests. However, there is little or no disadvantage in explicitly discussing a preference for a cooperative strategy when the other lawyer already has made a reasonable opening offer or meaningful early concessions.

d. *Active Listening*

Lawyers as negotiators are not computers programmed to respond to impulses from the other side; they are human beings with feelings generated by the negotiation. Negotiations usually begin as conflict situations and, as such, generate feelings of mistrust, fear and anger that are counterproductive to establishing a cooperative or problem-solving bargaining relationship.

The next several "cooperation facilitators" are designed to address the relationship between the two negotiators. If the negotiator uses techniques calculated to develop rapport with the other negotiator, the relationship necessary for cooperative or problem-solving negotiation strategies is facilitated without the negotiator "giving up" anything on the merits. In other words, interpersonal techniques that make the other negotiator believe the lawyer understands his concerns, and therefore facilitate cooperation, can be regarded as "the cheapest possible concessions." [15]

The most important of the interpersonal skills that can be employed as a cooperation facilitator in the negotiation context is *active listening*.[16] Active listening is the process of hearing what the other negotiator has said, understanding it and responding with a reflective statement which mirrors what the negotiator has heard. Assume that Gary Gerstein, the attorney representing Patrick Finney, has made an initial offer in the case against the Baltimore and Western Railroad of $2.2 million. He believes this is a reasonable opening offer given recent jury trends in his jurisdiction, his economists' and physicians' reports, and his careful review of all the circumstances. Roberta Martinez, representing the railroad, responds as follows:

1—Roberta: Don't be ridiculous. We can't even begin to talk about figures like that. I thought that we were developing a relationship during the discovery process where we could deal with each other in good faith. You're just like all the other plaintiffs' attorneys. You were "sand-bagging" me. When are you folks going to get real?

The normal human response at this point is to get defensive and to counterattack:

2—Gary: What are you talking about? Let's just look at the facts of the case for a moment and the experts' opinions. This number is carefully and fairly arrived at. You're the one who is playing games.

Assume, however, that Gary acts less defensively, breaks that fear/anger cycle, and employs an active listening response:

3—Gary: The high numbers are a surprise to you. You think I've been playing games with you and that this isn't a serious proposal.

Which response is most likely to result in Gary and Roberta engaging in serious dialogue about the value of the claim? In which case is serious consideration of the experts' reports more likely to occur during the remainder of the bargaining session?

15. I am indebted to my colleague Don Peters for this characterization.

16. *See* D. Binder & S. Price, *supra* note 6, at 20–37.

What has Gary really conceded through an active listening response? He has not conceded or admitted that his offer was too high, and he has not shared information that a competitive negotiator could use against him. Perhaps the only trade-off is that if he intended to use a pure competitive strategy/competitive style negotiation combination in which the essential message is "You'd better pay up with megabucks or I'm going to clean your clock at trial," initial use of the active listening approach is probably inconsistent with such an aggressive posture. However, few negotiators successfully use such a blatantly competitive style of negotiation with long-term success.

This example demonstrates the use of active listening to facilitate cooperative or problem-solving negotiation tactics. Active listening is used to convey that the negotiator has accurately heard and understood the other party's communications. The cooperative negotiator's active listening response is also *non-judgmental* about the other party's position. This does not mean the negotiator accepts the other party's position, or finds it substantively reasonable, but only that the negotiator recognizes that the other side can take the opposite position without being a monster or a lower form of life. Most people are inclined to be more trusting and cooperative when they believe that others have listened to them and have understood their message without rejecting them out of hand because of the message.

Three types of messages in negotiations can provide opportunities for active listening:

(1) facts as presented by the other negotiator;

(2) negotiation proposals or positions presented by the other negotiator; and

(3) feelings of the other negotiator.

One purpose of using active listening as a response to the facts and bargaining proposals of the other party is to be sure the negotiator has heard and understood them accurately. The emotionally laden and often frenetic atmosphere in which negotiation is typically conducted provides many opportunities for miscommunication. Negotiation where one party believes an agreement has been reached while the other party does not are common. Reflective statements capturing the essence of factual statements or negotiation proposals serve as a check on the potential for misunderstandings. Further, as discussed above, active listening responses to negotiation proposals or to the negotiator's emotional responses, as in the case of Gary and Roberta, facilitate the development of a bargaining relationship where cooperative and problem-solving negotiation is possible.

e. *Other Responses to Anger*

Anger is a frequently expressed emotion during a negotiation where goals are frustrated by the other party's negotiation behavior. Anger, unfortunately, obscures opportunities for cooperative and problem-solving bargaining. How should the negotiator who wants to

establish a cooperative or problem-solving negotiation atmosphere respond to anger?

Anger—or any other emotion being experienced by the other side
that is destructive to the bargaining relationship—often should be
acknowledged and explicitly addressed.[17] When verbal or non-verbal
communications lead the lawyer to believe that the other negotiator is
angry, the relationship frequently improves with direct empathetic
discussion of these feelings. The active listening response which Gary
used in the previous section is a good example.

The goal in responding to the other negotiator's anger is not to
respond substantively to the expression of anger, but instead to allow
him to express the anger directly so that it does not impair the
cooperative negotiation relationship in other hidden or subtle ways. If
Roberta Martinez is extremely angry at Gary Gerstein's initial offer, it
is unlikely that the negotiation will be productive until Roberta has a
chance to ventilate. However difficult it may be, the negotiator should
allow her angry counterpart to "let off steam" without responding
defensively or with interruptions. At the same time, the negotiator
should not allow such emotional outbursts to affect her substantive
positions or to cause her to lose confidence in herself or her case. In
fact, it is sometimes ill-advised for the negotiator to make any concessions or changes in her proposals immediately following an outburst by
the other side unless the negotiator can make it clear that the concession was not a response to intimidation brought on by the display of
anger.

D. PROBLEM–SOLVING ORIENTATION

This section focuses on the ways in which a negotiator using a
problem-solving strategy attempts to establish a relationship between
the negotiators which is different from the one preferred by the
competitive negotiator. This relationship is based on trust similar to
that used in the cooperative strategy. Further, the atmosphere in the
negotiation is one dedicated to finding mutual "solutions to problems",
rather than to making concessions and expecting the other side to
concede in return.

The techniques described in this section for achieving a negotiation
ambience hospitable to problem-solving are not necessarily designed for
use in the earliest stages of the negotiation. As described previously,
phases of a negotiation where cooperative or problem-solving techniques predominate frequently are preceded by more competitive
phases. If the other negotiator's initial approach is competitive, the
use of problem-solving tactics sometimes is not feasible until deadlock is
achieved and both negotiators recognize that little or nothing will be
accomplished unless their tactics change. Accordingly, the techniques

---

 17. *See* R. Fisher & W. Ury, Getting to
Yes: Negotiating Agreement Without Giving In 30–33 (1981).

described here for achieving a problem-solving orientation frequently are not profitably employed until the negotiation proceeds for some period of time and circumstances suggest that a change to a more problem-solving approach would be reciprocated.

When the opportunity is ripe, the lawyer using problem-solving tactics attempts to create an orientation between the negotiators that resembles the atmosphere created in the problem-solving pre-negotiation planning session with the client. The lawyer views the subject matter of the negotiation as the *problem* to be solved by the negotiators and not as an exchange of proposals.[18] The desired atmosphere is one where the negotiators attempt to maximize the joint gains of their clients, not divide a limited resource between the parties. The initial stage of a problem-solving negotiation, therefore, is to uncover, identify, and understand the parties' problems. This requires discussion of each side's underlying needs.

Success in the initial orientation of problem-solving negotiation depends upon achieving a psychological state characterized by the following:

(1) mutual trust between the negotiators;

(2) shared desire to achieve joint gains;

(3) open, honest communication between the negotiators; and

(4) adjustment to a negotiation process that is not a "one-party wins, one party loses" positional bargaining arrangement.

Trust between the parties facilitates problem-solving. A trusting atmosphere encourages accurate communication about each party's needs, and facilitates creative solutions. Without trust, each negotiator carefully controls the dissemination of information about her client's needs out of fear that such information will be used by a competitive opponent to disadvantage her client. A lack of trust also leads a lawyer to distrust communication from the other negotiator because she fears that he is acting competitively and is intentionally distorting the communication in order to gain a competitive advantage. Finally, the creativity needed to explore all possible solutions to a problem frequently dissipates if the negotiator does not trust her counterpart.

All of the techniques used to develop trust as a part of the cooperative negotiation strategy can also be used to establish the ambience necessary for problem-solving negotiation. Problem-solving bargaining additionally requires a motivation to achieve joint gains that flow from the realization that gains for the negotiator's client do not emanate exclusively from "losses" inflicted upon the other party.

Assuming that a negotiator can achieve an initial trusting relationship, what else must the negotiator do to facilitate a problem-solving approach to the negotiation opposed to a competitive or cooperative strategy? The key ingredient is to induce the other party to leave

---

18. For an excellent theoretical overview of the initial orientation in problem-solving negotiation, *see* R. Walton & R. McKersie, *supra* note 8, at 127–153.

behind his familiar habits of positional bargaining, whether in the competitive vein or the cooperative vein, and to move to a negotiation process which focuses on the underlying interests of the parties.

Pedantic lectures to a more experienced attorney on the virtues of a new type of negotiation—whether termed "problem-solving" or "principled"—are likely to be ineffective. Implicit in such assertions is a thinly veiled sense of moral superiority and a rejection of how the other negotiator has operated during his professional life. At best, such proselytizing behavior is ineffective and looks silly or naive; at worst, it is offensive.

Effective negotiators find more subtle ways to introduce problem-solving negotiation techniques. Assume that Dan Darrow, representing the Chestnut Development Corporation, demands a rental of $35 per square foot per month for the retail space desired by Banana Computer. How can Bev Bailey, representing Banana, move away from the other attorney's stated "position" and toward an exploration of the other party's underlying interests? [19] Initially, Bev should try to place herself in the position of the Chestnut Development Corporation and to understand what interests lie behind its stated position. She can also ask Dan directly, "How did your client determine this rental?" Note that in either case, Bev does not admonish Dan that positional bargaining is inappropriate or that there is a better way to do things. Assuming that Dan answers that the amount of the rental is necessary to guard against increased labor and insurance costs, this opens the door for Bev to ask more questions about those issues and to begin candid discussion of the "needs" of the Chestnut Development Corporation.

In addition to discovering the other party's underlying interests, the negotiator using problem-solving tactics explicitly communicates her client's underlying interests to the other negotiator. Recall that Banana Computer's underlying concern about the rental price was whether it would be able to afford the rates during the first two years of a new operation. If Bev uses a problem-solving strategy, she will clearly communicate this concern to Dan Darrow. Such explicit communication of needs eliminates any potential emotional reaction that Dan might have that "Banana is just trying to get away with a lower rent." It also clears the way for Bev and Dan to work together to find some solution similar to those discussed in the previous chapter, such as a rental that increases each quarter or that is tied only to the amount of store sales.

The statement of needs should be as specific and as concrete as possible. Often it is easier for parties to agree on specific solutions than on broad statements of general or abstract principles. Consider a labor negotiation between a health-care workers' union and a hospital over the issue of testing hospital workers for exposure to the AIDS virus. A broadly stated position of the hospital management might be:

19. *See* R. Fisher & W. Ury, *supra* note 17, at 45–51, 113–117.

"A regular program for AIDS testing of employees is absolutely essential in a health care facility where there is substantial contact between employees and patients." The union, fearing massive testing and immediate dismissal of employees with positive results, might respond with the position: "Mandatory AIDS testing violates the employees' civil liberties and invades their privacy." Not much room for compromise! However, a *specific* proposal from management far more likely to lead to an agreement would be one that is limited to employees with patient contact, ensures the privacy of those tested, and provides for alternative employment for those with positive test results.

The techniques for establishing a bargaining relationship conducive to problem-solving bargaining are critical, because many attorneys representing other parties enter negotiation with backgrounds in adversarial bargaining and are unfamiliar with problem-solving approaches. The next two chapters, covering initial proposals and information bargaining, include sections that continue the discussion of how specific problem-solving tactics can be employed in the early phases of negotiation to encourage an orientation in which the lawyers search for integrative solutions.

Chapter Six

INITIAL PROPOSALS

This chapter focuses on the lawyer's first attempts during negotiation to frame and present her proposals for issue resolution. At this early stage of bargaining, as throughout the process, the negotiator chooses between competitive, cooperative and problem-solving tactics. Before describing these three types of initial proposals, however, this text considers when the negotiator should make her first proposal.

A. TIMING OF INITIAL PROPOSAL

As previously described, sometimes the negotiation process begins with a proposal from one of the two parties. Typically, for example, personal injury negotiations begin with a "demand letter" from the plaintiff's attorney. In other cases, the negotiators refrain from making initial offers until they have negotiated for some time. Instead, the parties begin by exchanging information about their respective interests and needs, and about the transaction at hand. A proposal is made only after information is exchanged and the parties have an opportunity to evaluate each other.

When should the negotiator begin the bargaining with a proposal? When should she defer and either proceed first with information gathering, or encourage her counterpart to make the first serious proposal?

As a rule of thumb, the lawyer should not begin the negotiation with a serious proposal when she is uncertain about what constitutes a likely or reasonable range for the eventual agreement. Some attorneys have had the experience of suppressing the desire to make an initial demand in the negotiation, only to have the other party offer more in its initial bid than the amount the attorney's client required for settlement. For example, consider a university professor who has developed a new computer software system for predicting indemnity loss payment trends for liability insurance carriers. The professor, of course, knows that his software package is potentially valuable to insurance companies, but does not realize the considerable political value of his program in substantiating insurance company rate requests to various state regulatory authorities. On the other hand, the professor, unbeknownst to the insurance carrier, faces severe personal financial problems resulting from the cost of his children's college education and recent medical expenses. There is no "standard" price for such a software package. In a case like this, it is entirely possible that whichever party makes the first offer without extensive prior discussions will "lose" the negotiation. The professor does not fully understand the economic value of the software program to the insurance company, and therefore might make a first offer lower than what the insurance company happily would pay. The insurance company does not know the professor's current financial circumstances and pressing cash needs and, therefore, might offer more than necessary.

Inventor Thomas Edison reportedly experienced a similar situation.[1] After inventing the "Universal" stock ticker which was widely used by brokerage houses for several decades, Edison was asked by one General Lefferts, the President of the Gold & Stock Telegraph Company, how much he thought he should receive for the invention. Edison describes what happened:

> I had made up my mind that, taking into consideration the time and killing pace I was working at, I should be entitled to $5000, but could get along with $3000. When the psychological moment arrived, I hadn't the nerve to name such a large sum, so I said: 'Well, General, suppose you make me an offer.' Then he said: 'How would $40,000 strike you?' This caused me to come as near fainting as I ever got. I was afraid he would hear my heart beat. I managed to say that I thought it was fair.[2]

When the negotiator does not know the reasonable range of agreement between the parties, she has three options. She can:

(1) pursue information-bargaining before making an initial proposal;

(2) encourage the other party to make the first proposal; or

(3) make an extreme proposal which allows enough leeway to protect her if she underestimates the value of what she has to offer.

In many cases, information-bargaining should precede the negotiator's initial proposal. The reader is specifically warned not to draw a contrary conclusion just because this chapter on initial proposals precedes the next chapter on information exchange. Almost inevitably, information gathering precedes the initial proposal if the negotiator begins the negotiation with a problem-solving strategy; this is also often true with either the competitive or cooperative strategies.

1. *See* F. Dyer & T. Martin, Edison: His   2. Thomas Edison, quoted in *id.*
Life And Inventions 132 (1929).

B. WHO SHOULD MAKE THE INITIAL PROPOSAL?

There is no "rule" as to whether it is advantageous or disadvantageous to make the first offer or demand in the negotiation. In many negotiation contexts, custom provides that one party or another should make the first proposal. For example, in personal injury negotiation, it is typical for the plaintiff to make his initial demand before the defendant makes a first offer. In many other areas of negotiation, however, there is no strong convention as to who should make the first offer. Under these circumstances, deciding whether it is advantageous for the client to make the first proposal can be made only by applying the criteria discussed in this section to the particular negotiation problem. In some cases, these factors will point strongly toward either making or receiving the first proposal; in other cases the analysis will yield inconclusive results, suggesting merely that there are advantages and disadvantages to either approach.

The first proposal in negotiation, if credible and convincing, often becomes the focal point from which further bargaining proceeds. In some contexts, then, it is an advantage to make the first proposal because it establishes the probable bargaining range. To accomplish this objective, the negotiator should make the initial proposal appear formal and carefully considered. For example, in the lease negotiation with the Chestnut Development Corporation, Bev Bailey, Banana Computer's attorney, might present Dan Darrow, her negotiating counterpart, with a draft lease including all of the provisions desired by her client, including favorable rent provisions. The two attorneys probably will begin to bargain from these draft provisions. If they do, Bev has strongly influenced the bargaining range on various issues by making a credible first offer. In other bargaining situations, however, it is extremely unlikely that the opening proposal will strongly affect the bargaining range. For example, many personal injury negotiations begin with extreme proposals from both sides. Because of this lawyering tradition, even a realistic initial proposal generally is not viewed as establishing a focal point for serious negotiation.

The other major advantage of making the first proposal is to elicit the other negotiator's reaction. If Dan's reaction to the draft lease is to tell Bev that "The draft needs some work, but it's a good place to begin," that tells Bev that her proposal is reasonably close to being acceptable to Dan. On the other hand, if Dan cancels a scheduled meeting after receiving a copy of Bev's draft, a different message is communicated. The negotiator, however, must anticipate the possibility that her counterpart may feign an angry response to an initial proposal.

There are several disadvantages to making the first proposal. As suggested previously, the negotiator is generally ill-advised to make the first offer if she does not know enough about the case to predict the probable range of the eventual agreement. In the most extreme situation, such as Edison's, the negotiator's first proposal may be less favorable to her client than the first offer she would receive from her negotiating counterpart if she were more patient. In less egregious instances where the negotiator determines her initial proposal with inadequate information, she establishes a bargaining range less favorable to her client than is possible if she waits. By making the first proposal, the negotiator also gives her counterpart the opportunity to adjust his first offer after measuring hers. Finally, in some litigation contexts, an immediate offer to settle may be interpreted by the other attorney as a sign of weakness; that is, the negotiator is too willing to compromise her client's interests and is not ready to pursue vigorously her client's rights at trial.

The negotiator is ill-advised to engage in first offer "ping-pong" where the parties argue over who will make the first offer. However, in some instances she can encourage the other negotiator to make the first proposal. If there is pressure for her to make the first negotiating proposal without enough information, the negotiator may respond by making an extreme and obviously unrealistic offer, thus protecting her from making an offer which is unknowingly disadvantageous to her client.

C. COMPETITIVE FIRST PROPOSAL TACTICS

Competitive negotiation tactics, as described in Chapter Two, are designed to encourage the other party to enter into an agreement less advantageous to her client than she would have prior to the negotiation. Although additional principles of the competitive negotiation strategy relating to initial proposals are discussed below, the most important competitive tactic is to make an extreme, but not totally unrealistic, first offer or demand.

1. AMOUNT (LEVEL OF EXTREMITY) OF THE INITIAL DEMAND OR OFFER

The lawyer using competitive tactics usually begins the negotiation with a high initial demand. Empirical research repeatedly demonstrates a significant positive correlation between the amount of the negotiator's original demand and her payoff.[3] A competitive initial proposal, therefore, is one substantially more favorable to the negotiator's client than she would settle for, but not so extreme as to be blatantly unrealistic or ridiculous.

The principal purpose of the high demand or the low offer is to influence the other negotiator's perception of the eventual agreement between the parties. At the beginning of negotiation, generally there is uncertainty about the eventual range of agreement. In many in-

---

3. *See e.g.,* C. Karass, The Negotiating Game 18 (1970); Harnett, Cummings & Hamner, *Personality, Bargaining Style and Payoff in Bilateral Monopoly Bargaining Among European Managers,* 36 Sociometry 325, 342 (1973).

stances, an extreme—but credible—initial offer determines the range in which the parties will eventually bargain. From the competitive negotiation perspective, the high demand or low offer also serves implicitly as a threat to the other negotiator: "If you are not willing to bargain in this range, there will be no agreement." It may be that the extreme initial demand *should not* have this effect. If the other negotiator reasonably determines his minimum disposition, target, and initial offer, his counterpart's initial demand should have no effect. Nevertheless, negotiators frequently admit that their initial proposals were changed or modified after hearing their counterpart's first offer. In a similar vein, a high but realistic initial demand sometimes communicates to the other party that a negotiator will not be exploited and is going to be a tough bargainer.

An extreme initial offer also provides the negotiator with a margin of error to protect her against undervaluing her case at a time when she has incomplete information. For example, in the previously described negotiation between the professor and the insurance company concerning the sale of the software package, an extreme early proposal from either side would have protected that party from entering into an agreement less favorable than the one its negotiating counterpart would have been willing to concede. Further, the extreme but seemingly credible early negotiating position allows the negotiator to probe for more information and for a sense of the other party's minimum disposition before making a serious settlement proposal. If the negotiator uses an extreme initial proposal and the opposing counsel responds with a mild, "That sounds a little high, but it's in a reasonable range," the negotiator has learned that she will probably realize more from the negotiation than she had expected. Thus, the extreme early proposal enables the negotiator both to hide her own minimum disposition in the beginning stages of the negotiation and to learn something about her counterpart's.

According to proponents of the competitive strategy, the high demand or low offer also allows the negotiator to make a series of meaningful concessions during the negotiation and to obtain concessions from the other party in exchange. If the negotiator's initial proposal is too close to her minimum disposition, there is no room to bargain.

The most prevalent risk of a competitive initial proposal is that the other negotiator will ignore the initial proposal and give it no credence. This is not really a detriment by itself, it is simply an acknowledgment that the technique did not work. It may lead, however, to a shift in bargaining power if the opponent is able to force the negotiator to make a second, more realistic offer before he begins bargaining. This second offer is, in effect, a major concession at a time in the negotiation process when the relationship between the parties is fluid and still in the process of being established.

The possible disadvantages of the extreme initial proposal fall into three categories: (1) inviting retaliation, (2) risking deadlock and (3) causing a negative perception of the competitive negotiator.

A negotiator's early competitive tactics invite, and indeed virtually compel, the other negotiator to engage in similar behavior. If the other negotiator perceives the first offer as an extreme one, the appropriate response is probably to respond in kind. In addition, the extreme early offer may cause the other party to respond by concealing information and engaging in other competitive tactics, such as threats. Unless the negotiator successfully hides the extreme nature of the opening bid, she makes a competitive negotiation process likely.

An extreme initial offer also risks a walkout or early termination of the negotiation. The other negotiator may decide that the offer is so far out-of-line with what he could agree to that further negotiation would not be profitable. Further, an extreme opening proposal sometimes prompts the other party to decide that he does not want to do business with an unreasonable lawyer who negotiates in such a preposterous manner. In some cases, the walk-out or early termination of the negotiation process is itself a competitive negotiation behavior; in other cases, it is a sincere and final termination to the negotiation, attributable to a demand grossly in excess of the client's genuine needs and expectations.

If the other negotiator perceives the initial bid as totally unrealistic, the extreme bid may cause considerable damage to the bargaining relationship and the negotiator's reputation. The negotiator risks becoming known in the negotiating community as unreasonable. Further, inflated demands frequently are viewed as signs of inexperience or perhaps as evidence that the lawyer is not fully prepared.

2. FIRMNESS OF INITIAL PROPOSAL

The competitive negotiator's initial proposal most frequently communicates "firmness," that is, a commitment to that proposal and a reluctance to modify it. This appearance of firmness is an important aspect of the negotiator's campaign to convince the other negotiator that she is not going to change her initial position easily and that he must change his if he wants to avoid a negotiation stalemate.

In presenting the initial proposal, the language chosen is crucial. If Gary Gerstein, Patrick Finney's attorney, begins the bargaining to settle Patrick's personal injury claim for "something in the range of $1.2 million" or makes an initial demand of "$800,000 to $1.2 million," he has probably communicated too much flexibility. Any demand containing two figures indicates to the other side that the negotiator is willing to settle for the lesser amount. Similarly, if Dan Darrow, attorney for Chestnut Development Corporation, makes an initial offer of "$35 per square foot—negotiable," he similarly communicates a willingness to make substantial concessions. All blatant acknowledgments of a willingness to compromise are usually superfluous and dangerous. Implicit in any initial proposal is an implied commitment to further bargaining. Explicit restatement of this flexibility to bargain risks communication of an excessive desire to accommodate.

Walton and McKersie, in their definitive study of labor negotiations, provide an excellent analysis and an example of the importance of language in the initial proposal.[4] They argue that the degree of firmness of an initial proposal results from three factors: the degree of *specificity,* the degree of *finality* and the *consequence* that will flow from the party's commitment. To illustrate this point, Walton and McKersie describe a hypothetical demand by a union negotiator to the management during the final stages of a labor negotiation:

> "We must have the 12½–cent package and the seniority provisions which we proposed. We are prepared to strike, if necessary."

The provisions insisted upon, the "12½–cent package" and the "seniority provisions" are highly *specific,* according to Walton and McKersie. Less *firmness* would be communicated if the negotiator had demanded "the kind of package we have been talking about." Similarly the language "we must have" suggests a much higher degree of *finality* than a "suggestion" to management that it reconsider its position on these issues. Finally, the statement of the *consequences*—"we are prepared to strike"—is definitive. Substitute language such as "if you don't concede on these points, we are going to have a tough time selling this to membership" would have left more room to compromise at a later point in the negotiation.

3. JUSTIFICATIONS FOR THE PROPOSAL

The apparent level of the negotiator's commitment to her competitive initial proposal is also increased if she justifies the amount of the offer or counteroffer. For example, if Gary Gerstein, Patrick Finney's attorney, begins with an opening demand of $1.2 million which he has "picked out of the air" and cannot support with facts or reasonable arguments, the demand will probably have little effect on the railroad's evaluation of its case. On the other hand, if the opening demand is accompanied by a settlement brochure justifying both the liability and damage claims, the demand likely will have more persuasive effect on the negotiation. The demand in a personal injury case, such as Patrick Finney's, should ideally include a detailed breakdown of past and future medical expenses, rehabilitation costs, and past and future lost earnings. Even the demand for "pain and suffering" damages should be justified in some manner, such as comparison to awards in similar cases, or the use of a formula for calculation—for example, the product of the number of days of pain and suffering multiplied by an amount for each day. Such detailed justification lends an aura of legitimacy to the initial demand.

4. R. Walton & B. McKersie, A Behavioral Theory of Labor Negotiations 93–95 (1965).

At a later point in negotiation, this early articulation of the justifications for the demand provides an opportunity to explain changes in negotiation positions. As new information and arguments change the negotiator's evaluation of the factors originally used to justify a demand, she can make concessions and explain them as rational responses to new information and not the collapse of her bargaining will.

4. ESCALATION OF DEMANDS

Even among competitive negotiators, there is a general prohibition against either increasing the amount of an initial demand after it has been placed on the table, or adding new demands. In most negotiation contexts, this prohibition is a strong norm, and violating it probably will either anger the other party, or make the negotiator appear inexperienced.

Sound reasons support this negotiation norm. Effective negotiations are impossible when the negotiator starts to concede an issue to meet the other party's demands, only to have the other party suddenly withdraw his proposal. An initial proposal from the other negotiator implies that if its terms are acceptable to the lawyer's client, an agreement can be reached on that basis, and the negotiation concluded. This allows the negotiator to evaluate the other party's most recent bargaining position and make a decision on how, and whether, to negotiate further. Such evaluation is not possible if the other negotiator is continually and unpredictably increasing his demands. Further, the other lawyer's initial proposal contains the implicit message that these terms are acceptable to his client. How can the other lawyer subsequently argue with integrity and conviction that his own earlier proposal is now unacceptable to his client?

Every negotiation "rule" has its exceptions. Increasing the initial demand sometimes is appropriate if the negotiator warns the other party in advance and gives justifications for it. For example, the Baltimore and Western Railroad might announce that its $200,000 offer to pay Patrick Finney for his injuries will expire next month at the time when house counsel for the railroad turns the case over to retained trial counsel. The removal of the offer, an "escalation" from the defendant's perspective, could be justified on the grounds that the railroad faces additional expense when outside counsel is brought in, and also that trial counsel will make all offers of settlement after that point.

What happens when, during negotiation, counsel discovers a "smoking gun" which substantially increases her bargaining power? Is she precluded from making new demands or increasing the old demands? Or what about the possibility of adding a last minute demand, a "rider" to the agreement, when it is clear that agreement is going to be reached on the major points?

There is nothing illegal about increasing demands under these circumstances, and it is done. However, even these actions are regarded by many attorneys as violations of norms, except in extreme circumstances. Escalation tactics are unusually competitive ones. In most situations, when the negotiator increases her opening demand, she risks damaging ongoing and future bargaining relationships and her general reputation among lawyers.

5. FALSE DEMANDS

In addition to using extreme proposals as initial bids, the competitive negotiator sometimes also makes "false demands," that is, additional negotiation proposals insisting upon things which in reality have little interest or importance to her client. Why would any negotiator make such demands? To the extent that a false demand is made credibly and calls for concessions on important issues by the other party, the false issue becomes trade-bait. At a subsequent point in negotiation, the lawyer drops the false issue in exchange for a concession from the other negotiator on an issue she *does* care about. The value of the false issue in the negotiation depends upon how important the negotiator makes the issue appear to the other party. If the negotiator convinces the other party that dropping the issue is a great sacrifice, she can convincingly argue that she is entitled to a major concession in return.

However, the false issue strategy sometimes backfires. The other party occasionally decides to concede on the issue that the negotiator does not care about, and he expects a concession on another issue in return. The false issue strategy also damages the negotiator's future credibility and good will among other negotiators if it becomes apparent that she regularly employs this gamelike strategy.

The use of false demands raises ethical issues similar to those previously considered in the context of false statements about the lawyer's authority, or lack of authority, to enter into an agreement binding on her client.[5] To review, Model Rule of Professional Conduct 4.1 prohibits a lawyer from knowingly making a false statement of material fact.[6] The lawyer using a false demand tactic makes a false statement when she explicitly states the interest of her client in an issue for which the client has no concern. Nevertheless, false demands are routinely used in at least some negotiation contexts, such as collective bargaining. Presumably, false demands therefore fall within the exception for "certain types of statements ordinarily * * * not taken as statements of material fact" under generally accepted conven-

---

5. *See supra* Chapter Four, *Negotiation Planning,* at 70–1; *see also* White, *Machiavelli and the Bar: Ethical Limitations on Lying in Negotiation,* 1980 Am.B. Found.Research J. 926, 932 (1982).

6. Model Rules of Professional Conduct Rule 4.1 (1983); *see also* Model Code of Professional Responsibility DR 7–102(A)(5) (1987) for a similar provision in the *Code of Professional Responsibility.*

tions in negotiation.[7] Analytically, it is difficult to justify why demanding additional issues which are *relatively unimportant* to the client would be more ethically suspect than inflating the dollar figure of a demand in a quantifiable distributive issue above the client's minimum disposition. On the other hand, an arguably more serious ethical question arises when the client has *no interest* in the demands made by his attorney.

6. DEMANDS AS PRE–CONDITIONS FOR NEGOTIATION

Negotiators sometimes state a demand as a pre-condition for the "beginning" of negotiation. For example, Bev Bailey, in her role as counsel for Banana Computers, might refuse to even begin negotiations with Dan Darrow, representing the Chestnut Development Corporation, unless both parties agree that the eventual monthly base rental would be less than that called for in the standard Chestnut Mall retail store contract. Similarly, Gary Gerstein, Patrick Finney's attorney, could insist that the attorneys not meet unless Baltimore and Western is willing to concede liability.

One of the most famous examples of the reciprocal use of pre-conditions to bargaining is the continuing war of words between Israel and the Palestine Liberation Organization (PLO).[8] Israel has continually stated as a pre-condition to any negotiation with the PLO that the PLO recognize the right of Israel to exist as a nation. Because this admission, although certainly understandable from the Israeli point of view, conflicts with often articulated positions of PLO representatives, any agreement by the PLO to negotiate on these terms would involve a major concession. Conversely, the PLO implicitly states a pre-condition to negotiation by insisting that Israel negotiate with the PLO as a representative of the Palestinian people. Obviously, any willingness on Israel's part to negotiate with the PLO in this capacity involves a major concession.

Stating a demand as a pre-condition to negotiation serves several functions. First, if the other party accedes to the pre-condition in order to begin negotiations, the negotiator has gained substantively. This removes the issue from the bargaining session, and the negotiator is not required to make concessions in order to obtain the other party's agreement to this demand. Second, by agreeing to the pre-condition, the other party usually gives the negotiator a strong psychological advantage at the beginning of the negotiation. Finally, "impossible" pre-conditions often serve as a way of avoiding negotiation altogether

---

7. *Id.,* Rule 4.1 comment (1983).

8. *See* H. Kissinger, Years of Upheaval 197–99 (1982).

As this text was being printed, the Palestine National Council, the parliament in exile of the Palestinian movement, for the first time acknowledged, implicitly at least, the sovereignty of Israel. N.Y. Times, November 15, 1988, at 1, col. 6. The long term repercussions on diplomacy in the Middle East were unclear at that time. The Palestinian leadership regarded this acknowledgment as a major concession, but initially—at least publicly—both American and Israeli representatives sought to minimize its importance. Ibrahim, "In P.L.O. Eyes, a Big Step," N.Y. Times, November 16, 1988, at 1, col. 5.

when a party believes negotiation is futile or prefers other courses of action, but finds it necessary to explain to others his unwillingness to negotiate.

7. "BOULWARISM:" FIRST, FIRM, FAIR, FINAL OFFER

Although the typical competitive initial proposal consists of an extreme demand, an alternate competitive demand tactic exists. Under a tactic generally referred to as "Boulwarism," the party makes an initial offer that it believes is the basis for a reasonable agreement between the parties; in other words, this approach is directly opposite to the extreme initial proposal. The party making the offer then refuses to make any concessions or modifications of the initial offer: it is a "take-it-or-leave-it" proposition. There is no bargaining in the traditional sense.

The term "Boulwarism" is taken from the name of Lemuel R. Boulware, a vice-president of General Electric during the 1950's who pioneered the use of this bargaining technique in labor relations.[9] Under his direction, General Electric developed what it believed was a series of fair proposals regarding matters scheduled for consideration in collective bargaining. General Electric then bypassed the union representatives and publicized the proposals directly to the workers. Most importantly, it refused to make changes in its positions unless the union presented facts that it had overlooked.

The combination of these bargaining practices was ultimately found to be an "unfair labor practice" by the National Labor Relations Board [10] because it constituted a refusal to bargain in good faith that undermined the union's position and the integrity of the collective bargaining process. Nevertheless, the term "Boulwarism" is now applied to the negotiation approach of developing a "first, fair, firm, final" offer and then refusing to make concessions. Boulwarism is more than a historical footnote. Among others, a few insurance claims personnel sometimes use this approach. Frequently, prosecutors use this approach in plea bargaining and refuse to retreat from their original guilty plea offers to defendants.

Those who use Boulwarism as a negotiating tactic believe that it reduces the hassles, delay and expenses of the more typical bargaining dance, and also yields superior bargaining power for them. The first factor alone suggests that the use of Boulwarism is often justifiable on economic grounds in smaller cases. Further, Boulwarism arguably increases bargaining power because it effectively serves the competitive goal of convincing the other party that he can not obtain a better deal by using arguments, threats or other bargaining tactics.

However, using Boulwarism creates two substantial risks. First, it often leads to deadlock, particularly when the negotiators represent

9. NLRB v. General Electric Co., 418 F.2d 736, 740–746 (2d Cir.1969).

10. General Electric Co. and IUE, 150 N.L.R.B. 192 (1964), aff'd NLRB v. General Electric Co., 418 F.2d 736 (1969).

clients or other constituents. The expectation in negotiation is that both sides will compromise from their initial proposals and make concessions. When this does not occur, frustration results. This is especially important when the negotiator is bargaining on behalf of a client. When confronted with Boulwarism, the negotiator/attorney is not able to show her client that her representation during negotiation has accomplished anything. It is precisely this reasoning that led the National Labor Relations Board to declare Boulwarism an unfair labor practice, because it undermined the union as a representative of workers in the collective bargaining process. The possibility of damage to the attorney/client relationship when concessions are not made by the other party often causes the attorney to respond to the other negotiator with anger when he uses the "first, fair, firm, final" offer approach.

The second obstacle to the effective use of Boulwarism is credibility. The method fails unless the other party believes the negotiator when she says that her initial proposal is her firm and final offer. A negotiator who begins to use such an approach will likely be tested often in the early going, resulting in frequent trials or many broken deals. Once a negotiator begins using Boulwarism, she must never make concessions from the first proposal without a persuasive justification. Otherwise, future claims that her initial proposals are fair, firm *and final* will not be believed.

8. COMPETITIVE RESPONSES TO OTHER PARTY'S INITIAL PROPOSAL

The goal of competitive negotiation tactics is to undermine the other party's confidence in his evaluation of the negotiation situation. Therefore, the negotiator's visible response to the other negotiator's initial proposal is extremely important.

Assume that Patrick Finney's attorney, Gary, values his client's case at something in the $950,000 range. Further, Gary wants to obtain the highest possible settlement for his client, and plans to use a predominantly competitive negotiation strategy. Much to his surprise and delight, Baltimore and Western makes an initial offer conceding liability and offering to pay $975,000 to settle the case. How should he respond?

A larger than expected offer from Baltimore and Western indicates one of three possibilities to Patrick's attorney. The first is that he has substantially underestimated the value of the case. Second, Baltimore and Western may be using a cooperative negotiation strategy, employing a reasonable and moderate initial bid based upon a modestly overestimated value of the case. The third possibility is that Baltimore and Western intended to use a competitive tactic with an extremely low initial offer, but wildly overestimated the value of the case.

When the beginning negotiator actually receives a substantially-better-than-expected first proposal from the other party, all her instincts drive her to respond favorably or enthusiastically. She says something like, "I think we're close to reaching an agreement" or "That sounds reasonable." At best, like Thomas Edison,[11] she responds with dumbfounded silence. These responses forfeit any possibility of realizing additional meaningful concessions from the other party because the negotiator communicates implicitly that the first offer is near, or even exceeds, her minimum disposition. Further, the conciliatory approach often makes the other party realize that he has misjudged the case, and he may respond with belligerence.

How should the negotiator respond to the extremely favorable first offer? A basic choice must be made at this early point between pursuing a cooperative strategy or a competitive strategy. If the initial offer from the other party is already favorable to the client and the client desires either to maintain a favorable working relationship with the other party or to conclude negotiations quickly, a cooperative response is probably warranted. This cooperative response should be generally favorable, expressing recognition and appreciation that the other party is approaching the negotiation realistically, but should stress the need for further bargaining. The indication that there is more bargaining ahead mitigates the possibility that the other negotiator will believe that he has undervalued his case and will respond defensively.

How should the negotiator respond if she intends to employ a competitive strategy in this situation? It may be time for an Oscar-winning performance. Regardless of how delighted the negotiator actually is with the offer, should she react decisively *against* the proposal, claiming it is wholly inadequate and asserting that opposing counsel either does not understand the case or regards her as a fool. This specific competitive negotiation tactic warrants further reflection on the ethical and moral aspects of the lawyer as competitive negotiator. Is it wrong to enact a professional role-play designed to convince the other negotiator that what your client in fact regards as a favorable offer is wholly outrageous and unacceptable?

This question can be addressed at several levels. The only reasonably certain conclusion is that such deception violates neither formal professional rules nor prevailing norms. As previously described, Model Rule of Professional Conduct 4.1 provides that lawyers "shall not knowingly make a false statement of material fact or law to a third person"[12] but the comment to the rule indicates that "under generally accepted conventions in negotiation, certain types of statements ordinarily are not taken as statements of material fact."[13] The comment specifically provides that "a party's intentions as to an acceptable settlement of a claim"[14], which implicitly includes statements about authority to settle a case, lie within the exception. Further, in actual

11. *See supra* page 97.

12. Model Rules of Professional Conduct Rule 4.1(a) (1983).

13. *Id.* at Rule 4.1 comment.

14. *Id.*

practice misrepresentations of the attorney's bargaining authority appear to be frequent.

The underlying inherent ethical dilemma is that in distributive bargaining situations, achieving a result for the client that is more satisfactory than an agreement barely meeting his minimum requirements often requires deception, either by explicit statement or by omission, potentially at odds with at least the spirit of Model Rule 4.1. Yet the attorney's pursuit of zealous advocacy, coupled with her obligation to preserve her client's confidences—presumably including the client's minimum disposition—seems to sanction this behavior.[15] Within the parameters of the conduct allowed by professional rules and negotiation norms, personal ethical choices must be made. Is acting with outrage to an offer acceptable to your client consistent with your concept of yourself as a professional? As a person? If such conduct furthers your client's interests and is allowed by the profession's ethical code, can you refuse to use these tactics and be comfortable with yourself?

D.   COOPERATIVE INITIAL PROPOSALS

1.   AMOUNT OF OPENING OFFER OR DEMAND

Initial proposals under the cooperative negotiation strategy are designed to achieve the goals of that negotiation approach: to reach an agreement that is fair and just to both parties and to develop a relationship based on trust with the other negotiating party. The initial negotiation proposals of negotiators using cooperative tactics, therefore, differ in two important regards from initial competitive proposals. First, the amount of the negotiator's initial demand (the extremity of her proposal) is more moderate and reasonable than an initial competitive proposal. Second, the cooperative negotiator justifies her opening bid by reference to objective standards.

According to cooperative strategy proponents, the negotiator should begin bargaining, not with an extreme position, but rather with a more moderate opening bid that she regards as favorable to her client, yet barely acceptable to the other party.[16] In other words, the cooperative opening proposal should only exceed the negotiator's target point by a modest amount. On one hand, the initial proposal should be moderate enough to communicate clearly to the other party that the negotiator is trying to be reasonable and establish a cooperative bargaining relation-

---

15. Model Rule of Professional Conduct 1.6 provides that "[a] lawyer shall not reveal information relating to representation of a client unless the client consents after consultation, except for disclosures that are impliedly authorized in order to carry out the representation." Model Rules of Professional Conduct Rule 4.1(a) (1983). *See also* Model Code of Professional Responsibility DR 4–101 (1987). Disclosure of the client's minimum disposition arguably is "impliedly authorized in order to carry out the representation," but whether it falls within this exception merely restates the issue addressed in the text.

16. *See* Bartos, *Simple Model of Negotiation: A Sociological Point of View,* in The Negotiation Process: Theories and Applications 13, 19–20, 24 (I. Zartman ed. 1978).

ship. On the other hand, the initial proposal must contain enough of a cushion to allow the negotiator to make concessions so that she does not appear intractable in later phases of the negotiation.

The differences between competitive and cooperative initial bids cannot be readily quantified. More than anything else, the difference is in how the initial bids will be perceived by opposing counsel. As an example in the difference between the two approaches, consider again the initial demand on behalf of Patrick Finney in his case against the Baltimore and Western Railroad. If Gary Gerstein has concluded that from Patrick's perspective a reasonable settlement value of the case is between $900,000 and $950,000, the opening demand under the competitive strategy might be in the range of $1.8 million or more. On the other hand, the original cooperative offer is likely to be in the $1 million to $1.2 million range.

What are the advantages of the cooperative negotiator's moderate initial proposal? Experimental studies of opening moves in negotiation establish that early cooperative behaviors facilitate the development of trust and a mutually beneficial, cooperative relationship.[17] Further, the cooperative initial bid eliminates the disadvantages of the competitive initial bid previously described. In particular, the cooperative proposal minimizes the possibility that the bargaining will break off prematurely when, in fact, a mutually advantageous agreement could be reached. In his study of Phoenix attorneys, Williams found that competitive negotiators reached an impasse in 33 percent of their cases, compared with only 16 percent for cooperative negotiators.[18] Because more extreme competitive negotiating proposals often produce better results in simulated negotiations, it is important to remember that a majority of attorneys use a cooperative approach that includes moderate initial proposals. Williams found that 65 percent of negotiating attorneys used a cooperative approach, and these attorneys were more likely to be evaluated as "effective" than were their competitive counterparts.[19]

2. JUSTIFICATIONS FOR INITIAL PROPOSAL

The initial proposal under the cooperative strategy is justified by reference to objective criteria. Such justification serves to legitimize the initial proposal and to establish the basis for a fair and reasonable agreement between the parties. The sources of objective criteria are limited only by the negotiator's diligence and imagination. In a transactional negotiation, such as the lease negotiation between Banana Computers and the Chestnut Development Corporation, the "going rate," that is, the fair market value or fair rental value, is a well recognized standard. In lawsuit settlement negotiations, including the one involving Patrick Finney and the Baltimore and Western Railroad,

17. *See* J. Rubin & B. Brown, The Social Psychology of Bargaining and Negotiation 263–64 (1964). Rubin and Brown discuss a number of studies reaching this conclusion.

18. G. Williams, Legal Negotiation and Settlement 51 (1983).

19. *Id.* at 19.

comparable verdicts from the same or similar jurisdictions provide an obvious reference point. In either of these two cases, and in many others, the opinion of an impartial expert with good credentials serves to legitimize an initial proposal.

In addition to focusing on objective standards, cooperative negotiators strive to prove the proposal's fairness and reasonableness. As such, they rely heavily on the facts of the transaction or dispute, and the applicable law. They avoid threatening or undermining the other party.

3. COOPERATIVE RESPONSES TO THE OTHER PARTY'S INITIAL PROPOSAL

The negotiator who wishes to use a cooperative strategy faces her most difficult situation when she realizes that the other party is engaging in competitive negotiation tactics. As previously discussed, the success of a cooperative negotiation strategy depends entirely upon enticing the other party to engage in similarly cooperative behavior.

How should the negotiator who wishes to behave cooperatively respond to what she recognizes as a competitive opening bid from the other negotiator? First, she should expose the other party's initial bid as an extreme position, either explicitly or more tactfully. If she explicitly tells her counterpart that she recognizes that he is demanding more than he ever expects to realize, she risks making him defensive. A more subtle approach is to question the other lawyer about the justifications for his demand. How did he arrive at this figure? Can he verify it by reference to specific objective criteria? In this way, the negotiator moves the bargaining toward a discussion of the merits. This approach, however, risks giving some *credence* to an unreasonable opening.

The question of whether the negotiator should respond to an extreme demand with a proposal of her own is a more difficult one. In the best of all possible situations, she hopes the questioning process discussed above will lead the other party to acknowledge that his initial proposal was extreme. If he does, a genuinely cooperative response from the negotiator is in order at this point. In the more likely event that the other party sticks with his extreme opening proposal, the cooperative negotiator has three options:

(1) respond with an equally extreme initial proposal so that the midpoint between the offers is in the range regarded by the negotiator as being fair and reasonable;

(2) refuse to respond to such an extreme initial proposal until the other party displays reasonableness; or

(3) make a fair and reasonable offer.

The third approach is premised on the assumption that if the negotiator behaves cooperatively the other negotiator will trust her and respond in kind. The cooperative negotiator can probably afford to be this trusting *once, early* in the negotiation. If her confidence in her ability to make the other negotiator more cooperative proves to be unfounded, and the other negotiator does not make major concessions from his initial extreme proposal, the cooperative negotiator must STOP her cooperative behavior until she has evidence that the other negotiator is also prepared to cooperate.

The role of the negotiator who desires to use cooperative negotiation tactics is considerably easier when the other party begins the negotiation with a moderate and reasonable offer. Under these circumstances, the negotiator can acknowledge explicitly that she recognizes that the other party is being reasonable, and indicate that she hopes to respond in kind. When the other party makes a realistic initial bid, cooperative negotiation theorists suggest that the negotiator calculate her responding offer so that the midpoint between the two initial bids represents a fair and equitable outcome of the negotiation.[20]

E. PROBLEM–SOLVING INITIAL PROPOSALS

1. TIMING OF PROBLEM–SOLVING PROPOSALS

Before discussing the problem-solving approach to initial proposals, it is important to reiterate that the use of problem-solving tactics, including those involving initial proposals, often does not occur until later stages of the negotiation. Sometimes a negotiator is able to initiate a problem-solving approach to the negotiation from the earliest stages. In many other cases, however, the parties do not turn to problem-solving techniques until their initial competitive tactics yield mutual frustration. Therefore, even though the problem-solving approach for handling initial proposals is discussed at this early point in the text, a negotiator might not use problem-solving proposals until after a period of bargaining using predominantly competitive and cooperative tactics.

Initial proposals in a problem-solving strategy almost inevitably follow a period of information exchange. In contrast, recall that under the competitive and cooperative negotiation strategies, the initial proposal may come either before or after a phase of the negotiation characterized by the exchange of information. Information exchange precedes the initial proposals under the problem-solving method because information about each party's needs usually must be shared before viable solutions can be formulated.

Thus, proposals under the problem-solving approach frequently occur only after the parties have negotiated for a greater length of time and have exchanged more information than is necessary for competitive or cooperative initial proposals. Fisher and Ury, leading proponents of the problem-solving method, caution negotiators to "avoid

20. Bartos, *supra* note 16, at 21.

premature judgment." [21] The early articulation of bargaining positions, according to Fisher and Ury, endangers a collaborative working relationship between the parties. It can also lead to unnecessary rounds of proposals and counterproposals that may not meet the parties' needs because they are not based upon an understanding of their interests.

The full array of information-gathering techniques discussed in Chapter Seven, *Information Bargaining,* should be used by the problem-solving negotiator to determine the other party's underlying needs. Further, as discussed in that chapter, the negotiator must be willing to fully, accurately and specifically describe her own client's needs in the negotiation. This disclosure of her client's interests serves two functions. First, the other negotiator requires an understanding of her client's needs so that he can effectively participate in the process of proposing and evaluating solutions that meet both parties' needs. Second, the lawyer's disclosure of her client's needs encourages the other negotiator to reciprocate.

2. PROBLEM–SOLVING RESPONSES TO POSITIONAL BARGAINING PROPOSALS

When a lawyer who desires to use a problem-solving strategy negotiates with a counterpart who expects to bargain in a traditional fashion with opening demands and opening offers, she faces both a challenge and an opportunity. The challenge, of course, is to transform the negotiation—without sounding either naive or condescending—into something other than positional bargaining with the traditional dance of offer and counteroffer, concession and threat. The process of doing so often provides an opportunity to gain insights into the other party's underlying interests.

Let us return to the negotiation between Bev Bailey, the attorney representing Banana Computers, and Dan Darrow, negotiating on behalf of the Chestnut Development Corporation, as they attempt to reach agreement on a lease of retail space. Recall that Banana Computers believes its greatest problem is the likelihood that it will be unable to pay a standard rental fee during the early months of its operation. Here is an example of how Bev, faced with this seemingly intractable problem, might respond to Dan's presentation of Chestnut Development Corporation's initial negotiating position:

1—Dan: This is a copy of our standard retail store Lease Agreement. Our standard rate is a base rental of $35 per square foot plus six percent of all gross sales in excess of $500,000 and a charge of $8 per square foot to cover maintenance, insurance and common utility charges. We've figured your monthly rent on that basis.

21. R. Fisher and W. Ury, Getting to Yes: Negotiating Agreement Without Giving In 59–60 (1981).

2—Bev: I'll need, of course, to take a close look at the agreement and get back to you. My client did want me to find out something more about the methods we might possibly use to calculate the monthly rent. How did you arrive at the $35 figure?

3—Dan: It's a uniform rate. Everyone pays it.

4—Bev: Why has Chestnut decided on this policy of uniform rentals—is that universal with all shopping malls?

5—Dan: No, but it sure makes things considerably easier. We don't have one store griping about someone else paying less.

6—Bev: How was the $35 figure determined?

7—Dan: I'm not sure of the details. I'm sure it's what management believes is enough to pay expenses and make a decent profit. I know they're real concerned about escalating insurance rates and labor costs.

By constantly probing into the reasons behind Chestnut's position, Bev accomplishes two things. First, she gathers information about Chestnut's underlying needs. Later, this will assist her in making proposals which satisfy the legitimate interests of Chestnut, as well as those of her own client. Second, Bev transforms the discussion into a consideration of the needs of both parties rather than an exchange of negotiating positions. Her gentle "prodding" and constant use of "why" questions change the process into a problem-solving negotiation more effectively and subtly than would a mini-lecture on why problem-solving negotiation is superior to traditional negotiation approaches.

The change in the tenor of the negotiation can be accelerated if Bev engages in active listening and explicitly acknowledges the legitimacy of Chestnut's interests. Further, this conversation serves as an opportunity for her to raise her client's primary underlying concern that, although the base rental rate appears reasonable and is manageable for Banana over the long term, Banana probably cannot pay it for the first six months or so.

3. SEARCH MODELS

After exchanging information about the parties' requirements and aspirations, the lawyers using the problem-solving strategy search for solutions that satisfy the underlying interests of their clients. This process may proceed in either of two ways. First, the negotiator may present a previously developed proposal to the other negotiator for consideration. Second, the lawyers, often together with their clients, try to devise solutions that satisfy their respective interests.

This problem-solving process requires two steps:

(1) generation of potential solutions or proposals; and

(2) evaluation of such proposals.

Both the generation of possible solutions and their evaluation are informed by the facts which the negotiator has learned from her own client and from the other party.

Social scientists refer to the set of goals and other requirements which the bargainer uses to generate and screen alternatives as a *search model*.[22] A search model is used to evaluate known alternatives and to suggest additional approaches. If no identifiable alternatives fit all the aspirations and requirements of the model, the model is revised.

A lawyer can begin negotiation with a search model reflecting the aspirations and requirements of her client, as well as the known and anticipated requirements of the other party. As she learns more about the other party's preferences, the search model is revised. A search model for the negotiation between Banana Computer and Chestnut Development Corporation might contain the following requirements and aspirations:

Banana's Goals

(1) monthly rental of $60,000 or less for first six months.

(2) retail space in Chestnut Mall or other high retail traffic area west of town.

(3) lease period of between three and ten years.

(4) good security.

(5) adequate parking.

(6) at least 1500 square feet of space.

(7) central court area of mall.

(8) adequate electrical wiring.

(9) good management.

Chestnut's Goals

(1) rent adequate to cover expenses and reasonable profit, *e.g.*, $35 per square foot.

(2) uniform rental rate.

(3) fully rented space.

(4) reputable, solid tenants.

(5) protection against escalating overhead.

(6) stores that attract affluent customers to mall.

(7) stores that do not create undue demand on mall services.

(8) variety of retail offerings.

4. TYPES OF INTEGRATIVE AGREEMENTS

Regardless of whether or not the problem-solving negotiator consciously articulates a search model, she usually attempts to find a negotiated resolution that provides high joint benefit to both parties by satisfying their requirements and aspirations. Four basic types of integrative agreements are available for this purpose:

(1) *solutions which bridge* the parties' needs and satisfy both sets of underlying interests;

(2) solutions involving *logrolling*, or the trading of concessions on different issues;

(3) *cost-cutting* agreements that reduce the negative consequences imposed upon one party in making a concession necessary to satisfy the other party; and

22. *See, e.g.*, D. Pruitt, Negotiation Behavior 167–8 (1981).

(4) *compensation* agreements that provide substitute compensation for the party making a concession required by the other party for an agreement.

Each type of integrative agreement was previously described briefly in Chapter Four, *Negotiation Planning.* The last three types of integrative agreements involve the exchange of concessions on various issues or other methods to compensate a party for making concessions. Because lawyers often use these tactics to resolve the last remaining—and generally most troublesome—issues in a negotiation, they are discussed fully in Chapter Nine, *Closure.* They can, of course, be used earlier in the negotiation.

5. PRESENTATION OF BRIDGING PROPOSALS

The process of devising solutions which bridge the parties' interests is the heart of the problem-solving method. Chapter Four, *Negotiation Planning,* addressed how the attorney and her client can work together in counseling sessions, particularly by using "brainstorming techniques," to devise solutions providing high joint benefit. How should the proposals devised by the attorney and her client be handled during the negotiation?

When presenting problem-solving proposals to the other party, the negotiator can begin by acknowledging the legitimacy of the needs expressed by the negotiator and by showing that her client's proposal addresses these needs. Active listening responses to the other party's expressed interests often are an effective transition to discussion of the client's proposal. Consider Bev Bailey's presentation of the problem-solving proposal that she and her client, Banana Computers, have decided to present to the Chestnut Development Corporation:

1—Bev: Your client believes that over a ten year lease term, it must realize a base monthly rental of $35 per square foot. This is Chestnut's uniform rate, and it believes that any departure from this rate might cause tensions with the other retail tenants. Further, Chestnut is very concerned about providing a cushion in the rent so that it can handle escalating insurance premium and labor costs.

My client prefers to rent in your mall. Quite frankly, it's an ideal location for us. Our problem, as we've discussed with you, is the amount of rent during the first year.

I'm wondering whether we might work something out along the following lines. During the first year, Banana's rent would be 70 percent of the base rate you are asking; during the second year, Banana would pay the full rental; and during the third and fourth years, Banana would pay both the full rental plus an additional monthly amount equal to $\frac{1}{24}$ of the 30% discount you gave us the first year, plus interest calculated at the prime rate. This approach would enable your client to realize the required rate of return on its investment, but would enable my client to get through the difficult start-up period.

We also would agree to keep all of the terms of our agreement confidential, and our lease might even provide a liquidated damages clause if Banana breached the confidentiality clause.

The process of justifying bridging proposals is somewhat different than justifying either competitive or cooperative proposals. The negotiator explains why the proposal meets the other party's needs. Repeated active listening of the other party's needs as a part of the justification process allows the other negotiator another chance to correct any misunderstanding of his client's needs. It also builds rapport because it provides a further testimonial that the other party's needs have been heard and understood.

What follows then is a cyclical process of reaction to the proposal and subsequent refinement of the proposal. This process may occur several times. The other party's reaction to the proposal often provides additional information about his needs and aspirations. This process of proposal—reaction—refined proposal is a fundamental problem-solving method for coming closer to agreement. Accordingly, it is considered further in Chapter Eight, *Narrowing of Differences*.

6. DEVELOPMENT OF BRIDGING PROPOSALS

If the competitive negotiator's biggest fantasy is to have her negotiating counterpart capitulate immediately to an outrageous initial demand, then the problem-solving negotiator's fondest dream is to have both negotiators engage in a "brainstorming" session. In this utopian situation, both parties, knowing first-hand all there is to know about the dispute under negotiation and their clients' preferences, would sit down together and brainstorm. However, many attorneys are not familiar with brainstorming or other aspects of problem-solving bargaining. If the negotiator blatantly attempts to "educate" an attorney with decades of bargaining experience about a "different" way of negotiating, her efforts probably will not be greeted enthusiastically. Subtle approaches are usually more successful.

If the other attorney starts the negotiation with a negotiating "position" and appears headed toward traditional positional bargaining, the negotiator can respond by probing behind the articulated position to discover the other party's underlying interests. Recall how Bev Bailey inquired about the reasons for Chestnut Development Corporation's standard lease terms. If she is successful in encouraging the other negotiator to discuss his client's justifications for his initial proposal, this will lead naturally to an opportunity for Bev to explain her own client's requirements and aspirations.

When introducing a solution-generation process into the bargaining, the negotiator usually should not explicitly identify it as "brainstorming" (or "solution generation," for that matter). If Bev believes it is advantageous for the two attorneys to engage in a joint session of identifying possible solutions, instead of presenting those she and her client already have developed, she can introduce the solution-generation process by demonstrating an understanding of Chestnut's goals. She also can reiterate her own client's needs and interests. She might then proceed as follows:

1—Bev: We both understand what each other's requirements and goals are for this negotiation. It doesn't make much sense for me to make a demand for bargaining purposes, knowing that your client can't accept it.

I'm wondering whether we couldn't short-cut the process and together just throw out some ideas that we might use in the lease. If you come up with an idea, I'm not going to hold you or your client to it if it turns out that it is not acceptable to your client. What are your thoughts on how we might protect your client's interest in receiving a fair return on its investment at the same time we don't bankrupt my client during a start-up period?

Very informally, Bev suggests that the parties refrain from exchanging bargaining positions, but instead consider a variety of solutions. She explicitly focuses attention on the underlying needs of the parties. She attempts to separate the inventive phase of brainstorming from the evaluative or judgmental stage by indicating that neither party is bound by a proposal, thus avoiding premature judgment.

If the other negotiator begins the bargaining process by expecting Bev to make an offer, she can transform the process into a joint search for mutually beneficial solutions by tactfully refusing to engage in positional bargaining:

2—Bev: Rather than begin with a list of lease terms as a demand, let me tell you what my client really needs here. Banana Computer's situation looks like this * * *

This discussion of Banana's requirements and aspirations can then lead to Bev questioning Dan about his client's needs, as previously described, and eventually to a joint search for solutions.

The problem-solving negotiation strategy proceeds directly to the task of finding an agreement that satisfies both parties. Posturing is absent from this approach. As a result, it is important to reiterate that the timing of the introduction of problem-solving techniques into the negotiation must be right. Often the frustration of failed competitive tactics precedes meaningful problem-solving negotiation.

Chapter Seven

INFORMATION BARGAINING

A. A BROADER PERSPECTIVE ON INFORMATION GATHERING

No other aspect of negotiation is as important as the exchange of information between negotiators. Negotiation can be viewed as a process in which each negotiator learns enough about what the other party needs and wants to propose an agreement that is acceptable to both her client and the other party.

Frequently, when negotiators begin to discuss their needs and aspirations, and to exchange information, this signals the beginning of genuine bargaining. In many negotiations, particularly transactional ones, substantial information bargaining occurs prior to the time that the parties make their initial proposals. In other instances, substantial information exchange is deferred until after the initial proposals. In either event, information exchange usually is an ongoing negotiation subprocess which, once begun, takes place throughout the negotiation.

At the same time she is negotiating, the lawyer typically gathers information in a number of other ways, such as her own independent investigation of the facts, or discovery if there is litigation involved. If the lawyer is negotiating to purchase a small corporation owning a chain of nursing homes, and her independent inquiries establish that other parties who were once prospective purchasers are now no longer interested, this suggests that the owners of the corporation might accept less in exchange for their shares of stock. Further, under these circumstances the lawyer probably should investigate why the other prospective purchasers have backed away from the sale.

The progress of the negotiation itself also implicitly communicates information about the other party's needs and expectations. If the other party persistently refuses to change its position on a particular issue despite the negotiator's urging, the negotiator may infer that the other party values that issue highly, unless, of course, the other negotiator is pursuing a false demand tactic. This chapter, however, focuses on more direct and conscious attempts to gain information

119

during the negotiation process. Specific factual information about the matter being negotiated and the other party's attitude toward the transaction or the negotiation itself, as well as information about what he wants and expects from an agreement, all assist the negotiator in proposing an agreement that is both acceptable to the other party and advantageous to her client.

This chapter discusses information exchange from both "offensive" and "defensive" postures. Tactics for gathering information from the other party and tactics for disclosing or concealing information are both considered. First, however, the differing perspectives of the competitive, cooperative and problem-solving strategies on information exchange are described briefly. The three strategies suggest different approaches to the three key issues of (1) information gathering, (2) information concealment and (3) information disclosure.

B. THE COMPETITIVE STRATEGY AND INFORMATION EXCHANGE

Because competitive tactics are designed to achieve an agreement most beneficial to the client at the expense of the other party, the purpose of competitive information gathering tactics is to determine what the other party's "bottom line" is, that is, what are the terms least satisfactory to the other side which he will accept. Thus, the competitive negotiator seeks information which either directly or indirectly indicates the "opponent's" minimum disposition. She typically believes her opponent also is approaching the negotiation competitively; she assumes he will try to conceal information from her. Consequently, obtaining information becomes a game, albeit one with important implications for the parties.

Conversely, it is a competitive tactic to conceal from the opponent information which indicates, directly or indirectly, the negotiator's own minimum disposition, or which weakens her bargaining power. Information that indicates to the opponent that the negotiator's own minimum disposition is an agreement less advantageous to her client than the one which she articulates during negotiation, or the one that the other party previously perceived was her minimum disposition, weakens the negotiator's bargaining power. Similarly, it is a competitive tactic to conceal from the opponent information that would induce him to change his minimum disposition to one even less advantageous to the negotiator than the opponent's original minimum disposition.

The competitive strategy does not suggest that all information be concealed. Information suggesting to the opponent that the range of the eventual agreement is more favorable to the lawyer's client than he previously thought increases the lawyer's bargaining leverage and should be disclosed.

There are substantial limitations on the ability to conceal information from the other negotiator in the real world. First, there are practical limits on the ability to make "one-sided" information disclosure in negotiation. Even using the variety of subtle techniques described below to conceal information, at some point the competitive negotiator's efforts to disclose favorable information while concealing unfavorable information become obvious. In the event that the negotiator temporarily succeeds in one-sided disclosure, her credibility may be severely impaired if the other negotiator subsequently realizes the extent of the uneven and potentially misleading disclosure. Second, in litigation negotiation, the widespread availability of discovery makes it more difficult to conceal information. However, full discovery is not always economically feasible. Indeed, negotiation can be used as an alternate form of discovery in those cases in which the full array of discovery mechanisms either is not feasible (smaller cases) or is not available (criminal cases in most jurisdictions).

C. THE COOPERATIVE STRATEGY AND INFORMATION EXCHANGE

Cooperative information bargaining tactics differ from competitive ones. The cooperative goal in information bargaining is to encourage and facilitate a full and accurate exchange of information so that the parties efficiently may achieve an agreement that is fair and just to both parties. In terms of information gathering, therefore, the cooperative approach functions similarly to the competitive approach—to gather as much relevant information as possible—but with a different purpose, a fair and just agreement.

The key difference between the two approaches to information exchange lies in the willingness of the cooperative negotiator to reveal information within her possession, even if it is potentially disadvantageous to her bargaining leverage. She risks this diminution of her bargaining position for two reasons. First, if the best possible negotiated result for the two parties is to be achieved, both parties require full and accurate information about the matter being negotiated, and about which issues each party values most. Second, revealing information is used as a tactic to obtain information from the other party. A cooperative information bargaining tactic is to reveal information and to expect the other party to reciprocate. In other words, the expectation is to assume that the parties will trade information, just as they exchange concessions.

D. THE PROBLEM–SOLVING STRATEGY AND INFORMATION EXCHANGE

Problem-solving information bargaining, like its cooperative counterpart, encourages the free flow of information between the parties. Full information about the parties' needs, goals and motivations is required if the negotiators are to devise bridging solutions to address the parties' underlying problems. The negotiators also must exchange information about their client's priorities among the issues if they are to engage in logrolling and trade concessions on different issues in a manner that maximizes joint gains.

E. INFORMATION GATHERING

Information gathering is an indispensable element in any negotiation strategy, regardless of whether it employs predominantly competitive, cooperative or problem-solving tactics. After a brief introduction describing the pervasive nature of information gathering, this section describes a variety of specific information gathering techniques.

1. TYPES OF INFORMATION TO BE OBTAINED

The negotiator wants to know everything possible that might affect the other negotiator's bargaining behavior and the eventual negotiation results. Specifically, she wants to know anything that suggests directly or indirectly what the other party's requirements and expectations are for an agreement, and what are his alternatives to a successful negotiation. Therefore, her bargaining should include attempts to fill in information gaps about the matter being negotiated, as well as to ascertain the other party's perceptions of the negotiation situation. In addition, other kinds of information are relevant to the negotiation process itself instead of to the transaction or dispute being negotiated. Is the other negotiator too busy or inexperienced to handle the negotiation properly? Is he scared to go to trial if the negotiation breaks down? An extremely competitive negotiator might want to know when the other lawyer intends to take a vacation with his family, so she can use the date of the approaching vacation to create an artificial time deadline.

Consider Bev Bailey's information gathering in the negotiation between Banana Computer and the Chestnut Development Corporation. Bev tries to obtain information which indirectly tells her something about Chestnut's minimum disposition and its negotiation target. Are there other promising commercial tenants interested in leasing the same space? The terms and conditions of leases with other tenants would be informative, as would knowledge about the underlying cost structure for mall operations. Information about renewal rates and why other tenants have elected not to renew their leases might yield valuable bargaining leverage. Does Chestnut Development Corporation believe that it harms the business of other stores to allow a retail space to remain vacant for a significant period of time, or is Chestnut typically patient, willing to wait for extremely desirable tenants?

Similarly, consider information gathering in the negotiation between Patrick Finney and the Baltimore and Western Railroad. In addition to facts affecting the merits of the negligence case and the railroad's opinion of the liability and damage issues, Gary Gerstein, Patrick's attorney, also is interested in the amount of any insurance coverage, because this may affect the willingness of the defendant and its insurer to settle the claim within a given range. In addition, he wants to know the amount of reserves the carrier has established for this case, and how the carrier determined this amount. This information helps Gary determine both the limits of the opposing attorney's negotiation authority and the likelihood that it can be modified.

Information gathering can begin substantially in advance of any "formal" negotiation sessions. Off-hand comments by an attorney, complaining about her busy schedule when asking for leave to file an answer or a motion on a delayed basis, suggest that she may not have the time to properly prepare and litigate every issue if opposing counsel pushes the case forward quickly. References by an attorney to her experience or lack of experience in similar cases, or about her lack of enthusiasm for a difficult client, also are important facts that may affect settlement value and negotiation strategy.

2. QUESTIONING

The most effective way to gain information during negotiation is the most obvious—ask questions. Most individuals are socialized at a very early age to answer politely questions addressed to them, and such conditioning is reinforced by law school professors and judges who ask questions and expect answers. It is difficult to refuse to answer a question without giving a reason, and many negotiators feel uncomfortable about declining to answer questions even when they do give reasons. Even if a negotiating attorney finds ways to fend off a question without answering it, either her client or an expert who is present often will not have the poise or experience necessary to parry the question without answering it.

In some negotiations, direct questions about issues going to the heart of the matter often produce spontaneous and surprisingly revealing answers. Such questions include "What's your bottom line here?" or "What's it going to take to resolve this?" Direct questions are most likely to prompt accurate and meaningful answers if posed early in the negotiation, particularly if asked of an inexperienced negotiator, or as part of a negotiation the other lawyer regards as being a "small matter."

When the other negotiator declines to answer a direct question or answers it evasively, slight variations in the same question frequently produce more information. For example, consider Patrick Finney's personal injury settlement talks with the Baltimore and Western Railroad. The most direct and blunt question to be asked by Gary Gerstein would be "What's your client's bottom line?" or "Let's stop fooling around, how much will it take to settle this thing?" In all likelihood, that question will be answered evasively or dishonestly. The slightly more indirect variation of the same question would be "What do you expect the jury will do with this case?" The answer to this question may yield significant information for Gary about the railroad's minimum disposition both because it is likely to produce quantifiably *more* information than the earlier question and perhaps because it will produce a more honest response. There may be a kind of implicit assumption that if the other negotiator is forward enough to ask directly about the negotiator's "bottom line," deceit is perfectly acceptable, but that misleading the other negotiator about trial predictions is less professionally acceptable. Finally, the negotiator can ask an even more indirect variation of the question, such as "What evidence do you expect to use at trial to prove your case?" Once again, the answer to this question tells the negotiator something indirectly about what the other attorney expects the results at trial to be, and therefore about what constitutes his minimum disposition. By inquiring even more indirectly, however, the last question frequently produces both greater detail in the information and greater honesty than the questions described previously.

The negotiator should use varying *forms* of questions depending upon the following factors: how forthcoming the other negotiator is, the stage of the negotiation, and whether the parties are using predominantly competitive or predominantly cooperative and problem-solving negotiation tactics. The form of the question—that is, whether it is an open-ended, narrow or specific, or leading question—may affect the behavioral response of the other negotiator.[1] Once again the best known example of this is the advice to novice trial attorneys to use leading questions during cross-examination, not only because the rules of evidence allow them, but also because such questions are most likely to control the content of the witness's testimony.

Open-ended questions are questions posed to the other negotiator which allow him to choose the topic, or which aspect of a broadly defined topic, to discuss. For example, Gary Gerstein, Patrick Finney's attorney, might ask the following open-ended questions in his negotiation with the attorney representing Baltimore and Western Railroad:

"How does your client view this case?"

"Why do you think this is a no liability situation?"

Open-ended questions posed to the other negotiator are productive when he is openly sharing information previously unknown to the negotiator and at least some of the information is relevant and useful. Open-ended questions are most likely to yield worthwhile information when the negotiators are using predominantly cooperative or problem-solving negotiation tactics, and therefore are committed to sharing information with each other. Incidentally, open-ended questions themselves facilitate the use of cooperative or problem-solving tactics by assisting in developing rapport between the negotiators. They build rapport by allowing the other negotiator to choose the topics he is discussing and giving him the sense that his client's interests in the negotiation are being fairly considered. Finally, open-ended questions

1. For an excellent discussion of the forms of questions and their effects on the individual being questioned, *see* D. Binder & S. Price, Legal Interviewing and Counseling: A Client–Centered Approach 38–47 (1977).

usually are most productive early in the negotiation when the negotiator has wide-ranging information gaps, and needs to gain general knowledge about the matter being negotiated and the other party's attitude toward it.   Later in the negotiation, when the negotiator already has most of the information she needs, frequent use of open-ended questions probably is inefficient.

Specific or narrow questions are questions in which the negotiator chooses the specific subject matter that she wishes the other negotiator to discuss.   Examples of specific questions which Patrick Finney's attorney might ask the railroad's attorney during the negotiation include the following:

"How fast was the train going at the time of the accident?"

"What procedures has Baltimore and Western established for keeping its crossings clear of overgrown brush and weeds?"

"When did the engineer first notice the truck approaching the tracks?"

The negotiator should ask specific questions when her information needs are well defined or when the other negotiator is not sharing relevant information openly.   Specific questions are much more difficult for the other negotiator to evade than are open-ended ones.   Thus, they are recommended when competitive tactics are predominant in the negotiation.   Further, specific questions often are more fruitful later in the negotiation when the lawyer largely understands both the subject matter of the negotiation and the other party's views on the matter being negotiated, but still has information gaps about specific issues.

A leading question is an extreme form of a specific question that makes a statement and asks the other negotiator to confirm it.   Strings of leading questions similar to those posed to hostile witnesses in a courtroom during cross-examination are seldom, if ever, appropriate during negotiation.   A courteous and cooperatively phrased leading question, however, may enable a negotiator to pin-down a point during bargaining.   For example, consider the following questions interspersed by Gary Gerstein in his conversation with the railroad's representative:

"So the engineer did not see the truck on the tracks until he was 80 yards away from the crossing?"

"You're telling me then that there wasn't any program of regular inspection of crossings to identify visibility problems.   Is that right?"

3. ACTIVE LISTENING FOR CONTENT

The use of *active listening* as a cooperation facilitator in negotiation previously was considered in Chapter Five.   It will be recalled that *active listening* was defined as a process of hearing what the other negotiator has said, understanding it and responding with a reflective statement which mirrors what the negotiator has heard.   In addition to the use of active listening primarily as a cooperation facilitator to reflect the other negotiator's *feelings*, active listening also can be applied to mirror factual statements by the other negotiator. When active listening is employed in this vein, it serves as a "content check" to assure the lawyer that she accurately has heard and understood the other negotiator. Thus, active listening for content is closely related to the non-combative cross-examination techniques described in the previous section.

Consider the following sequence in the negotiation between Gary and Roberta:

1—Gary: Tell me what measures your client took to be sure that visibility at crossings was not obscured by overgrown brush and weeds?

2—Roberta: My client's regular train crews were responsible for reporting whenever brush and weeds obscured vision at crossings.

3—Gary: So there was no other regular process for regularly inspecting crossing visibility.

4—Roberta: That's right.

In segment number 3, Gary uses *active listening* to check his understanding that Baltimore and Western relied upon their train crews to report weeds and brush obscuring visibility and had no other regular inspection process. Roberta's response to his *active listening* consolidates this admission by Baltimore and Western.

4. SILENCE

The most overlooked information gathering tactic in negotiation is silence. Particularly because many negotiators frequently experience bargaining sessions as high anxiety events, it feels unnatural and awkward for there to be long pauses in the discussion. Accordingly, many negotiators are prone to fill gaps in the conversation by talking— and when they talk, they reveal information. The negotiator should not feel obliged to respond to every point made by her counterpart if his conversation is providing information helpful to her. The negotiator, however, needs to guard against the possibility that her counterpart will gain a real or perceived psychological dominance of the bargaining session by monopolizing the conversation.

5. DIRECT CHALLENGES

Another approach to obtaining information that the other negotiator is reluctant to yield is to "bait" him, or directly attack or challenge him in a way that yields a defensive outpouring of information. Assume in Bev Bailey's negotiation with the Chestnut Development Corporation that Chestnut has been evasive about revealing its current and expected labor and insurance costs, despite its claim that it is very concerned about increases in these costs. Both direct and indirect questions have failed to solicit this information. Another approach would be for Bev to directly challenge Dan Darrow, the attorney for Chestnut:

1—Bev: (with obvious frustration after a long bargaining session)

Dan, you keep telling me that your client needs a higher rental to cover increased insurance and labor costs. Yet you're unwilling to share your records showing such cost trends with me. It almost makes me wonder whether your management has a cost accounting system which can produce this kind of information.

2—Dan: (testily)

You can be sure that our accounting systems are state of the art, and that the applicable shares of the costs for labor and insurance can be allocated to each retail space.

3—Bev: If you are going to continue to justify your higher demand for rental on the basis of high wages and insurance, I think I'm entitled to see your supporting documents.

In this case, Bev combines the direct challenge in the first statement with another information gathering tactic, the demand for inspection of documents, in the third statement. A demand for inspection of documents or files following unproven factual assertions by the other negotiator puts considerable pressure on the other party to release the files or reports. If shared with the negotiator, such documents often include a variety of other information.

6. INTERPRETING PARALINGUISTICS AND NON–VERBAL COMMUNICATIONS

The ability to interpret non-verbal communication and paralinguistics can play a critical role for the negotiator. Paralinguistics are content-free vocalizations and pauses accompanying speech.[2] They include vocal qualities such as pitch and loudness, as well as speech disturbances such as stutter, omission, repetition, hesitation and unfilled pauses. Non-verbal communications, of course, refer to facial expressions, hand movements and body language.

The ability to read non-verbal communication and paralinguistics sometimes allows the negotiator to detect when the other party is using competitive tactics behind a collaborative smoke-screen. In choosing between competitive or collaborative tactics, the most important factor is to predict accurately whether cooperative or problem-solving tactics will be reciprocated. The biggest danger for the negotiator is taking seemingly accommodative actions at face-value when, in fact, competitive tactics are being used. The ability to recognize and interpret

2. *See* D. Druckman, R. Rozelle & J. Baxter, Nonverbal Communication: Survey, Theory and Research 43–44 (1982).

paralinguistic signals and non-verbal communication is often the most effective way to expose the competitive negotiator who seeks to mislead with a cooperative style. The ability to read such communication also can expose specific substantive examples of deception and evasion by a competitive counterpart.

There is no simple Rosetta Stone or index that tells the negotiator that a particular non-verbal communication invariably has a certain meaning. Individual non-verbal communications must be interpreted in the context of other non-verbal clues, the negotiation situation, and what is being verbally communicated. On the other hand, interpreting non-verbal communications is not as complex or difficult as it first sounds because most people consciously or unconsciously interpret non-verbal messages on a regular basis.

No other part of the body is more expressive than the eyes—a fact frequently commented on by poets and proven by empiricists.[3] "Inquisitive looks," "icy stares," "shifty eyes," and "seductive stares" are all interpretations of mental states based upon visual cues. If the negotiator understands visual nonverbal communication, she often can use it to interpret the other negotiator's "eye messages." On the other hand, if the negotiator consciously focuses on her own visual behavior, she probably can manipulate, at least to some extent, her own visual messages.

Visual contact between the negotiators serves at least three functions. First, visual behavior is used subconsciously to signal to the other person when it is time to speak and when it is time to listen.[4] For example, when the other lawyer establishes direct eye contact with the negotiator during a conversation, it often signals his desire to speak. As a general rule, the negotiator has more eye contact with the other lawyer when she listens to him than when she speaks to him. The second function of looking at the other negotiator is to obtain information about him.[5] Research shows that frequency of gaze is an index of information-seeking. Those who seek information about the other while controlling information about themselves—a description fitting the negotiator using competitive tactics—frequently use short, frequent gazes. More sustained looks are characteristic of those who want to gather information about the other party, while disclosing information themselves—such as negotiators willing to use cooperative or problem-solving tactics.

How can a negotiator become more effective by consciously controlling her own visual behavior? Studies suggest that a high degree of eye contact causes a presentation to be viewed as more authentic and a

3. *See id.* at 73–84 for a survey of research involving visual behavior.

4. *See* Argyle & Ubgham, *Gaze, Mutual Gaze, and Proximity,* 6 Semiotica 32–49 (1972); Duncan, *Some Signals and Rules for Taking Speaking Turns In Conversations,* 23 Journal of Personality and Social Psychology 282–92 (1972); Kendon, *Some Functions of Gaze–Direction in Social Interaction,* 26 Acta Psychologica 22–63 (1967).

5. *See* Foddy, *Patterns of Gaze in Cooperative and Competitive Negotiation,* 31 Human Relations 925–938 (1978).

speaker to be seen as more poised.[6] Once again, however, the validity of this generalization depends upon the circumstances. Certainly sustained staring often backfires and looks very awkward. Further, differences in the sex, race or cultural backgrounds of the negotiators sometimes mean that sustained eye contact may produce feelings of discomfort or even hostility.

Eye contact with another person also serves to communicate a willingness to collaborate—in the context of this text, either to engage in cooperative or problem-solving negotiation tactics. The average length of gaze (eye contact) and mutual gaze have been found to be greater for cooperators than for competitors, while the frequency of gaze and mutual gaze were the same for both groups.[7]

The negotiator also learns by watching for other non-verbal communications from her counterpart, including facial expressions and body language. Facial expressions probably convey the most specific information about the other negotiator's attitudes and emotions, but are more susceptible to conscious control by him.[8] *Kinetics*, or body language, including gestures, postural shifts and movements of the hands, head, feet and legs, has been extensively studied and classified.[9] Most often, body language conveys broad psychological states rather than specific intentions and emotions. Thus, patterns of body language may help reveal whether the other negotiator is behaving generally in a competitive or a collaborative manner, but they reveal little about a specific message from the other lawyer.

Perhaps the most relevant research for negotiation students is a study by Druckman, Rozelle and Baxter, that measures the differences in non-verbal communications between subjects who were honest, evasive and deceptive.[10] The results of their research suggest that if the negotiator can observe her counterpart's degree of eye contact, frequency of leg movements and fidgeting with "objects" (*e.g.*, pen, pencil, or jewelry), she may be able to predict whether he is being honest, deceptive or evasive. Subjects who were deceiving others were found to have a higher number of speech errors, such as stuttering, repetition of phrases, broken phrases and insertions of nonsubstantive phrases. "Deceivers" also spoke more rapidly and in a higher pitch. In addition, deceivers were more likely to "fidget" with objects and to avoid looking at the other party. Those who evaded answering questions were found to have more leg and foot movements than other subjects and to engage

---

6. Kleck & Neussle, *Congruence Between the Indicative and Communicative Functions of Eye Contact in Interpersonal Relations,* 7 British Journal of Social and Clinical Psychology 241–46 (1968); Le-Compte & Rosenfeld, *Effects of Minimal Eye Contact in the Instruction Period on Impressions of the Experimenter,* 7 Journal of Experimental Social Psychology 211–220 (1971).

7. Foddy, *supra* note 5, at 936.

8. *See generally* D. Druckman, R. Rozelle & J. Baxter, *supra* note 2, at 52–64; G. Nierenberg & H. Calero, How to Read a Person Like a Book 28–34 (1971).

9. *See generally* D. Druckman, R. Rozelle & J. Baxter, *supra* note 2, at 64–73; G. Nierenberg & H. Calero, *supra* note 8, at 36–134.

10. D. Druckman, R. Rozelle and J. Baxter, *supra* note 2, at 109–175.

in more side-to-side head shaking, particularly early in the interaction. "Evaders" also avoided eye contact by gazing and fidgeting, particularly in the later phases of the interaction.

Negotiators often experience anxiety, discomfort, or defensiveness during bargaining. These emotional states may result either from deception or evasion in negotiation behavior, or from other factors. In addition to some of the non-verbal communications previously described as characteristics of deceivers or evaders, other commentators have noted the increased frequency of throat-clearing and the presence of hands covering or positioned near the mouth among those experiencing anxiety or discomfort.[11] In addition, arms crossed on the chest are a typical sign of defensiveness. Picture a manager leaving a dugout at a baseball game, rushing onto the field to dispute a call by the first-base umpire. How will the umpire respond? If sufficiently provoked, probably by ejecting the manager. Before things get to that point, however, the fans are likely to observe the umpire fold his arms across his chest.

Few negotiators will master the interpretation of all subtle non-verbal communication clues. One signal that most negotiators often can detect, however, is incongruity between the verbal message and the non-verbal communication. Assume that the response to the negotiator's demand is a slight pause or hesitation in the conversation and perhaps hints of a subtle smile by the other negotiator. When he then erupts with a statement that the demand is "OUTRAGEOUS" and that it is clear the negotiator is "wholly unrealistic about the case," the negotiator should not take these verbal statements at face value.

What other non-verbal behaviors may suggest a willingness of the other negotiator to engage in cooperative or problem-solving tactics? Perhaps the most obvious non-verbal behavior signaling openness or sincerity is "open hands" with the palms extended and facing up. The author once taught Torts to a class that included a hearing impaired student who had become extremely adept at reading non-verbal communication. During one class, the student stopped her answer to a Socratic question in mid-sentence. When later asked about her unusual behavior, she responded that the author almost always displayed "palms-up" and even pulled his hands toward himself when he thought that the student's answer was a worthwhile contribution to class discussion. Conversely, she reported, the author usually turned his hands over into a "palms-down" position when the student's answer did not please him. Thus, when her professor turned his hands "palms-down" during her answer, she concluded that there was no reason to complete her answer!

Other gestures may indicate a readiness to engage in serious bargaining or to use cooperative or problem-solving tactics. Nierenberg and Calero suggest, for example, that if the other negotiator is literally

---

11. *See* G. Nierenberg & H. Calero, *supra* note 8, at 44–104 for a fuller description of the specific non-verbal communications described in this section.

sitting on the edge of his chair, this signals a "readiness for action." [12] On one hand, this "action" may be a willingness to conclude the negotiation; on the other hand, it is also possible that the position indicates that the individual is about to walk out of the negotiation. However, if the other negotiator makes a "final and last offer" in this position, it is more likely that the offer is in fact "final and last" than it would be if he were leaning back from the table with his hands behind his head. Similarly, according to Nierenberg and Calero, if the other negotiator's hand or finger touches his chin or another part of the face, this often is an "evaluation gesture" suggesting that he is in fact seriously engaged in evaluation, hopefully of the lawyer's latest proposal.[13]

Any visual clues suggesting the other negotiator's degree of confidence obviously also are important. If the other negotiator is pursuing competitive tactics, non-verbal displays suggesting poise or confidence indicate that he believes his negotiation tactics are working. Conversely, if the negotiator herself is using competitive tactics in an attempt to undermine the confidence of the other negotiator, his body language may indicate whether her competitive tactics are working. Probably the most clearly defined non-verbal communication suggesting confidence is "steepling," a hand position in which an individual joins the fingertips from one hand to the corresponding fingertips on the other hand to form a figure resembling a "church steeple." Nierenberg and Calero recommend that if you are playing poker and one of the players is steepling, "unless you have a very good hand, get out of the game." [14] Another gesture typically indicating confidence is leaning back with two hands laced behind the head. If the other negotiator displays these confident gestures, it suggests either that his confidence is not being undermined by the negotiator's competitive tactics or that he believes his own competitive tactics are working.

Like non-verbal communication, paralinguistic variables—content free vocalizations and pauses associated with speech—also can be used to detect anxiety. The frequency of speech disturbances, such as "ahs" and repetitions of words or phrases, increase with anxiety, whether that anxiety is caused by deception or other factors. In addition, the pitch or vocal frequency frequently becomes higher when a subject is lying.

The words chosen by the lawyer in negotiation also may communicate unintended messages. For example, when the other negotiator begins a statement about the limits of his authority with the preface "To be perfectly honest * * * " or a similar phrase, the lawyer should be careful. Experience suggests that such statements frequently precede lies. "When somebody tells you it isn't the money, it's the principle of the thing," Artemus Ward once said, "It's the money." Similarly, careful listening can help the lawyer distinguish what actu-

---

12. *Id.* at 44–47.

13. *Id.* at 77–79, 81–83.

14. *Id.* at 93–104.

ally was said from what the other negotiator hoped or expected that she would infer from the statement. Often negotiators will be careful not to tell a direct lie, but will purposely use words to mislead. For example, consider again the negotiation between Gary Gerstein and Roberta Martinez. Initially, the following statements by Roberta may appear to be saying the same thing:

(1) "My client cannot and will not pay more than $250,000."

(2) "I am not authorized to pay more than $250,000."

(3) "I am not authorized to offer more than $250,000 *at this time*."

The first statement obviously is more absolute than the other two statements, posing less opportunity for subsequent changes in negotiation position. The second statement communicates implicitly that although the railroad attorney is not authorized to pay more, the amount of the settlement authority could be changed. The third statement is even more explicit, and virtually invites a suggestion that the attorney return to her client to seek further authority.

The brief discussion of non-verbal communication and paralinguistics presented here is not exhaustive, and will not make you an expert overnight. It is intended only to make you conscious of non-verbal communications and paralinguistics. Unconsciously, you have always read non-verbal communications. Greater concentration on the other negotiator's non-verbal communication may assist you in answering the critical question of whether the other lawyer is acting competitively or collaboratively.

7. ADDITIONAL PROBLEM–SOLVING INFORMATION GATHERING TACTICS

The information gathering tactics previously discussed can be used as a part of the problem-solving strategy, as well as in competitive or cooperative bargaining. One additional major information gathering approach for the problem-solving negotiator was previously discussed in Chapter Six, *Initial Proposals*. When the other negotiator begins with a traditional bargaining position, it was suggested that the problem-solving negotiator respond by asking her counterpart which of his client's interests are served by the proposal. In other words, she should ask "Why?" The answer to such an inquiry is likely to reveal the underlying interests of the other party. In addition, if the negotiator's own proposal is summarily rejected, she can ask "why not?"

Another information gathering, or more accurately, information sharing technique, is for the negotiators to engage in informal problem-solving discussions outside the framework of formal negotiation sessions.[15] For example, labor negotiators frequently discuss the needs

---

15. *See* D. Pruitt, Negotiation Behavior 98–99 (1981). In their book entitled *A Behavioral Theory of Labor Negotiations: An Analysis of a Social Interaction System*, Walton and McKersie discuss the effect of "off the record" conversations on the 1964 automobile industry negotiations. With both sides free to pursue alternatives in these conversations, tentative solutions were proposed and explored without fear of

and interests of the union and of management more openly away from the formal, public bargaining sessions. They often do so with the understanding that such conversations are "off the record" and that they will not be held publicly accountable for any opinions or views expressed when the proposals are discussed.

F. INFORMATION CONCEALMENT

Information concealment is a competitive tactic. A competitive negotiator often avoids revealing information to conceal his minimum disposition or to prevent erosion of his bargaining leverage. By definition, problem-solving and cooperative information tactics involve disclosure, not concealment. However, even negotiators using predominantly problem-solving or cooperative tactics sometimes conceal information, such as when it is apparent the other negotiator wants the information solely to weaken the negotiator's bargaining position.

This section begins with a discussion of the professional responsibility issues inherent in concealing information from the other negotiator or even misleading him. It then discusses a variety of techniques available to the lawyer to avoid answering the other negotiator's inquiries.

1. ETHICAL CONSIDERATIONS

Competitive tactics for concealing the client's minimum disposition, and even misleading the other negotiator about the client's interests in the negotiation, pose the primary set of ethical issues for the lawyer as negotiator. Model Rule of Professional Conduct 4.1 explicitly provides:

> In the course of representing a client a lawyer shall not knowingly:
>
> (a) make a false statement of material fact or law to a third person; or
>
> (b) fail to disclose a material fact to a third person when disclosure is necessary to avoid assisting a criminal or fraudulent act by a client, unless disclosure is prohibited by Rule 1.6.[16]

The Model Rules thus address the negotiator's deception whether accomplished with an affirmative misstatement of fact (subsection (a)) or through concealment (subsection (b)).

The provisions of the Model Code's predecessor, the Disciplinary Rules, arguably are even more ethically demanding. Disciplinary Rule 1–102 states generally that "[a] lawyer shall not * * * engage in conduct involving dishonesty, fraud, deceit or misrepresentation." [17] Further, the Disciplinary Rules prohibit the lawyer from knowingly advancing claims or defenses unwarranted under existing law or from

later accountability. R. Walton and R. McKersie, A Behavioral Theory of Labor Negotiations: An Analysis of a Social Interaction System 158–160 (1965).

16. Model Rules of Professional Conduct Rule 4.1 (1983). *See generally* C. Wolfram, Modern Legal Ethics 719–27 (1986).

17. Model Code of Professional Responsibility DR 1–102(A)(4) (1987).

concealing or knowingly failing to disclose that which she is required by law to reveal.[18]

The proper application of these seemingly straightforward prohibitions to the lawyer as negotiator remains obscure, but perhaps not as obscure as the existing prevalence of misrepresentation in negotiation would lead one to believe.[19] The inherent dilemma for the negotiator using competitive tactics is how does she comply with the ethical constraints and simultaneously deceive the other lawyer regarding her client's minimum disposition.

Certain types of statements used by the negotiator to deceive can be readily identified as falling on one side or the other of the ethical line. A statement by Gary Gerstein that Patrick Finney's past medical expenses were twice as great as they really were is clearly a forbidden misrepresentation of material fact, as would be a false account of Chestnut Development Corporation's expenses. An extremely high initial demand by Gary Gerstein, on the other hand, although calculated to deceive, is permissible. Similarly, "puffery" or misstatements of opinion about value are not misstatements of material facts under convential bargaining norms and therefore are permissible,[20] as are misrepresentations of the lawyer's authority to bind her client.[21] False demands also are a traditional and arguably inherent part of multiple issue negotiation and thus probably do not constitute an ethical violation.[22] Finally, a negotiator presumably can argue a plausible interpretation of the law during negotiation, just as she can during argument to the court, at the same time she entertains private doubts about whether the law applies to the instant case.[23]

This list of exceptions to the prohibition against misrepresentation does not provide a clear standard against which to test the ethical propriety of the innumerable possible variations of deceptive state-

18. The relevant portions of Disciplinary Rule 7–102(A) state:

(A) In his representation of a client, a lawyer shall not:

* * * (2) Knowingly advance a claim or defense that is unwarranted under existing law, except that he may advance such claim or defense if it can be supported by good faith argument for an extension, modification, or reversal of existing law.

(3) Conceal or knowingly fail to disclose that which he is required by law to reveal.

(4) Knowingly make a false statement of law or fact.

Code of Professional Responsibility DR 7–102(A) (1987).

19. A survey of lawyers conducted by the University of Michigan Law School in conjunction with the American Bar Foundation reportedly found that 18 percent of the national attorneys and 28 percent of Michigan attorneys surveyed believed that lawyers regularly or frequently make representations during negotiation that they believe are false. *See* R. Haydock, Negotiation Practice 201–02 (1984).

20. Model Rules of Professional Conduct Rule 4.1 comment (1983); *see also* White, *Machiavelli and the Bar: Ethical Limitations on Lying in Negotiation,* 1980 Am.B.Found.Res.J. 921, 931 (1980).

21. *See supra* Chapter Four, *Negotiation Planning,* at 70–1, for a full discussion of the ethical issues involved in a false denial of authority to settle a claim.

22. *See supra* Chapter Six, *Initial Proposals,* at 104–5, for a comprehensive discussion of the ethics of false demands.

23. *See* White, *supra* note 20, at 931.

ments during negotiation. Some commentators assert that bargaining conventions governing acceptable levels of deception vary from heterogenous urban areas to more homogeneous rural communities where greater good faith in negotiation is required.[24] Further, they contend that traditional practice provides for a higher standard of ethical conduct in certain substantive practice contexts, such as securities practice, than in others, like personal injury practice. These practice differences arguably suggest that standards governing professionally acceptable levels of deception in negotiation vary according to the negotiation context.[25] Other commentators have proposed articulated standards of truthfulness in negotiation which are far more demanding and which would effectively prohibit many competitive negotiation tactics.[26] For example, Professor Steele has suggested a rule providing, in part, that "each lawyer owes the other an obligation of total candor and total cooperation to the extent required to insure that the result is fair."[27]

The questions regarding the ethical necessity to disclose certain kinds of information in negotiation are perhaps even more difficult than those relating to affirmative misrepresentations. Generally a negotiator is under no affirmative obligation to disclose or volunteer information which harms her bargaining position. What is Gary Gerstein's obligation to the other lawyer, however, when Patrick Finney informs him that some of the medical expenses he claimed earlier are fictitious? Well-established law governing misrepresentation makes it clear that the party who fails to correct the earlier misstatement commits a misrepresentation actionable as a tort.[28] Model Rule of Professional Conduct 1.6, however, provides that unless the lawyer receives the client's permission to correct the earlier statement, she cannot reveal it in negotiation except under the most unusual circumstances.[29] In a variety of other contexts, the lawyer's obligation to reveal information in order to prevent an ethical violation is debatable.[30]

24. *See* Guernsey, *Truthfulness in Negotiation,* 17 U.Rich.L.Rev. 100–01 (1982); White, *supra* note 20, at 929–30.

25. White, *supra* note 20, at 931.

26. Rubin, *A Causerie on Lawyers' Ethics in Negotiation,* 35 La.L.Rev. 577 (1975); Steele, *Essay: Deceptive Negotiating and High–Toned Morality,* 39 Van.L.Rev. 1387 (1986).

27. Steele, *supra* note 26, at 1400.

28. Restatement of Torts Second § 551(2) (1965); W. Keeton, Prosser and Keeton on the Law of Torts 738 (5th ed. 1985).

29. Model Rule of Professional Conduct 1.6 permits a lawyer to reveal information relating to the representation of a client either when the client consents or when the lawyer reasonably believes disclosure to be necessary "to prevent the client from committing a criminal act that the lawyer believes is likely to result in imminent death or substantial bodily harm." Model Rules of Professional Conduct Rule 1.6(b)(1) (1983).

30. *See* Guernsey, *supra* note 24, at 113–121; Hazard, *The Lawyer's Obligation to Be Trustworthy When Dealing With Opposing Parties,* 33 S.C.L.Rev. 181, 185–96 (1981); White, *supra* note 20, at 935–38.

2. TACTICS TO AVOID REVEALING INFORMATION

As noted previously, there are practical, as well as ethical, limits regarding how one-sided even the competitive negotiator can expect the information exchange process to be. No experienced negotiator will reveal substantial information without reciprocity. Further, the tactics outlined in this section to conceal information succeed only if the other negotiator lacks the ability, persistence or desire to follow up on his initial questions and to press for the information requested.

A complete array of tactics to avoid answering questions can be observed in any press conference held by a high government official or politician. Some of these tactics include:

(1) *Don't Answer the Question and Shift to Another Topic*

Consider the following example from the Banana Computer/Chestnut Development Corporation negotiation:

> 1—Bev: How much rent is the jewelry store that just began operations last month paying?
>
> 2—Dan: I'm glad you mentioned Goldstone's. I think their success really points out the advantage of the location near June's Department Store. They have had nearly double the number of customers they were expecting during the first month. How many "lookers" and how many "buyers" are you projecting?

Dan avoids answering the question asked about the amount of rent charged Goldstone's and uses the mention of Goldstone's as a transition to the discussion of another topic, store location.

(2) *Answer a Different Question Than the One Asked*

An example from the negotiation between the attorneys for Patrick Finney and the Baltimore and Western Railroad illustrates this tactic:

> 1—Gary: How many other car-train accidents have you had at this crossing?
>
> 2—Roberta: In all my years representing the railroad, we've never had a lawsuit from that crossing.

Roberta does not answer the question about the number of *accidents* at the crossing; instead, she answers the very different question of how many *lawsuits* have resulted from accidents at the same crossing.

(3) *Answer Incompletely*

This evasive tactic is similar to the last one, as suggested by its application to the same situation:

> 1—Gary: How many other car-train accidents have you had at this crossing?
>
> 2—Roberta: To the best of my knowledge, there has never been one.

By limiting her answer to her own knowledge, Roberta answers incompletely. Gary does not learn the answer to the question, and unless he pursues the topic, Roberta is under no obligation to investigate the answer to the question.

(4) *Answer Only If Information Sharing Is Reciprocated*

The negotiator agrees to answer the question, but only if the other party is prepared to answer a corresponding question. For example, let's consider again the negotiation between Banana and Chestnut:

1—Bev: How much rent is the jewelry store that just began operations last month paying?

2—Dan: I appreciate your interest in reaching a fair deal based upon all the facts. My client would be prepared to share that information if your client will share with us the rates being quoted to you by other shopping centers and commercial landlords in this area.

(5) *Delay*

When asked a question she wishes to evade, the negotiator can promise to get the answer to the question and supply it at a later date. Somehow, however, she never does, and unless the information is important, the other negotiator frequently will not follow up on his request. The question has been effectively evaded.

(6) *Refuse to Answer and Explain Why*

Frequently, a negotiator simply rules a question out-of-bounds. When asked how much authority she has from a client, she states, "That's between me and my client." When asked about the rates being paid by other tenants at the Chestnut Mall, Dan Darrow might respond that the leases with the other tenants are confidential, and therefore he cannot disclose their terms.

(7) *Beware of the Outright Lie*

The Model Rules of Professional Conduct clearly state that misstatements of fact by attorneys during negotiations are prohibited and constitute violations of professional ethics.[31] Unfortunately, it is clear that some members of the bar do intentionally misrepresent facts during negotiation.

(8) *Say Little*

If asked a specific question, it usually is not professionally or socially acceptable behavior to remain silent and say nothing. Over the course of a negotiation session, however, one of the best ways to reduce the amount of information being revealed to the other negotiator is to stay quiet and do little talking. As previously discussed, many

---

31. Model Rules of Professional Conduct Rule 4.1 (1983).

lawyers representing other parties will fill silence by talking. Not only does the negotiator gain information while the other negotiator talks, during the time she listens, she also does not reveal any information to him.

(9) *Calculated Ignorance*

One way to avoid sharing any information with the other negotiator is to avoid knowing anything. For example, Roberta Martinez, attorney for the Baltimore and Western Railroad, might make a calculated decision not to have any substantive conversations with representatives of her client prior to her first meeting with Gary Gerstein, Patrick Finney's attorney. A more extreme example is the law firm that sends an associate to a negotiation who knows very little about the case and who has no authority to settle it.[32]

G. INFORMATION DISCLOSURE

It is difficult to conceive of any negotiation which concludes without both negotiators sharing at least some information with their negotiating counterparts. Unless the negotiator either discloses new information or demonstrates in new ways how the facts previously available to the other party support her own proposals and arguments, there is no reason for the other negotiator to change his initial proposal. Therefore, even the negotiator using predominantly competitive tactics discloses information that supports her proposals.

The negotiator using cooperative or problem-solving tactics goes further and discloses even information that conceivably could be used to harm her client's bargaining interests. The cooperative approach to information exchange is to encourage full and accurate disclosure of facts from both parties so that the negotiators together can determine what constitutes a fair and just agreement. One specific cooperative tactic is to initiate this sharing process by disclosing information and expecting reciprocation. The cooperative negotiator initially should choose carefully those items of information to be disclosed, so that if the other negotiator fails to reciprocate and instead seeks to use the disclosure to the detriment of the negotiator's client, any damage to the negotiator's bargaining position is limited.

Information disclosure during negotiation also occurs as the lawyer presents *arguments* in an effort to influence the other negotiator to alter his bargaining position. Arguments will be considered more fully in the next chapter. For now, recognize that arguments call for the other negotiator to reach conclusions based upon inferences from certain facts. Accordingly, the negotiator must present facts as a basis for her argument. For example, assume that Chestnut Development Corporation prefers Banana to lease the more expensive location adjacent

32. Some judges, perhaps responding to this tactic, now require attorneys attending pre-trial conferences either to have full settlement authority or to be accompanied by a client representative who does.

to the center court of the mall rather than another location at the far end of the facility. To convince Banana of the desirability of the center court location, Chestnut presents comparable pedestrian traffic counts for the two locations. From this data, Chestnut's attorney argues that the center court location is the more desirable available space. This argument discloses to Banana pedestrian count information for both possible locations, including the less attractive facts about the more remote store that Chestnut otherwise might have been somewhat reluctant to reveal. Argument is probably the most important and frequently used form of factual disclosure during negotiation.

Information disclosure in negotiation sometimes takes the form of elaborate oral or written presentations. Some plaintiffs' personal injury attorneys prepare "settlement brochures" that provide a comprehensive and well documented presentation of the plaintiff's case on liability and damages. Similarly, a party to a transactional negotiation sometimes prepares a "prospectus" outlining the advantages to the other party of a sale of the business, merger or other continuing relationship.

Like cooperative tactics, successful problem-solving bargaining requires full and accurate information about each party's needs and preferences. Problem-solving information exchange occurs in two stages. First, the negotiators exchange considerable information about each party's requirements before they initially suggest bridging solutions or logrolling exchanges of concessions. At a later point, the negotiators again freely exchange information about their preferences regarding each of the solutions that have been proposed.

In both cooperative and problem-solving information exchange, it is critical for the lawyer to determine if the other negotiator is sharing information fully and accurately, or whether he continues to withhold or misstate information. Some of the most effective competitive bargaining comes clothed as cooperative or problem-solving bargaining. Again, the issue is whether the other negotiator really is using cooperative or problem-solving tactics or is simply masking competitive tactics in a cooperative style, hoping to deceive his counterpart. The competitive negotiator wearing cooperative or problem-solving clothing attempts to exploit the other party by uncovering her minimum disposition and potential sources of leverage against her.

Chapter Eight

NARROWING OF DIFFERENCES

A. INTRODUCTION

Initial negotiation proposals are on the table. Each side attempts to learn more facts about the matter being negotiated and the other party's requirements and expectations. How do the parties move from initial proposals to agreement?

The process of narrowing the differences between the parties, more than any other aspect of negotiation, resembles the traditional stereotype of "bargaining." Each lawyer uses tactics intended to induce the other negotiator to accept an agreement favorable to her client; usually the final terms are vastly different than those suggested by the original proposals. In addition, this phase often is time consuming. In predominantly competitive negotiations, the process is characterized by arguments, threats and frustration—the symbols of traditional "haggling." Eventually the expectations of the parties change as realism sets in. In short, narrowing the differences between the parties is the work of negotiation.

It is important to reiterate that "narrowing of differences" is not a "stage" of negotiation mutually exclusive of information bargaining or new proposals. While the negotiators are narrowing their differences, they continue to gather information and generate new proposals.

The negotiator has two complementary goals during this convergence process. First, she seeks to induce the other negotiator to agree to terms that are favorable to her client. Regardless of the strategy employed by the negotiator, she possesses some leverage over the other party, because the negotiating relationship is almost always a voluntary one. Although each party needs or wants something from the other, the lawyer retains the option of walking away from the negotiating table. Because this would frustrate the other party's hopes, it gives the lawyer some influence over the other party. She uses this influence by communicating her client's interests during the narrowing of differences phase—either directly by using *arguments* or indirectly by conceding on some issues and not on others.

As she participates in narrowing the differences between the parties, the negotiator's second goal is to determine what terms are acceptable to the other party. Information gathering tactics obviously address this goal. At the same time, by observing the other party's modifications of his original proposals, the lawyer also learns about the other party's level of resistance to modifying his initial proposal or the relative importance he attaches to various issues. For example, the negotiator sometimes attempts to monitor her counterpart's concession behavior to determine if there is a pattern that suggests the other party's "bottom line."

B. COMPETITIVE TACTICS FOR NARROWING DIFFERENCES

When using competitive convergence tactics, the negotiator attempts to convince the other party that she will not enter into an agreement substantially less advantageous than her original proposals. Further, she seeks to persuade the other negotiator that his alternatives to a negotiated agreement are not as favorable as he believes. Taken together, these two messages are designed to convince the other negotiator that it is in his client's best interests to yield, that is, to "concede" more in negotiation than he originally believed necessary.

A concession is defined as any modification of a negotiator's bargaining proposal making it less advantageous to her client. Because the competitive negotiator believes that all gains for her client come at the other party's expense, she tries to force the other negotiator to concede. One way to do this is to convince the other negotiator that if there is to be an agreement, he must do most of the conceding. To achieve this end, the negotiator should show reluctance in making concessions—she should concede infrequently, and in small increments. These concession tactics are described below in the section entitled "Limiting the Negotiator's Own Concessions."

The other primary methods the negotiator uses to induce the other party to make substantial concessions are (1) arguments and (2) threats. To augment the effect of threats, the negotiator can use other competitive tactics including displays of anger or a staged "walk-out" or premature termination of the negotiation.

1. ARGUMENTS

An *argument* is the invocation and reasoned elaboration of norms and their application to the subject matter of the negotiation. An *argument* is used either to support the lawyer's proposal or to critique the other negotiator's proposal. Arguments can be used as competitive, cooperative or problem-solving tactics. However, each variety of argument is different. Consider how Gary Gerstein, the plaintiff's lawyer in Patrick Finney's case against the Baltimore and Western Railroad, would use the same liability expert for different purposes, depending upon whether he wanted to use competitive or cooperative tactics. If

Gary uses the competitive argument tactic, he would take the approach, at least implicitly, that "I have an expert who will testify to these conclusions at trial, and as a result your client is certain to lose." In contrast, if he uses cooperative tactics his approach would be that "My liability expert's objective analysis suggest that the fairest way to resolve the liability issue is to agree that * * *" Finally, argument occurs as part of the evaluation process in problem-solving negotiation. When there are a variety of proposals on the table for consideration instead of two polar positions, the expert's analysis is then used to evaluate the advantages and disadvantages of the various proposals. This too is a form of argument.

Argument in negotiation is different from argument experienced in appellate court or trial court proceedings.[1] After studying patterns of argument in legal negotiation, Professor Condlin describes it as "more akin to analysis than oratory."[2] He suggests that to avoid having a detailed argument come across as an awkward soliloquy that would be viewed suspiciously by the other negotiator, the lawyer should advance her arguments conversationally. A conversational tone suggests spontaneity, as opposed to the premeditated style of a well prepared appellate argument.

Even for the competitive negotiator, the goal of argument is rarely, if ever, to browbeat her counterpart into confessing error and openly acceding to the negotiator's viewpoint. After all, the other lawyer's professional duty is to represent as effectively as possible his party's interests. Instead, effective competitive argument undermines the other negotiator's confidence in his own analysis and in his negotiating posture. The most effective arguments, therefore, are ones that bring new facts or interpretations of facts to the other negotiator's attention, not predictable ones.

Conclusory and one-sided arguments, even if presented with great emotional vehemence, are unlikely to convince anyone who does not already agree with the negotiator—particularly someone who is paid to analyze the situation from the other party's viewpoint. To be effective, argument in negotiation should be detailed and balanced. The negotiator should begin her argument with facts, law, settlement procedures or principles that are difficult to dispute, and argue inferences from these details. In this manner, she is usually better able to persuade the other party of the validity of her position than by simply using conclusory statements with no stated basis in fact. In most instances, competitive arguments presented in a cooperative style—calmly, not angrily or sarcastically—are more likely to have an impact. There may be times, however, when it is to the negotiator's advantage to use

1. For a comprehensive description and analysis of argument in negotiation, *see* Condlin, *"Cases on Both Sides": Patterns of Argument in Legal Dispute–Negotiation,"* 44 Md.L.Rev. 65–136 (1985). The reader is cautioned that Condlin classifies arguments into "cooperative" and "competitive" categories using different criteria than those used to make that distinction throughout this text.

2. *Id.* at 129.

anger when presenting an argument. Displaying anger as a competitive negotiating tactic is discussed below.

2. THREATS

A *threat* is a conditional commitment by a negotiator to act in a way that appears detrimental to the other party unless the other party complies with a request. The most common type of negotiation threat is the threat to terminate the negotiation unless the other party makes specified concessions. The cooperative analog of the threat is the *promise,* a conditional commitment to act in a way that appears beneficial to the other party if the other party complies with a request. For example, a negotiator might agree to drop one demand if her counterpart would make significant concessions on another issue. Promises, and their relationship to exchanges of concessions, are discussed more fully in the next section on "Cooperative Tactics for Narrowing Differences."

Threats serve two functions in negotiation. First, and most importantly, threats induce the other negotiator to concede and enter into an agreement more favorable to the negotiator's client than his previous bargaining position suggested would be possible. Second, threats serve as a means of communicating the negotiator's own commitment to her bargaining position. If, for example, Dan Darrow threatens to break off negotiation with Bev Bailey and her client unless Bev agrees to a 15 year lease, Dan sends a strong message to Bev that the length of the lease is an important issue to his client, the Chestnut Development Corporation.

Although implicit threats are present throughout negotiation, explicit threats should be used carefully and sparingly. Empirical studies suggest that while a negotiator's threats do lead to more concessions from the other negotiator, they also increase the degree of hostility between negotiators and the probability of negotiation breakdown and impasse.[3] Threats frequently elicit counterthreats. As a result, many negotiators use threats only when they cannot exert influence in other ways.

When the negotiator does decide to use a threat, she may be able to minimize these potential risks by stating the threat calmly and rationally, in a cooperative style. Sometimes the negotiator can soften the threat by "blaming" the client or another party. For example, Dan might say, "I am really sorry, Bev, but Chestnut's manager has just told me that if you don't agree to this package this afternoon, I am to stop negotiating with you."

A threat may involve issues over which the parties are negotiating or matters extraneous to the negotiation. Potential threats involving issues within the negotiation include not only a threat to terminate the

3. J. Rubin & B. Brown, The Social Psychology of Bargaining and Negotiation 278–87 (1975).

negotiation as a whole, but also a commitment not to make concessions on specified issues unless the other party complies with the negotiator's demand. An example of an external threat would be an announced intention never to do business with the other party again.[4]

Most often, the value of a threat is lost if it must be carried out. As an extreme example, consider the presence of American military personnel in western Europe. Although these few personnel are clearly an insufficient force to defend against a full-scale Soviet invasion of Europe, the implicit threat is that a military attack on Western Europe will be regarded as a military attack on the United States. Appropriate American responses might include the use of nuclear weapons. When the threat is carried out, the threat has failed! The threat's value lies in increasing the probability that the other negotiator will accede to a request, or in this case, that the Soviet Union will not invade western Europe.

To be effective, threats must be credible, and the impact of carrying out the threat on the other party must be significant. If the other party does not believe in the reality of the threat, the threat fails. If the other party understands the reasons for the threat, he is more likely to view it as credible. Therefore threats are not credible when they are disproportionate to the issues at stake. The attorney who threatens to take her client's small claims action "all the way to the Supreme Court" generally is not believed unless she can demonstrate that the issue is one of great personal conviction for her or her client and that they have the time and resources to pursue it.

The most important factor affecting the credibility of a threat is the past record of the negotiator. If she has said twenty times before that she "must have" a specified sum of money or she "would break off negotiation and set the case for trial," and each time she has avoided trial and settled for a lesser amount, her twenty-first threat is not credible.

Similarly, the negotiator sometimes takes steps during the negotiation demonstrating her willingness to carry out threats. For example, a negotiator can openly prepare to carry out her threat. Suppose that Dan Darrow, the attorney for the Chestnut Development Corporation, tells Banana Computers that unless Banana agrees to a lease by May 1, he will terminate discussions and advertise the availability of the rental space to other prospective tenants. Dan makes his threat more credible if he announces he has reserved space in retail trade journals beginning May 1 or if he schedules meetings on May 2 with other prospective tenants.

---

4. The lawyer is ethically prohibited from using many forms of extraneous threats. *See* C. Wolfram, Modern Legal Ethics 714–19 (1985). For example, the lawyer in a personal injury negotiation who threatens to publicize photographs of the defendant's embarassing (but unrelated) marital infidelities, commits criminal extortion. ALI Model Penal Code s 223.4(c) (Proposed Official Draft 1962). Threatening criminal prosecution in negotiation of a civil matter is similarly prohibited. Model Code of Professional Responsibility DR 7–105 (1987).

The same result is accomplished by breaking down a major threat into a series of incremental threats, and then carrying out several of the initial threats. Suppose Gary Gerstein has threatened to break off negotiation on behalf of his client Patrick Finney and to try the case unless the Baltimore and Western Railroad quickly agrees to his assessments of the liability issue and the amount of appropriate compensation for medical bills and lost wages. When counsel for Baltimore and Western does not respond to his demand, Gary could schedule the dates for the final depositions, the final pre-trial conference, and the trial.

Threats are also more credible if the negotiator suggests that she cannot back away from her commitment or undo the threat, as when her client has given her or a third party binding instructions. Assume that just before leaving on a four week trip to Tibet where she would be out of communication, Maria Mortimer, the President of the Chestnut Development Corporation, gives Dan Darrow binding instructions to break off negotiation with Banana Computer on May 1 unless Banana has agreed to certain specified terms. Dan's threat to Banana based upon these facts would be quite credible!

Threats often can be made more credible if blamed on the client's intransigence. "My client is adamant about it, Roberta," Gary Gerstein tells counsel for the Baltimore and Western Railroad, "Unless you offer $950,000 by next Thursday, he wants me to set it for trial as quickly as possible."

A negotiator also makes a threat more credible if she ties it to her own reputation or to her concern about setting a precedent. For example, Chestnut Development Corporation might threaten to break off negotiations unless Banana stops demanding reduced rental during the first six months of the lease. To increase the credibility of this threat, Chestnut can stress the precedent that such reduced rental would set for other lease negotiations. In addition, the negotiator's own strong personal commitment can lend credibility to a threat, as in the case of the legal services attorney who is willing to appeal a small claims case all the way to the United States Supreme Court, if necessary, because of her strong belief that her client has been unjustly wronged.

3. BREAKING–OFF NEGOTIATION

One type of threat that is both common and extreme, the threat to break-off negotiations, deserves special attention. Sometimes this "threat" is accomplished when one of the negotiators walks out of a bargaining session. Her expectation is that the other negotiator will make concessions in order to entice her back to the bargaining table; she gambles on the other negotiator's willingness to make concessions to avoid a deadlock. Further, walking out tells her whether the other negotiator's apparent unwillingness to concede is firm, or whether it is a negotiating tactic. Walking-out may be risky behavior, however; the other party might elect not to resume negotiations again. Accordingly, walking-out as a concession-inducing tactic should be used only when the negotiator strongly believes that concessions will be forthcoming or when favorable alternatives to a negotiated agreement exist.

4. DISPLAYS OF ANGER—REAL OR FEIGNED

Real or feigned displays of anger sometimes accompany competitive arguments or threats. Negotiators frequently express anger, effectively suggesting to the other negotiator that a threat or a particular position should be taken seriously. Depending upon the psychological make-up of the other negotiator, the display of anger can sometimes intimidate him and induce concessions.

Anger, particularly real anger as compared with feigned anger, also has its risks in negotiation. For one thing, it is likely to elicit similar outbursts from the other party, thus contributing to a cycle of hostility and fear in the negotiation. Also, when genuinely angry, most people do not think as clearly as they do in calmer moments. When angry, negotiators are likely to make threats they will not carry out, thus decreasing their credibility. They may also disclose information or make other negotiating errors they would not make if they were in control of their emotions.

5. READING CONCESSION PATTERNS

The competitive tactics described above are intended to induce the other party to make concessions. The competitive negotiator's objective is to reach an agreement with the other negotiator that is as close as possible to the other's minimum disposition. The information gathering tactics previously described in Chapter Seven aid the negotiator in determining the other party's minimum disposition. The negotiator may find additional clues to the other party's minimum disposition by observing his concession pattern.

Suppose that Patrick Finney's attorney, Gary Gerstein, originally demanded $1.8 million in his Complaint against the Baltimore and Western Railroad. Several months later, after pleadings and initial motions were filed, Gary offered to settle for $1.4 million "to avoid the risks of litigation." After fifteen months of discovery, Gary reduced his demand to $1.1 million, acknowledging that depositions produced a weaker case than anticipated. With the beginning of serious bargaining, Gary's subsequent concessions went to $1 million, then to $975,000, then to $960,000, and, finally to $955,000. What is Patrick Finney's minimum disposition? Probably $950,000. How does the negotiator know? Because the concessions fit into a pattern of decreasing magnitude, converging on a settlement figure of $950,000.

Concessions typically decrease as bargaining continues. Sometimes, by observing this pattern, it is possible to determine the other party's minimum disposition. However, some negotiators who are aware that concession patterns can be read, avoid revealing their true minimum disposition by creating a pattern of decreasing concessions around a "false minimum disposition." For example, Gerstein might sequentially concede to $1.4 million, $1.25 million, $1.15 million, $1.12 million, with the intention of misleading his sophisticated counterpart—who has learned the tricks of the trade—into believing that his minimum disposition is $1.1 million.

6. LIMITING THE NEGOTIATOR'S OWN CONCESSIONS

The negotiator using competitive tactics not only seeks concessions by the other party, but also seeks to concede as little as possible herself. Her reluctance to concede serves another function: it is the single most important factor convincing the other party he must make more and larger concessions if an agreement is to be reached.

Strictly speaking, any concession is a cooperative negotiation tactic; only a refusal to concede is described accurately as a competitive tactic. Even negotiators using mostly competitive tactics, however, find it necessary to make concessions. Accordingly, this section focuses on competitive tactics for limiting the frequency and magnitude of concessions.

Most often, lawyers think of concessions in terms of dollars. For example, Patrick Finney originally demanded $1.8 million in satisfaction of his personal injury claims; later he "conceded" and indicated his willingness to accept $1.4 million. Concessions, however, do not necessarily involve dollar amounts. Consider Banana Computer's initial desire to occupy the retail space in the "center court" area of the Chestnut Mall where pedestrian traffic is heaviest. Banana's subsequent willingness to locate in another vacant space is a negotiating "concession" on its part that does not involve a cash amount.[5]

Two reasons support the competitive negotiator's reluctance to make concessions. The first is *position loss*, the abandonment of a negotiating position that is more favorable to the negotiator and her client than her position after the concession. Because negotiating norms generally make it impossible to withdraw a concession once made, when the negotiator concedes, she loses any chance at an agreement based upon her earlier bargaining position that was more satisfactory to her client. Further, the negotiator "uses up" a concession, and cannot later trade that same concession for a reciprocal concession favoring her client. In addition to *position loss*, the second disadvantage in making concessions is *image loss*. The negotiator's concession often leads the other negotiator to believe that if he just "hangs tough," the negotiator will concede again. Accordingly, it may encourage him to engage in further competitive tactics.

Even the negotiator pursuing predominantly competitive tactics, however, recognizes the necessity of making concessions. The two most important reasons to make concessions are:

5. *See* D. Pruitt, Negotiation Behavior 23–24 (1981).

(1) to prevent premature termination of the negotiation or deadlock; and

(2) to encourage the other to make reciprocal concessions.

In addition to preventing premature breakdowns in negotiation, timely
concessions may also prevent either the client or the other party from
becoming so "locked-in," or emotionally committed to a position, that
appropriate concessions at a later point in the negotiation become
impossible.

Concessions also have the advantages that have been discussed
previously in the context of general cooperative tactics. Concessions
are often necessary to preserve a good future working relationship
between the parties. In addition, at times a negotiator who wants to
demonstrate her reasonableness to a third party (such as a judge who
encourages settlement or a mediator) concedes. Finally, concessions
can speed the resolution of a negotiation. Sometimes when a negotiation is stalemated, or when the issue at stake does not warrant
extended haggling, the negotiator who begins making concessions expe-
dites the negotiation process.

The competitive approach to the necessary evil of making concessions is to concede as infrequently as possible, and in amounts as small
as possible. Patience is a key for the competitive negotiator. The
uncertainty that characterizes negotiation is frequently anxiety-produc-
ing, particularly for inexperienced negotiators. When matched against
a competitive negotiating counterpart, a negotiator usually ends up
with a less advantageous agreement if she expresses a strong desire to
settle early in the process. Consider, for example, the negotiation
between Gary Gerstein, Patrick Finney's attorney, and Roberta Martinez, counsel for the Baltimore and Western Railroad. In the actual
case upon which this hypothetical is loosely based, the defendant denied
any liability and refused to pay anything other than "court costs" for a
period of years. Discovery continued and motions were heard, but still
the defendant continued to "stonewall" it, even past the point of the
pre-trial conference immediately preceding trial. Not until one week
prior to trial did the defendant finally make an initial offer of several
hundred thousand dollars and begin serious bargaining. Personal
injury cases frequently do settle literally on the courthouse steps. The
attorney who attempts to bargain seriously too early in the process may
disadvantage her client.

Similar testimonials to the virtues of patience are present in labor
negotiation and international diplomacy. Labor agreements frequently
settle after 72 hour marathon sessions; the negotiator who makes a
reasonable offer well in advance of a strike deadline may disadvantage
her client.[6] The 1978 Camp David Peace Accords entered into by Egypt
and Israel were not agreed to until President Carter had "confined"

6. *See* R. Walton & R. McKersie, A Behavioral Theory of Labor Negotiations 90–
91 (1965). The trend in recent years has
been for labor and management to reach
agreement earlier in the collective bargaining process.

President Sadat of Egypt and Prime Minister Begin of Israel at Camp David for a period of thirteen days.[7]

a. Justifying Concessions

The competitive strategy suggests that the negotiator accompany each concession with two explanations:

(1) the reason why the negotiator is willing to concede and change her previously articulated position; and

(2) the reason why the negotiator cannot and will not make a greater concession than the one articulated.

The importance of such explanations lies in their tendency to counteract image loss. As stated previously, one of the risks in making concessions is reinforcing the competitive tactics of the other negotiator by convincing him that additional concessions are forthcoming. Concessions may make the negotiator's previous bargaining position look arbitrary, and suggest that, once begun, concessions will continue indefinitely. An explanation of a concession dispels the notion that the concession resulted from the other negotiator's competitive tactics or his lack of concessions. The negotiator's preferred justification, explaining why this concession is the last, is designed to counteract the impression that one concession will lead to another, since now it is clear the negotiator will not "stick to her guns."

Consider again the Patrick Finney personal injury negotiation. Assume that the previous demand of Patrick's attorney, Gary Gerstein, was $1.4 million and that he now intends to lower his demand to $1,050,000:

1—Gary: As you know, Roberta, we've now completed fifty-four depositions in this case, and it's set for trial next month.

2—Roberta: It certainly looks like we'll be going to trial. You're still asking $1.4 million in a case in which my client believes it faces little exposure.

3—Gary: I'm glad to hear that after all those depositions you recognize that your client does face some risk of liability. Discovery has given us both a pretty good idea of what is going to happen at trial. I think you'll agree that we have plenty of evidence of negligence on the part of the railroad—not keeping the shrubs, tree branches and weeds cleared so that vehicular passengers could see a train coming—to get to the jury. I will admit, however, that there is some risk that the jury will reduce the damages because they might find that my client was also negli-

7. *See* J. Carter, Keeping Faith: Memoirs of a President 327–37 (1982).

gent in moving onto the railroad tracks. Patrick says he stopped at the crossing and looked as carefully as he could. But your engineer claims that Patrick did not stop. Because of the risk we face on that issue, I'm willing to attribute 25 percent of the fault to Patrick and reduce my prior demand to 75 percent of $1.4 million, or $1,050,000.

4—Roberta: It's most generous of you to allocate 25 percent of the fault to your client who drove his truck out in front of a roaring locomotive.

5—Gary: I choose that figure because of a recent verdict in Ohio, with facts very similar to these, in which the jury allocated fault 75 percent to the railroad and 25 percent to the driver.

In this dialogue, Gary provides both a reason to concede and a reason to limit his concession. In segment number 3, Gary justifies his concession on the basis of the facts uncovered during discovery—that is, the factual dispute as to whether Patrick did or did not "stop and look" before proceeding across the tracks. The engineer's testimony was new information to Gary, not available at the time he formulated his earlier demand. Later, in segment number 5, Gary provides a reason for the amount of his concession and why the concession is not larger. He discloses that the jury in a comparable case allocated the fault between the railroad and the driver on a 75 percent–25 percent basis. In other words, he makes an argument that, based upon the facts of Patrick's case and a similar verdict from another court, his demand is justified.

Two other aspects of this dialogue are worth noting. First, Roberta's opening comment in segment number 2 that her client believes it "faces little exposure" may be a significant concession if the Baltimore and Western's previous posture had been that this was a "no liability" case. In segment number 4, Roberta's comment that allocating 25 percent of fault to a plaintiff who drives his truck in front of his train is "generous" is both strategically competitive and also stylistically competitive, *i.e.,* sarcastic. Roberta's competitive response, of course, is not necessarily indicative of how she might answer Gary's concession later in the negotiation.

b. Positional Commitment

Patience in making concessions, and providing credible reasons why the negotiator cannot concede further, are both competitive tactics to express *commitment* to bargaining positions. Walton and McKersie, in their study of labor negotiation, define *commitment* as the taking of a bargaining position with some implicit or explicit pledge regarding a future course of action.[8] *Threats,* therefore, are one form of commit-

8. R. Walton & W. McKersie *supra* note 6, at 82.

ment, because they promise detrimental consequences unless the other negotiator responds as demanded. A second form of commitment is a *positional commitment* where the negotiator pledges an inalterable bargaining position and no more concessions.

Positional commitment is the quintessential competitive tactic. If the negotiator's positional commitment is believed by the other party, then the other party is limited to the options of accepting the negotiator's current proposal or forgoing an agreement. Professors Lax and Sebenius of the Harvard Business School go so far as to claim that any negotiation in a distributive context "can be 'won' by the side that first commits credibly and irreversibly to a preferred settlement." [9] Credible positional commitments, however, also carry a high risk of negotiation breakdown or stalemate. The negotiator should be careful when using positional commitments to avoid unintended negotiation breakdowns in cases where the client's interests suggest continued negotiation.

The negotiator can use the same methods to make positional commitments credible as she uses to make threats credible. For example, the negotiator or her client can take actions consistent with the positional commitment, that is, she can visibly prepare for a negotiation breakdown. She also should demonstrate that she is under minimal time pressure to conclude the negotiation, thus suggesting that she has no need to make concessions to resolve the negotiation quickly. For example, when negotiations began in Paris between diplomats from the United States and North Vietnam, the Vietnamese delegation reportedly rented a house with a two year lease. Finally, as with a threat, a positional commitment can be justified on the basis of the intransigence of the client or the attorney's personal commitment to the bargaining position.

c. Avoiding Consecutive Concessions

That concessions will be reciprocated is a typical norm in many legal negotiations. After all, a negotiator's concession accomplishes nothing for her client unless it also brings the other party closer to an acceptable agreement. Therefore, the negotiator should always be wary of making consecutive concessions. A pattern of unreciprocated concessions could indicate that she needs to take a stronger stand to avoid being pushed around.

Some negotiators use the norm of reciprocated concessions to engage in a competitive negotiation tactic best described as *disingenuous consecutive concessions*.[10] For example, assume that Roberta Martinez, representing the Baltimore and Western Railroad, admits—after an extended period of discovery—that her client faces some exposure of liability, and she offers to pay $150,000 to settle Patrick Finney's

---

9. D. Lax & J. Sebenius, The Manager as Negotiator: Bargaining for Cooperation and Competitive Gain 124 (1986).

10. *See* C. Craver, Effective Legal Negotiation and Settlement 131–32 (1986).

claims. Following the trial court's denial of her motion for summary judgment, she offers $190,000 and explains her concession on the basis of the denial of her motion. Subsequently, she concedes again to $200,000. At this point, she claims indignantly that she has made "three consecutive concessions" and has not received anything in return. Obviously, the magnitude of the later two concessions was minor, and she could just as easily have offered $200,000 instead of $150,000 in the first instance. Instead, she sought to use the "reciprocated concession norm" to force Gerstein to respond meaningfully to her last two concessions. The negotiator should not react to such a ploy and should focus on the cumulative magnitude of the concessions instead of solely on their frequency.

C. COOPERATIVE TACTICS FOR NARROWING DIFFERENCES

1. CONCESSIONS BEGET CONCESSIONS

The negotiator using cooperative tactics views the concession as an affirmative tool, not just as a necessary evil. The primary cooperative tactic for encouraging the other party to concede is for the negotiator to make a concession herself, believing that her own concessions will lead to reciprocity. In fact, research suggests that the negotiator who makes concessions is more likely to elicit cooperation from the other party than the negotiator who uses competitive tactics.[11]

The tendency for the negotiator's concessions to beget concessions by the other party results from strong bargaining norms that concessions should be reciprocated. More generally, as previously discussed, most people are socialized to cooperate with those who cooperate with them. When one of their friends, co-workers or family members "makes a concession," most individuals are unlikely to see this as a sign of weakness to be exploited by using even more competitive tactics. It should not be surprising, therefore, that attorneys who have negotiated with each other throughout their careers make concessions, realistically believing that they will encourage the other lawyer to reciprocate. Once again, it is important to reiterate that Williams found that 65 percent of the attorneys described in his survey were "cooperative," and that "willing to move from original position" was one of their characteristics.[12]

2. PROMISES

The *promise* is the cooperative counterpart of the threat. A promise is an expressed intention to act in a certain way that appears beneficial to the interests of the other party.[13] Thus, it commits the

---

11. *See* D. Pruitt, *supra* note 5, at 59–60; J. Rubin & B. Brown, *supra* note 3, at 269–78. More than thirty studies reaching this conclusion are cited in these two texts.

12. G. Williams, Legal Negotiation and Settlement 18, 21 (1983).

13. J. Rubin & B. Brown, *supra* note 3, at 278.

negotiator to an affirmative or cooperative action, as contrasted with a threat which commits the negotiator to take harmful action.

Most often the promise can be predicated on the other negotiator taking some action which would benefit the negotiator's client. For example, Dan Darrow, representing Chestnut Development Corporation, might promise "to look more closely at a lower rent during the first six months of the lease if Banana were willing to rent in a location other than the vacant store adjacent to the Mall's 'center court' area." Similarly, Roberta Martinez might promise to accept Gary Gerstein's calculations on Patrick Finney's economic damages—wage loss and medical expenses—if Gerstein becomes more realistic regarding the percentage of fault attributable to his client. In this manner, the promise serves effectively as a means of initiating the reciprocal concession process; the negotiator promises to make a concession on the condition that the other negotiator either concedes on a certain issue, reexamines his position, or takes other action favorable to the negotiator's client.

Empirical evidence supports the effectiveness of promises as negotiating tactics.[14] Studies show that negotiators use promises more frequently than they use threats in simulated negotiations. These same studies show that promises tend to result in immediate concessions by the other party. Further, their use increases the likelihood of reaching a mutually satisfactory agreement, while the use of threats decreases that likelihood. Finally, as would be expected, the use of promises, instead of threats, produces better interpersonal relationships between the negotiators.

3. ARGUMENT AS A COOPERATIVE TACTIC

The nature of argument as a negotiating tactic and the essential difference between competitive and cooperative arguments were previously discussed in this chapter. The purpose of cooperative argument is to establish the basis for a fair and just agreement, generally using objective criteria or norms. Objective criteria used by the cooperative negotiator include those previously discussed: trial results in other cases, settlement results, fair market values, or principles like equal sharing. To transform the bargaining session into a discussion of what constitutes a fair and just agreement, Fisher and Ury suggest asking the other negotiator to articulate the reasons why he thinks his negotiation proposal is a fair and just one.[15] Further, Fisher and Ury suggest that the lawyer first seek an agreement with the other negotiator on a principled basis for deciding what constitutes a fair and just agreement before they apply such an agreed upon standard to the specific issue at hand.

14. *See generally id.* at 278–88; D. Pruitt, *supra* note 5, at 76–81.

15. R. Fisher & W. Ury, Getting to Yes: Negotiating Agreement Without Giving In 91–96 (1983).

4. COOPERATIVE TACTICS TO PROTECT AGAINST COMPETITIVE EXPLOITATION

The risk inherent in making concessions and in using other cooperative tactics is that instead of reciprocating the lawyer's cooperation, the other negotiator will seek to exploit the negotiator's tactics through an even more competitive stance. This section describes a number of cooperative tactics that can be used to protect against competitive exploitation.

a. Limiting the Risks of Concessions

If the negotiator concedes and there is no reciprocal concession by the other party, the negotiator has impaired her client's interests without gain. How can the negotiator protect herself against the unreciprocated concession?

One method is for the negotiator to communicate flexibility on an issue without making a concession. This enables her to test the other negotiator's response to her expressed flexibility before deciding whether to proceed with the concession. She hopes that her indication of a willingness to concede will induce the other negotiator either to begin with a concession or at least to offer a statement of flexibility similar to her own. For example, Gary Gerstein might indicate that he would be willing to "look again at" the issue of his client's degree of fault in the crossing collision if Roberta Martinez, representing Baltimore and Western, would do likewise.

Obviously, expressing flexibility is inconsistent with a posture of extreme commitment to the prior negotiating position. After the negotiator states her flexibility on an issue, she usually cannot convincingly assert that there will be no further concessions on that issue. Nevertheless, by merely stating flexibility rather than actually conceding, the negotiator experiences no *position loss* unless the other party reciprocates. At some point in the future, for example, Gary will still be able to trade a concession on his client's degree of fault for a concession from Roberta that benefits his client. At the same time, however, the negotiator who expresses flexibility affords the other negotiator an opportunity to break-out of a competitive stalemate.

The second tactic that the negotiator can use to protect against the unreciprocated concession is the "disownable concession." Recall that negotiation norms establish rather clearly that concessions once made cannot be withdrawn. However, assume that an ambiguous communication from the negotiator to the other party appears to contain a concession. If the other negotiator responds by reciprocating the concession, the negotiator can affirm that the original ambiguous message did indeed contain a concession. On the other hand, if the other party does not respond cooperatively, the negotiator can argue an interpretation of the ambiguous message that denies that a concession was made.

Consider the following exchange between Gary Gerstein, representing Patrick Finney, and Roberta Martinez, counsel for the Baltimore and Western Railroad. Remember that Gary earlier referred to a similar case in Ohio in which fault had been assessed 75 percent to the railroad and 25 percent to the driver of the vehicle. Assume that prior to the following exchange, this Ohio verdict had been the only prior case regarding the parties' respective degrees of fault that the lawyers had discussed:

1—Roberta: The biggest obstacle to our settling seems to me to be your highly inflated value for pain and suffering damages. If you were willing to accept a value of $275,000 for pain and suffering, to be discounted by your client's percentage of fault, I think I could convince my client to resolve the division of fault issue consistent with the way it's been handled in similar cases in other jurisdictions.

2—Gary: I certainly can't accept your pain and suffering figure. Get serious. This is a young man who is now a paraplegic for the rest of his life. I'm going to have to stand with my demand for $725,000. I am encouraged, however, that you have agreed that your client's share of the fault will be assessed at 75 percent in accordance with the Ohio case.

3—Roberta: No, I'm sorry. You've misunderstood. I've uncovered settlements in two other virtually identical cases in California and Michigan. One assesses the railroad's fault at 30 percent and the other assesses it at 15 percent.

In segment number 1, Roberta obviously expresses her willingness to agree to the 75 percent–25 percent division of responsibility referred to earlier, if Gary agrees to a substantial concession on the amount of pain and suffering damages. Both parties understand tacitly the terms of the exchange of concessions being offered. Gary responds competitively, however, and refuses to make the concession, at the same time that he tries to capture the concession that Roberta offered. Instead, Roberta, in segment number 3, reacts by suggesting that Gary misunderstood her and that she was not willing to accept the 75 percent degree of responsibility, but was only referring to additional cases from other jurisdictions. When her offer to exchange concessions was not accepted, Roberta "disowned" her original concession. She has sustained *image loss*—Gary now realizes that she may accept the 75 percent liability figure. On the other hand, she has suffered no *position loss* and subsequently should be able to extract a concession from Gary in exchange for her agreement that her client will pay 75 percent of the damages.

A third cooperative tactic to reduce the risk of unreciprocated concessions is the use of "fractionated concessions." [16] Instead of making one large concession and awaiting the other negotiator's response, the negotiator divides the issue into a series of small concessions, where if any one is unreciprocated, there is little damage to the negotiator's position. One limited concession is made, and the negotiator awaits a response from the other negotiator. If he responds cooperatively, the negotiator then proceeds with the next in the series of concessions.

When the object of the negotiation is division of dollars between the parties, it is easy to see how fractionated concessions work. They also can be employed, however, on less quantifiable issues. Consider Chestnut Development's Corporation's demand that Banana pay a proportional share of increased labor and insurance costs. Banana might concede on the issue of increased insurance costs and await a reciprocal concession from Chestnut before making a proposal designed to address the issue of increasing labor costs.

b. Negotiation Breaks to Limit Concessions

The use of negotiation breaks or "walk-outs" as a competitive tactic to induce the other party to make concessions was discussed previously in this chapter. Calling a temporary halt to negotiations also can be used "defensively" when a negotiator senses that the negotiation is not going well from the perspective of her client or that she is being otherwise "swept away." This can occur under several different circumstances:

(1) she perceives an emotional shift in the climate of the negotiation against her client;

(2) she is confronted with unexpected new information or negotiating positions from the other party;

(3) her own negotiating tactics are not having the effects she anticipated; or

(4) she is confused or tired.

A recess under any of these conditions often breaks the psychological momentum against the negotiator and gives her a chance to reassess her evaluation of the case and the posture of the negotiation.

c. Responding to Extremely Competitive Tactics

All negotiators, particularly inexperienced ones and ones who attempt to use cooperative or problem-solving tactics, sometimes become targets for extremely competitive tactics from more traditional negotiators representing opposing parties.[17] These tactics include personal attacks, escalating demands, artificial deadlines and extreme

16. Pruitt originated the use of this term. See D. Pruitt, supra note 5, at 99–100.

17. This section was influenced substantially by the teaching of my colleague

Don Peters. See also R. Fisher & W. Ury, supra note 15, at 134–49.

threats. For example, how should Bev Bailey respond when Dan Darrow informs her that the manager of the Chestnut Development Corporation has instructed him to break off negotiations with Bev unless agreement is reached by April 1 when Bev knows that the space to be rented will not be available for several months? First, Bev should ask "why" the seemingly artificial deadline is being established. If Dan is not able to articulate a credible reason, then her inquiry confirms her suspicion that the deadline is a competitive negotiating tactic and not a legitimate requirement. Second, Bev should let Dan know that she recognizes that he is using a competitive tactic:

> 1—Bev: Dan, I have the sense that you're trying to pressure me into reaching an agreement quickly.

Third, Bev should let him know that the tactic will not work:

> 2—Bev: I just want to let you know that I've discussed this with my client and we've agreed that we will not rush into any agreement until we've had a chance to evaluate other options and all the terms of the agreement.

In this portion of her response, Bev tells Dan both that the tactic will not be successful and, that if Dan continues to pursue the tactic, he risks alienating Bev and her client. This dialogue may then lead naturally into an explicit discussion of the negotiation process and the actual time pressures under which the parties are bargaining.

D. PROBLEM–SOLVING TACTICS FOR NARROWING DIFFERENCES

1. DELAYED INITIATION OF PROBLEM–SOLVING BARGAINING

It is important to reiterate at this point that problem-solving bargaining can "break out" at any point during the negotiation. On one hand, negotiators sometimes use problem-solving tactics with great success during the earliest stages of the negotiation. As previously suggested, however, in many other negotiations competitive phases of bargaining precede problem-solving phases. Frequently, problem-solving tactics are effectively initiated precisely when the parties are becoming most frustrated with the exchange of arguments, threats, and limited concessions that leave their bargaining positions far apart and make their differences seem insurmountable. Accordingly, it is sometimes at this "stage" of the negotiation that parties may begin to devise bridging solutions or to share information about their interests and needs more openly. If this occurs, the grouping of problem-solving tactics with competitive and cooperative tactics in this book may no longer be in tandem. In other words, after using arguments, threats and the other competitive tactics described in this chapter, the negotiators may begin using the problem-solving tactics for initial proposals described in Chapter Six or the problem-solving methods of information gathering analyzed in Chapter Seven.

In simulated negotiation exercises, many students personally experience the frequent frustrations resulting from competitive tactics. Now is an excellent time to go back and review, as a somewhat more sophisticated and experienced negotiator, the opportunities offered by problem-solving methods. This chapter builds upon the analysis presented in earlier chapters of the problem-solving approaches to planning, information sharing and solution-generating processes.

2. EVALUATION OF BRIDGING PROPOSALS

For negotiators using problem-solving tactics, the narrowing of differences occurs in a conceptually different manner than it does for negotiators using predominantly either competitive or cooperative tactics. Negotiators who employ problem-solving tactics intentionally avoid beginning with two polar positions and then converging on a compromise middle position. Instead, as previously discussed, problem-solving negotiators devise numerous potential "solutions" to the problems faced by their clients. These solutions are developed either by the lawyer and her client during counseling conferences or by the two negotiating attorneys during bargaining sessions. Sometimes clients also participate in these sessions. With problem-solving tactics, the narrowing of differences through a convergence of bargaining positions, characteristic of the competitive or the cooperative strategy, is replaced with a process for deciding which proposal, among the many identified possibilities, best meets the needs and expectations of the parties.

During this process of evaluating *bridging solutions,* the negotiators should consider together the potential solutions previously developed and evaluate how well these solutions meet their respective needs. Professor Menkel–Meadow, in her analysis of problem-solving negotiation,[18] identifies the following six criteria, among others, for evaluating the quality of any proposed solution:

1.   Does the *bridging solution* address the client's needs and goals?

2.   Does the *bridging solution* address the other party's needs and goals?

3.   Does the proposal facilitate the desired relationship with the other party?

4.   Have the negotiators explored all possible alternatives that might either make both parties better off or one party better off with no adverse consequences to the other party?

5.   Is the proposal feasible and realistic or will it create additional problems?

6.   Is the solution fair and just?

18. Menkel–Meadow, *Toward Another View of Legal Negotiation: The Structure* *of Problem Solving,* 31 UCLA L.Rev. 755, 760–61 (1984).

The negotiators' evaluation of bridging proposals requires both additional information sharing between the parties and the use of arguments. Recall that prior to developing potential bridging solutions, the negotiators using problem-solving tactics shared information about their underlying interests. At this later point in the process, problem-solving negotiators exchange information again. They tell each other how well each of the proposed bridging solutions satisfies their respective clients' interests and which of the possible options their clients prefer.

The negotiators also use *arguments* to assist in evaluating bridging solutions. A negotiator might argue, for example, that one specific proposal fits her client's needs best. She might also identify for the other counsel the respective advantages and disadvantages of the various proposals as her client views them. Because the other negotiator previously has informed the lawyer of his client's needs and interests, the negotiator additionally is able to assess and argue how each of the proposals satisfies the other party's interests.

How would this evaluation process work in the negotiation between Chestnut Development Corporation and Banana Computer? In order to keep this analysis manageable, this section will do something that a good problem-solving negotiator would never do: focus on only a single issue, the monthly rent amount. Remember the brief solution-generating (brainstorming) session between Bev Bailey and Jeff Walton, manager for the Banana store. Together they identified ten options to meet their concern about Banana's probable inability to pay the regular rental rates during the early months of the lease: [19]

1. Base monthly rental (dollars per square feet) at a reduced rate;

2. A contingency clause increasing rent if labor or insurance costs rise dramatically;

3. Periodically increasing rent;

4. Rent tied solely to revenues, no base rent;

5. A series of short-term quarter to quarter leases with periodic adjustment of rent;

6. Purchase of the mall;

7. Leasing a less desirable location within the mall at a lower rent;

8. Leasing space at a shopping center across the street;

9. Leasing a smaller store within the mall if available;

10. Providing computer services to the mall in exchange for reduced rent; and

11. Chestnut's subsidization of Banana's start-up costs, including refurbishing costs and promotional expenses.

---

19. *See supra* Chapter Four, *Negotiation Planning*, at 56–8.

Several of these proposals would never be introduced into the negotiation and would not receive a full-fledged evaluation by the negotiators. The parties will not seriously consider Banana buying the mall, and a series of short-term leases is probably not advantageous to either party. Renting space at the shopping center across the street is not appropriate for mutual evaluation by the negotiators, although it might be used as a threat.

Several other proposed solutions can be disposed of expeditiously in a problem-solving negotiation procedure analogous to a summary judgment. Chestnut can quickly indicate whether it has any interest in a computer services exchange and whether there are smaller stores in less desirable locations available at reduced rents. The standard lease with a reduced rental is probably not attractive to Chestnut unless Banana is willing to trade other concessions for a reduced rent in a logrolling process. Of course, Banana would also be able to obtain a standard lease with reduced rent if the respective alternatives to a negotiated agreement of the two parties suggest that Banana had considerably more bargaining power than Chestnut, *i.e.*, there were no other parties interested in leasing the vacant space. In that event, the resolution of the rent issue would be a strictly distributive one.

The remaining five proposals are:

1. rent tied solely to store revenues—no guaranteed base rent;

2. a contingency clause increasing rent in event of labor or insurance costs rising dramatically over a specified amount;

3. periodically increasing rent;

4. subsidization of start-up costs by Chestnut; and

5. leasing a less desirable location away from center court.

These are the proposals that the two negotiators should evaluate seriously. Without knowing the full range of information available to the two negotiators, it is difficult to predict how the evaluation process would proceed from this point. Certainly the business prospects for a computer store in the mall, and the percentage of its revenues that Banana is willing to commit to rent, will strongly influence Chestnut's reaction to alternative number 1. Chestnut's evaluation of alternative number 2 depends upon Chestnut's actual degree of concern about increased labor and insurance costs. Banana obviously needs information about these costs, available only from Chestnut, in order to evaluate that alternative.

At this stage of the problem-solving negotiation, the evaluation process should be a joint analysis where the two lawyers try to decide what alternative meets the requirements and aspirations of both their clients. The lawyers may have begun the negotiation process with competitive tactics. Now, however, threats and arguments no longer resonate in the negotiation chambers, and the lawyers participate in a far different joint analytical process to find an agreement satisfactory to their clients' interests. In whatever manner the bargaining began, this is how many negotiations end.

3. REFINEMENT OF BRIDGING PROPOSALS: INCORPORATION

As described in Chapter Six, the development of bridging proposals during negotiation is a continuing and cyclical process.[20] As new information about the parties' preferences is shared, the proposals originally advanced are modified to reflect a better understanding of the parties' needs.

Two very different variations of this "proposal—response—refined proposal" cycle are described by social psychologist Dean Pruitt.[21] The first, *incorporation,* involves adding to the negotiator's own proposal some element or proposal made by the other party. Consider, for example, Bev Bailey's problem-solving proposal regarding the rental terms between the Chestnut Mall and Banana Computer. Bev originally suggested an agreement containing the following provision for periodically increasing rent:

1. during the first year, Banana would pay as base rent 70 percent of the market rate being requested by Chestnut;

2. during the second year, Banana would pay the full rental; and

3. during the third and fourth years, Banana would pay both the full rental plus an additional monthly amount equal to $1/24$ of the 30 percent discount Banana had received during the first year plus interest calculated at the prime rate.

In evaluating this proposal from Chestnut's perspective, Dan Darrow might respond with two objections. First, Chestnut would be better off investing its money in bonds or money market accounts where there would be less risk. Second, Dan might assert that this proposal really does not protect his client against dramatically higher insurance and labor costs. He would suggest that Bev's proposal does not require Banana to pay its proportionate share of any increased insurance and utility costs.

Bev, recognizing the reasonableness of Dan's concerns, could then incorporate a modified version of Dan's suggestion into her original proposal. Her client's interests in keeping the rent as low as possible during the initial start-up period prevents her from adopting Dan's proposal outright. Instead, her revised proposal, incorporating Dan's suggestion, delays any reimbursement by Banana for higher insurance and utility costs until after the initial two years of the lease:

Bev: We could add to my original proposal that Banana would reimburse you, during the third and fourth years, for our share of any increased labor and insurance costs attributable to the first two years of the lease, as well as subsequent

---

20. *See supra* Chapter Six, *Initial Proposals,* at 117.

21. *See* D. Pruitt, *supra* note 5 at 169–85.

years. In this way, we could ease your client's concerns about dramatically escalating costs.

To address Dan's concerns about the relatively low interest rate included in her original proposal, Bev might offer that her client would pay interest at a rate significantly greater than the prime rate.

4. REFINEMENT OF BRIDGING PROPOSALS: HEURISTIC TRIAL AND ERROR

Pruitt designates the second method for refining bridging solutions as "heuristic trial and error." Using this technique, the negotiator makes frequent variations in her own proposal that only gradually reduce her level of satisfaction. These changes do not necessarily respond to any explicit information from the other negotiator; on the contrary, they are often proposed without any idea as to how the other negotiator will react. Accordingly, *heuristic trial and error* is not a conscious, planned attempt to have the refined proposal meet the underlying interests of the other party. Instead, the negotiator only learns how well her proposal meets the other party's needs when the other negotiator reacts to each of the series of modifications of the original proposal.

The *heuristic trial and error* approach can be an important tool for the problem-solving negotiator when the other negotiator is unable or unwilling to communicate fully and accurately concerning his client's interests, how well each negotiating proposal meets these interests or his client's preferences among the various proposals. *Heuristic trial and error* is particularly important in multiple issue negotiation when the negotiator is unclear as to which of the issues is most important to the other party. Sometimes even the other party himself is not able to consciously rank or prioritize the importance of the issues. In these cases, his responses to a wide variety of proposals on a trial and error basis may be the best indicators of what issues are most important to him. For example, one variation of a proposal might include a concession on one issue; a second variation would concede a different issue. The other party's responses to these two variations implicitly, but reliably, communicate his preference.

5. OTHER PROBLEM–SOLVING TACTICS

The problem-solving negotiation sub-processes described in this chapter and the next overlap with each other. At the same time that the problem-solving negotiator evaluates and refines bridging solutions, she usually also employs *logrolling, cost-cutting* and *compensation* techniques. Each of these techniques facilitates concessions either by arranging exchanges of concessions that promote high joint benefit or by lessening the disadvantages of the concessions. These tactics frequently are employed to enable the parties to "close the deal." Accordingly, they are considered in a comprehensive fashion in the next chapter.

Chapter Nine

CLOSURE

A. INTRODUCTION

The negotiation processes described in previous chapters are collapsed occasionally into a two minute conversation between prosecutor and defense attorney in the courthouse halls. More often, the investigation, meetings, phone calls and exchange of correspondence last for months, or even years. Ultimately, however, whether an agreement is reached often comes down to what is said and done in a few minutes.

By this time, the negotiators usually have substantial information about each other's requirements and expectations for an agreement. It is theoretically possible that one negotiator may obtain everything from the negotiated agreement that her client could ever have hoped for. Such a result occasionally occurs if the lawyer has relentlessly pursued purely competitive tactics, and the other negotiator lacks the bargaining power, the negotiating ability or the will to adequately protect his client's interests. Bridging solutions that wholly satisfy both parties' interests may lead to an outcome similarly utopian from the client's perspective. More likely, however, both parties will give up something in the final stages of negotiation.

This chapter begins with a description of competitive tactics used to bring the negotiation to a conclusion. It then analyzes various aspects of making the final concession, a cooperative tactic critical to the final stages of negotiation. Finally, problem-solving tactics for concluding the negotiation—specifically how to reach an agreement with high joint benefit even if it is necessary to make concessions—are described.

B. COMPETITIVE CLOSURE TACTICS

1. DEADLINES AND ULTIMATUMS

Frequently, negotiators become considerably more cooperative as deadlines approach.[1] Labor negotiations, for example, often settle during the proverbial "eleventh hour bargaining" as the strike deadline looms.[2] Personal injury actions, much to the frustration of judges and sometimes clients, often settle only "on the courthouse steps." As a deadline approaches, it puts pressure on the parties to state positions as close to their minimum dispositions as possible in order to avoid a negotiation failure. Sometimes parties even are forced to change their minimum dispositions to reach an agreement. Further, the use of competitive tactics decreases as the deadline approaches. Empirical research repeatedly demonstrates that time pressures increase the likelihood of agreement and tend to reduce the aspirations of negotiators, their levels of demands and the amount of bluffing.[3]

Why does so much agreement take place at the last possible moment? Basically, because the negotiator using predominantly competitive tactics sees bargaining as the proverbial game of "chicken." The longer the negotiator holds out in the face of possible negotiation breakdown, the more likely it is that the other negotiator will yield and come closer to her position. Also, if both negotiators use predominantly competitive tactics, information about the parties' true underlying interests will be exchanged slowly, grudgingly and incompletely throughout the bargaining process. As a result, the negotiator never knows what constitutes the best agreement she can obtain for her client.

At some point, however, the negotiator using competitive tactics believes that she has enough information about the other side's minimum disposition and that she is never going to get a better deal. At that point, she puts the other negotiator under a genuine or artificially imposed deadline to respond to an offer. Genuine deadlines include approaching trial dates, strike deadlines or deadlines imposed by third parties. As an example of a deadline created by a third party, consider the negotiation between a sub-contractor and a contractor who intends to bid on a government project. The deadline for bids for the government contract creates a somewhat earlier deadline for the contractor and sub-contractor to reach agreement. Artificial deadlines can be attributed to the insistence of the negotiator's client or the negotiator's expressed need to begin to pursue other options to an agreement if bargaining stalls. For example, Gary Gerstein might establish a deadline in his negotiation with Baltimore and Western Railroad based

1. *See* J. Rubin & B. Brown, The Social Psychology of Bargaining and Negotiation 120–24 (1975).

2. During the 1960's, perhaps *most* labor negotiations concluded at the last pos-
sible moment. More recently the trend is for labor and management to reach agreement earlier in the bargaining process.

3. *See* J. Rubin & B. Brown, *supra* note 1, at 123.

upon his need to begin extensive trial preparations if agreement cannot be reached.

The setting of a deadline often is accompanied by a "final offer" or ultimatum. The negotiator should rarely designate the final position an "ultimatum" because yielding to an ultimatum involves loss of face. In order to be credible, final positions or ultimatums usually cannot be announced too early in the process. When the negotiator announces an ultimatum too quickly, she finds it difficult to convince the other negotiator that she has exhausted her attempts to compromise and that she has no further room to concede. Another reason for delaying any "final" offer is the other negotiator's increased motivation to achieve an agreement later in the negotiation when he already has invested considerable time and effort in the bargaining process.

In order to be effective, the ultimatum must be supported by reasons. By justifying the ultimatum, the negotiator makes it more credible and decreases any loss of face the other party will experience in yielding to the ultimatum. To avoid the ego threat to the other negotiator, the final position should be stated in a cooperative style. Sometimes it can be attributed to the negotiator's client: "This is absolutely the most that the railroad claims manager will allow me to offer," Roberta Martinez informs Gary Gerstein. In other cases, the negotiator can offer the other party two or more choices, both of which serve her client's interests. Offering the other party a choice may mitigate the ego threat to the other party at the same time that either choice serves her client's interests.

2. CONSOLIDATION OF THE AGREEMENT

When a negotiator is ready to close the deal, she should repeat all the elements of the agreement in summary form. Like active listening for content, such summarization serves to check for mutual agreement or understanding on each issue. Often the attorneys reduce the agreement to writing in a summary form and initial it on the spot. In more complex cases or cases with multiple issues where it may not be possible to draft a memorandum of agreement immediately, it is advisable to follow an oral agreement promptly with either a letter summarizing the terms of the agreement or a brief memorandum stating the "agreement in principle." At a minimum, the lawyer should draft a memorandum to her file stating the terms of the agreement. Experience teaches many lawyers that "If it isn't in writing, it doesn't exist."

The negotiator should volunteer, where possible, to draft any written agreement to be signed by the parties. The language chosen by the lawyer in drafting is unlikely to be identical to the words her counterpart would use, particularly if the agreement is long and complicated, or when the bargaining has been competitive. This is not to suggest in any way that the drafting lawyer should modify the terms agreed upon, or add or delete any provision of the agreement. Such an artifice constitutes unprofessional conduct and would create considerable professional damage within the bargaining community.

Most often, however, minor details and exact language have not been specifically negotiated. Counsel for the other party actually may appreciate the attorney's willingness to draft the agreement. Some counsel representing other parties will not engage in hair-splitting if minor points, not expressly negotiated, are drafting in a manner favorable to the negotiator's client. Conversely, drafting the agreement also protects the negotiator against "shading" of provisions by the other lawyer. If the other lawyer does draft the agreement, the negotiator should always compare the agreement and her own notes of the oral agreement. Optimally, the negotiator has developed a negotiating "record" throughout the bargaining process by drafting a continuous stream of memoranda "to the file" covering her contacts with the other lawyer. She should not hesitate, in these days of word processing equipment, to insist upon corrections of any imperfections in the statement of the agreement or any "shading" of the terms.

Finally, the negotiator should refrain from suggesting to either the other negotiator or to a third party that she "won" the negotiation. Lawyers tend to negotiate with the same negotiators in future dealings. If the other negotiator hears that the lawyer thought she took advantage of him in a prior negotiation, it makes later negotiations with him considerably more difficult.

C. COOPERATIVE CLOSURE TACTICS

1. FINAL CONCESSIONS

As in other phases of the negotiation, cooperative tactics during the concluding stages do not consist of threats and ultimatums, but instead focus on initiating the reciprocal exchange of concessions. There are two variations of this basic tactic in the final stages of the negotiation. The first is for the negotiator to announce a final concession and invite reciprocation. In Gary Gerstein's negotiation with Roberta Martinez, Gary might initiate an exchange of final concessions as follows:

> 1—Gary: We started a long way apart in these talks. It's been two years and we've taken fifty-four depositions. The case is set for next Tuesday, but I think we're close enough that we ought to be willing to settle our differences. Your last offer was $780,000, and my last demand was $965,000. I've talked with my client and we are willing to settle this thing for $875,000. But he's made it clear that he will go no further. If you can't accept $875,000, we'll go to trial.

A second method for initiating the final exchange of concessions is for Gary to tell Roberta that if she were willing to pay $875,000, he "thinks it would be acceptable to his client." Without actually making the concession, Gary tacitly communicates his client's willingness to accept a settlement of $875,000.

How large should the final concession be? As previously discussed, during most negotiations, the amounts of concessions decrease during the bargaining. Accordingly, one would expect a final concession to be small. A disproportionately large concession in the latest stages of the negotiation may suggest to the other negotiator that the lawyer has not reached her minimum disposition and probably can concede further. On the other hand, the final concession should arguably be larger than the concessions immediately preceding it in order to be a dramatic and symbolic gesture of closure.

A negotiator frequently proposes a final exchange of concessions by suggesting that the parties "split the difference." Empirical evidence suggests that negotiations tend to reach agreement near the midpoint between the parties' respective bargaining positions once two realistic offers are on the table.[4] However, the negotiator should not use "splitting the difference" as a justification for making a concession early in the negotiation process. At that early stage, concessions should always be justified on grounds related to the substance of the matter being negotiated so that the negotiation process does not become only a game of willpower yielding arbitrary results. In the final stages of negotiation, however, when the differences between the parties are modest, "splitting the difference" is an acceptable justification for resolving the remaining discrepancies. This assumes that the proposed agreement exceeds the client's minimum disposition and is agreed to by the client.

The negotiator should be careful to be sure that the other lawyer has not manipulated the result of "splitting the difference" by his concession pattern during the last several rounds of bargaining. If, during these prior rounds, the lawyer has made concessions diminishing her client's level of satisfaction with the agreement substantially more than the other lawyer's concessions have reduced his client's satisfaction, then "splitting the difference" is no longer an equitable means of compromise.

2. CREATING CONSTRUCTIVE AMBIGUITIES

Traditionally, good lawyers are taught that a contractual agreement should anticipate every possible contingency and resolve them in an unambiguous manner. Unfortunately, disagreement about minor or peripheral points occasionally jeopardizes an agreement when all major issues have been resolved. One way to deal with this situation is "to agree to disagree" and to include in the agreement a "constructive ambiguity."[5] Ambiguous language on a peripheral point may enable each party to believe he has accomplished his objective. Frequently,

---

4. Bartos, *Simple Model of Negotiation: A Sociological Point of View,* in The Negotiation Process: Theories and Applications 13, 19–24 (I. Zartman ed. 1978).

5. *See* C. Craver, Effective Legal Negotiation and Settlement 100–101 (1986).

the issue in question will never become an object of dispute between the parties. If it does, the parties to a transactional negotiation probably will have been working together under the agreement long enough to have established sufficient rapport to resolve minor disagreements as they arise. Sometimes it may be desirable to add an explicit provision to an agreement concerning disputes or general interpretation, providing for resolution either by arbitration or by a decision of some other specified third party. Occasionally the results of the negotiation include a "reopener agreement" indicating that upon the occurrence of certain conditions, specific provisions will be re-negotiated by the parties.

3. DETERMINING WHEN THE OTHER PARTY'S "FINAL" OFFER IS FINAL

To protect herself from exploitation by a negotiator using the competitive tactics of ultimatums and final offers, the negotiator needs to ascertain when an offer designated by the competitive negotiator as "final," really is *final*.

The credibility of the statement that an offer is "final" can be judged by many of the same factors that suggest the credibility of other *threats* and *commitments*. The negotiator should consider the language used by the other negotiator in stating the ultimatum. Was it in absolute terms, or were there qualifiers or conditional statements which may allow room for future bargaining? For example, a statement that "my client and I have decided this is the best we can do based upon all the information we have" indicates a willingness to change the final position if additional facts are forthcoming. The lawyer should analyze any non-verbal communications or paralinguistic vocalizations which she might have observed as the other negotiator delivered the ultimatum. Further, whether or not the "final" position appeared to be a logical culmination of extended bargaining or whether it occurred too early in the negotiation process is an important indicator of its actual finality. The negotiator should also practice "role reversal" to decide whether it makes sense from the other negotiator's perspective to offer a "take it or leave it" deal. Finally, did the ultimatum occur in the heat of battle? Was it an inadvertent reaction to the course of the negotiation or even the result of the lawyer's emotional involvement in the situation instead of a genuine final offer?

Even when the other negotiator claims that his offer is "final," he usually modifies his position or compromises to some extent before the negotiators conclude an agreement. How can the negotiator respond to a final offer which is unacceptable to her client when she believes that it is in both parties' interests to continue the negotiation?

If the negotiator believes that the other lawyer has legitimately reached her limits and is not engaged in a competitive bluffing tactic, she can use *active listening* to express understanding of the other negotiator's inability to negotiate further, as in the statement "You feel you've gone as far as you can." Then she can restate the other party's final offer in a way that makes it a firm position, but not a final one. By diffusing the tension inherent in "final offers," the negotiator opens the door to the use of several additional tactics. First, she can respond with her own concession, even if it does not match the other negotiator's final demand. Consider Roberta Martinez's response to Patrick Finney's "final demand" of $950,000:

1—Roberta: I understand that $950,000 is the best you can do. I knew we were close to loggerheads, so I took the same attitude in talking again with my client. My client indicated its willingness to agree to $900,000, but absolutely refused to pay more. We may be stalemated, but why don't you take the $900,000 figure back to your client?

Notice that Roberta links her final concession with an explicit request that Gary take the new offer back to his client.

Another approach is for the negotiator to express her understanding that this is a final offer, but then continue to ask "why." If Roberta asks Gary "why?" his position is a final one and Gary responds, Gary's answer continues the dialogue on the merits at a time when Gary had intended to present a "take it or leave it demand" and stop further discussion. In addition, it will be difficult for Gary to find a reasonable explanation for a willingness to accept $950,000, but to refuse adamantly to accept $900,000.

The negotiator can also deflect a final offer by responding with new information or by advancing a new perspective on information previously considered by the parties. If genuinely novel, such additional input arguably justifies reconsideration of a final position because it was not considered when the other lawyer and his client formulated their "final" position.

The negotiator can also respond to a final offer on a specific issue by deferring consideration of the issue until later in the negotiation. If the parties are able to agree upon other issues, it increases the pressure on both of them to compromise on the stalemated issue. Finally, the negotiator can respond to a final offer by suggesting that the negotiation be recessed until later. This competitive response communicates that one party or the other is going to have to change its evaluation of the situation before agreement can be reached. The recess may be accompanied by a suggestion that the lawyers talk with their clients.

4. REOPENING DEADLOCKED NEGOTIATIONS

When a lawyer seeks to reopen a negotiation that has broken down, the other negotiator often views her as being overly anxious to settle. To propose new discussions, therefore, risks *image loss*. The lawyer's willingness to resume negotiation, without a change in circumstances, often leads the other lawyer to believe that her earlier "toughness," that led to the breakdown, was mere bluffing and that she can be pressured into further substantial concessions. To counter this perception, where possible a lawyer should justify the resumption of bargaining by bringing forth new information, obtained through investigation or discovery, that may change the parties' evaluations of the situation. Often, however, the only change since the breakdown of the heated negotiation is that tempers have cooled. Under these conditions, the lawyer proposing the reopening of negotiation should forthrightly offer her opinion that the best interests of both parties would be served by resuming bargaining.

D. PROBLEM–SOLVING CLOSURE TACTICS

1. AGREEMENT ON A BRIDGING SOLUTION

Prior chapters discuss the process of inventing bridging solutions that satisfy both parties' underlying interests.[6] As described, this process can occur either between the attorneys during bargaining sessions, or between the lawyer and her client during counseling sessions before or during the negotiation process. In either case, the lawyers ultimately evaluate any proposed solutions from the perspectives of their respective clients during a bargaining session.[7] Closure in the bridging process occurs when the lawyers agree that one of the bridging solutions is preferable to the others because it best satisfies their clients' underlying interests. Bridging solutions which totally satisfy all of the aspirations and requirements of both parties, without compromise or diminished expectations, occasionally occur, but are quite rare.[8] In most cases, agreement on a bridging solution requires one or both of the parties to concede on peripheral issues or to some extent to have their initial expectations frustrated.

2. LOGROLLING

The most common technique used to achieve final agreement in negotiation is the problem-solving tactic of *logrolling*, which has been previously described. To review briefly, *logrolling* occurs when the parties exchange concessions on different issues; each party concedes on the issue he cares least about, thus creating high joint benefit. Most negotiations involve multiple issues, and in final bargaining the negotiators frequently offer to concede on one issue in exchange for a concession on an issue more important to her client. For example, Banana Computers, in its lease negotiation with the Chestnut Development Corporation, might offer to pay its proportionate share of Chestnut's increases in labor and insurance expenses in excess of eight percent during the lease term. Chestnut stressed this issue as a priority throughout the negotiation. In exchange, Chestnut might

6. *See supra* Chapter Four, *Negotiation Planning,* at 55–60 and Chapter Six, *Initial Proposals,* at 117–8.

7. *See supra* Chapter Eight, *Narrowing of Differences,* at 158–61.

8. *See* D. Pruitt, Negotiation Behavior 157 (1981).

agree to accept a lower minimum rent during the first year of the lease, provided that such lower base rent is coupled with a supplemental rent based on a higher percentage of gross sales than is typical. This provision addresses Banana's highest priority, its need for lower fixed rent during the initial start-up period.

Notice in this example that logrolling is coupled with a bridging solution. The rent provision calling for a lower fixed rent initially and a higher percentage of gross sales is an unusual lease provision designed to address both Banana's concern about meeting its expenses during the first year and Chestnut's interest in an adequate return on its investment over the entire lease term. Logrolling frequently can be used simultaneously with any of the other problem-solving closure tactics—bridging solutions, compensation or cost-cutting. Even when the negotiators resolve an issue using one of these other problem-solving tactics, the expectations of one party or the other frequently are frustrated to some extent. In a logrolling compromise, the party's acceptance of the agreement reached on a specific issue through the use of bridging solutions, compensation or cost-cutting, is conditioned upon a favorable resolution of another issue which has a higher priority for him. Any frustration resulting from the resolution of the first issue is outweighed by his enthusiasm for the advantageous resolution of the second issue.

3. COST–CUTTING

In order for the lawyer and the other negotiator to reach an agreement meeting all the requirements of the lawyer's client, it is often necessary for the other party to make concessions that reduce his level of satisfaction with the agreement. To encourage such a concession, the negotiator may seek to reduce the costs or detriments experienced by the other party in making the concession. Pruitt refers to this process as "cost cutting." [9]

Cost-cutting is any method that reduces the disadvantages to the other party of agreeing to a proposal which benefits the negotiator's client. Two specific forms of cost-cutting, however, are common. The first addresses the other party's concern that if he concedes on an issue during the current negotiation, his concession will set a precedent for future dealings. For example, Chestnut might fear that if it agreed to a reduced base rent during the first year of the lease that Banana would expect a similar concession when it came time to negotiate a renewal. Bev and Dan could easily address this problem through an exchange of correspondence indicating that the lower base rent was being agreed to only because this was an initial lease. In this manner, the lawyers "decouple" present conduct from future conduct. Similarly, Chestnut would be concerned that such a provision in its lease with Banana Computers could be a precedent for leases with other retail

---

9. *Id.* at 142–48.

stores in the mall. The lawyers could avoid this problem by agreeing to a confidentiality clause.

The second common method of cost-cutting is to find a way to reduce the image loss, or slighting of ego, that either the other lawyer or his client may experience when making a concession. Frequently, the other lawyer experiences a sense of diminished status when making a critical concession. For example, if Gary Gerstein were a young attorney and he made a large concession at the end of the negotiation with Roberta Martinez, he might perceive a loss of professional esteem. To mitigate the ego damage, Roberta might comment that at the beginning of negotiation when he had demanded $1.4 million, Gary was not aware of the strong evidence undermining Patrick Finney's case. Through this comment, Roberta suggests that, in her eyes, neither Gary's initial high demand nor the subsequent large concession resulted from Gary's inexperience. She might also refer to future negotiation between them "when it will be her turn" to make the final major concession.

4. COMPENSATION

As previously described, *compensation* is a problem-solving tactic which indemnifies the other party for making concessions.[10] In exchange for a concession that her client requires for an agreement, the negotiator provides the other party something in return. Logrolling is a form of compensation in which the consideration for the concession is a concession on a different issue. As another example of compensation, consider the negotiation between Chestnut Development Corporation and Banana Computer. In exchange for conceding to a reduced base rental figure for Banana Computers, Banana might agree to provide the Chestnut Development Corporation with computer hardware and software of equivalent value. Although computers and software were not originally items to be negotiated, Banana may find it cheaper to supply them as a means of "compensating" Chestnut for a reduced base rent, than it would be for Banana to pay a higher base rent.

E. ACHIEVING CLOSURE ON LEARNING ABOUT THE NEGOTIATION PROCESS

Closure marks the last of the negotiation processes. It is possible that in multiple issue negotiation closure may be achieved on one issue while other issues remain in stages characterized by "narrowing of differences" tactics or even information gathering tactics. Despite the unevenness of issue development in a particular negotiation, this discussion of closure does complete this book's analysis of the basic negotiation process between lawyers representing two parties. The next chapter describes the added complexities of multiple party negotia-

---

10. *Id.* at 148–53.

tion and a few new tactics primarily suited for use in these negotiations.

This is an appropriate point, however, to stress that every negotiator uses tactics from each of the three negotiating strategies in virtually every negotiation. The negotiator who uses only competitive tactics and never concedes, for example, will find that all of her negotiations terminate prematurely without agreement. Conversely, the cooperative negotiator who never holds the line and never threatens either implicitly or explicitly to terminate negotiation, does not negotiate—she only capitulates to demands. The negotiator who always seeks to find bridging solutions and who fails to realize the distributive nature of many issues will soon learn that all negotiators must compromise.

People go through life using a mixture of competitive, cooperative and problem-solving tactics in day-to-day human relationships. If you now consciously recognize some of your own behaviors as negotiation tactics, then this text succeeds. Such recognition allows you to make deliberate choices regarding tactical decisions in legal negotiation. None of us has perfect instincts for choosing the most effective tactics in every legal negotiation. Conscious analysis helps.

Chapter Ten

MULTIPLE PARTY NEGOTIATION

A. INTRODUCTION

The previous chapters have focused upon negotiation as an interaction between two participants. Many negotiations, however, involve more than two parties. For example, multiple defendants increasingly are joined in litigation. Consider a construction dispute between the owner of a building and the general contractor. Ultimately the negotiation may involve attorneys representing architects, engineers, subcontractors and various parties' sureties. Similarly, labor negotiations frequently include multiple unions and bargaining units, and in corporate bankruptcy reorganizations, various creditors usually negotiate. Even decisions of public agencies, such as where to locate a hazardous waste disposal site, typically involve protracted negotiations among various interest groups.

In the arena of international diplomacy, an extreme example of multiple party negotiation was the Law of the Sea negotiation.[1] Between 1973 and 1980, 160 nations negotiated complex financial arrangements for deep sea mining. Many other international negotiations, such as those concerning trade agreements or the restructuring of debts of a financially impaired nation, include multiple parties. Despite the prevalence of multiple party negotiation, there is a dearth of empirical studies and other academic literature covering this topic.

The analysis of the negotiation process described in previous chapters generally applies to multiple party negotiation. In these negotiations, the participants choose among *competitive, cooperative* and *problem-solving* tactics. Multiple party negotiation, however, is a more complex process than two party negotiation. As the number of negotiating parties increases, frequently so do the number of issues to be resolved and the time it takes to reach an agreement.

Even in the planning stages, the increasing complexity of multiple party negotiation influences the negotiation process substantially. The

---

1. *See* H. Raiffa, The Art and Science of Negotiation 275–87 (1982).

client's alternatives to a negotiated agreement among all the parties include the possibility of reaching agreements with some, but not all, of the negotiating partners. Conversely, the number of possible alternatives to a negotiated agreement for the other parties is increased by the prospect of some group of these parties reaching an agreement among themselves, but excluding the negotiator's client. Therefore, an analysis of bargaining power in multiple party negotiations must include consideration of the negotiator's ability to reach agreements and form coalitions with a subset of the parties, and the other parties' ability to do the same.

The lawyer chooses between two basic approaches when negotiating with multiple parties. The first is to seek intentionally to build coalitions or bargaining alliances between her client and other negotiating parties, and then to bargain on behalf of the coalition with the remaining parties. The second approach is for all representatives of all the parties to negotiate together in an attempt to identify a proposal or package of proposals that satisfies all the parties' underlying interests. Viewing multiple party negotiation as a process of constructing bargaining coalitions which then bargain with each other follows naturally from the *positional* conception of negotiation inherent in the competitive and cooperative strategies. This process is analyzed in the next section of this chapter. Conversely, the second approach, in which the parties simultaneously seek a solution satisfying their interests, is related closely to the problem-solving strategy.[2] This chapter includes a general discussion of how to structure simultaneous problem-solving bargaining among multiple negotiators, and specific consideration of the "single text" procedure.

Just as the use of *competitive* tactics does not preclude the use of *problem-solving* tactics at another point in the negotiation, the tactics outlined in this chapter are not mutually exclusive. For example, a coalition formed among Western industrialized nations in trade negotiations might prepare a "single text" for presentation to all other nations as a part of an ongoing negotiation. Further, it is important to reiterate that all the tactics described in previous chapters can be used in multiple party negotiation.

B. COALITION FORMATION

1. AN OVERVIEW OF COALITIONS AND NEGOTIATION

The primary characteristic of multiple party negotiation is the formation of bargaining coalitions among some or all of the negotiation partners.[3] A *coalition* is the joining of power or resources of two or

2. *E.g.,* R. Fisher & W. Ury, Getting to Yes: Negotiating Agreement Without Giving in 118–22 (1981).

3. *See* J. Rubin & B. Brown, The Social Psychology of Bargaining and Negotiation 64–79 (1975); Wilke, *Coalition Formation*

From A Socio–Psychological Perspective in Coalition Formation 115–72 (H. Wilke ed. 1985); *see also generally* H. Blalock & P. Wilken, Intergroup Processes: A Micro–Macro Perspective 394–96 & 405–08 (1979); J. Kahan & A. Rapaport, Theories of Coali-

more parties so that they have greater ability to determine the content of the negotiated agreement.

In most legal negotiations, bargaining alliances emerge sooner or later. When entering into such coalitions, the parties typically agree upon what each needs to receive in order to be satisfied with a negotiated agreement. Therefore, the process of entering into a coalition with another party is much like any other negotiation between two parties. The negotiation to form a coalition includes the use of *problem-solving, cooperative* and *competitive* tactics. This coalition then proceeds to negotiate with other coalitions or with a party who has not joined a coalition. Once again, in these negotiations, the negotiators use competitive, cooperative and problem-solving tactics. In short, multiple party negotiation is perceived as a series of two party negotiations.

The bargaining among coalition members includes elements of the *counseling process,* as well those of the negotiation process. When each party to the coalition is representing its own interests in the intra-party bargaining among members of the coalition, the parties use traditional negotiation tactics. When, however, the members of the coalition together consider what bargaining positions and tactics to use in negotiation with other coalitions or lone parties, this process resembles the pre-negotiation planning process between the attorney and client described in Chapter Four. The two processes are intertwined.

2. A THEORETICAL PERSPECTIVE ON COALITION FORMATION

Most research regarding coalitions focuses on the variable of power and its effect on coalition formation.[4] This research suggests that coalitions tend to form when parties perceive that they lack the bargaining leverage necessary to obtain the results they desire without such alliances. Coalitions thus favor weaker parties at the expense of stronger parties.

Somewhat surprisingly, the research finds that when there are three negotiating parties, the two less powerful parties tend to form a coalition instead of either of them joining forces with the stronger party.[5] Each of the weaker parties apparently fears exploitation by a more powerful coalition partner. A party's decision to join a coalition thus is influenced not only by the potential coalition's prospects for success in the negotiation, but also by how it will fare in the "intra-coalition" bargaining when the benefits to be "won" by the coalition in the negotiation are divided. On one hand, the ideal coalition partner is strong enough to add the bargaining leverage required to succeed in the negotiation. On the other hand, the prospective partner should be

tion Formation (1984); Miller, *Coalition Formation in Characteristic Function Games: Competitive Tests of Three Theories,* 16 Journal of Experimental Social Psychology 61–76 (1980).

4. *See e.g.,* H. Blalock & P. Wilken, *supra* note 3, at 394–95, 405–08; J. Rubin & B. Brown, *supra* note 3, at 64–74.

5. *See e.g.,* J. Rubin & B. Brown, *supra* note 3, at 73–74.

weak enough to allow the negotiator to dominate the bargaining among coalition members. The spoils of a coalition's negotiation "victory" are likely to be shared in a manner proportional to the bargaining coalition member's perceived power.

Social scientists' analysis of coalitions in multiple party negotiation suggests that under two conditions, coalitions will usually not be formed.[6] First, coalitions do not form when it is useless to do so because one party would still possess overwhelming bargaining power even after coalition formation. Second, a party with strong bargaining power may actively attempt to prevent coalitions from forming among other negotiators by establishing a counter-coalition with one of the weaker parties or by instigating divisiveness or contention among these parties.

A party's attractiveness as a coalition partner is influenced not only by its bargaining power, but also by its perceived status and the bargaining ability of its lawyer or other negotiator. In addition, the party's reputation for success in past negotiations and its track record for honoring its past commitments to its coalition partners often play a role.

3. APPLICATION TO LEGAL NEGOTIATION

How does the theoretical work of scholars regarding coalition analysis apply to multiple party legal negotiation? This section applies coalition analysis to two legal negotiations; the first is a litigation example and the second is a transactional negotiation.

Consider hypothetically a medical malpractice case filed on behalf of the estate of Lee Buccarelli. Lee died during an operation, allegedly because of a reaction to the anesthetic. The executor of Lee's estate has filed suit against the anesthesiologist, the attending surgeon and the hospital. During discovery, plaintiff's attorney learns that the patient's death probably resulted from an excessive dose of anesthetic caused by a malfunctioning valve in a piece of equipment manufactured by Medical Devices, Inc. (hereinafter "MD"). Accordingly, MD is joined as a defendant.

Prior to discovery, the defendants in Lee's lawsuit probably view themselves as belonging to a bargaining coalition, with the plaintiff standing alone on the other side of the case. As in most cases, the defendants here begin with common interests in denying liability and in minimizing the amount of damages to be paid to the victim. Further, the attorneys representing the various health care providers may have worked with each other in the past; they also probably share a certain ideological and psychological perspective when their clients are sued by malpractice claimants.

As the lawsuit progresses, however, this initially defined alignment of parties changes. The anesthesiologist and the surgeon both possess

6. *Id.* at 71–73.

knowledge about the operating room incident helpful to the estate's attorney in establishing a case against MD Inc. or even against the hospital. Conversely, the plaintiff's attorney has the "bargaining power" to grant the physicians what they desire—a quick release and exit from the lawsuit without substantial payment. Therefore, favorable conditions exist for the building of a *coalition* between the estate of the plaintiff and the two defendant physicians. In exchange for their testimony and cooperation against MD, the product manufacturer, or against the hospital, the physicians obtain dismissals from the litigation.

How might the attorneys for MD Inc. or the hospital prevent the formation of this coalition? As suggested by coalition theory, counsel for these defendants might attempt to form a "counter-coalition," focusing upon denial of liability or minimization of the plaintiff's damages. Similarly, these attorneys might seek to instigate divisiveness or contention among the plaintiff and the two physicians; for example, in communicating with the physicians' attorneys, counsel for MD would stress the lack of merit of the plaintiff's case as a whole.

A second coalition example is a transactional negotiation involving the management and various creditors of "Omigosh Mfg. Co." [7] Omigosh is insolvent and seeks to prevent involuntary liquidation in bankruptcy by reaching an agreement with its creditors to continue the business. The various creditors and owners all stand to lose—most substantially—if the business is sold for liquidation value. On the other hand, all parties must give up some of their rights—creditors must defer receiving payment, or even loan new money—if Omigosh is to survive.

The negotiation is chaired by an attorney representing Omigosh, and includes attorneys representing the shareholders who own the corporation and who recently advanced personal funds to enable the corporation to meet its payroll; the Certain Insurance Company that is owed $4 million on a fifteen year note secured by a first mortgage on all the corporation's real estate, plant and equipment; and the Unsure Financial Corporation, the short-term lender whose $6 million revolving line of credit is secured by a lien on accounts receivables and inventory. Further, a single attorney represents the more than 300 unsecured creditors, mostly "trade" creditors who supply parts, supplies and essential raw materials, and who are owed a total of $2.75 million. Finally, a tax consultant hired by management attends the meeting and advises the lawyers about both a multi-million dollar tax refund that may be owed the corporation and overdue payroll taxes. Not represented in this creditors' meeting is an injured judgment debtor

7. This example is taken from the transcript of a fascinating mock creditors' meeting presented on August 2, 1983 by the Commercial Financial Services Committee of the Section on Corporation, Banking and Business Law of the American Bar Association and reprinted in Poscover, *The Business in Trouble—A Workout Without Bankruptcy*, 39 Bus.Lawyer 1041 (1984). I would like to thank my colleague Skip Williams for bringing this example to my attention.

who recently obtained a $3 million products liability verdict against Omigosh, that the company's attorneys believe will be upheld on appeal, and various labor unions representing the company's employees.

Negotiation in the Omigosh case proceeds in a manner typical of bargaining among creditors in this situation. Despite its weak financial condition, Omigosh has considerable bargaining power, because the creditors' alternatives to a negotiated agreement are so unattractive. During the creditors' meeting, two secured creditors, Unsure and Certain, form a *coalition*. Unsure, the accounts receivable and inventory lender, indicates its willingness to extend further credit provided that it is given a second lien on the company's fixed assets. Certain, unwilling to extend additional funds itself, agrees to accept a second lien on the real estate, plants and equipment that is subject to the first mortgage, so long as Unsure agrees not to initiate foreclosure proceedings. By entering into this agreement, Unsure has improved its priority in regard to the fixed assets when compared with the interests of all other creditors. The two secured creditors, Unsure and Certain, thus form a bargaining *coalition* in opposition to the interests of the unsecured creditors that also is capable of further bargaining as a unit with Omigosh management. In the intra-coalition bargaining between Unsure and Certain, it is Certain who has the stronger bargaining position as a result of its fully secured status. As predicted by coalition theory, it is Unsure, therefore, who concedes and agrees to advance additional funds.

This *coalition* of Certain and Unsure then proceeds to negotiate with the company for other new priorities and an increased voice in company management. Ultimately Certain agrees to defer collection of principal repayment under its loan from Omigosh in exchange for increased rights to monitor the business and for the principal shareholders' personal guarantees to stand by the corporation's debts. Together the two secured creditors have more bargaining leverage than either one would have alone, and more than enough to extract concessions from Omigosh and its shareholders. Eventually, the unsecured creditors, with little bargaining power, join the agreement in exchange for modest concessions. Parties not represented at the creditors' meeting, most notably the labor unions and the product liability judgment creditor, receive no concessions, but are still probably better off than if the company is liquidated.

C. STRUCTURING MULTIPLE PARTY NEGOTIATION

In some ways, the two party negotiation dyad is a relatively uncomplicated social interaction. As more and more parties become involved in bargaining, however, the issue of structure or organization becomes more important. In purely logistical terms, how do 160 nations negotiate an agreement as parties to the Law of the Sea

Conference?[8] How is an agreement reached to handle hundreds of large personal injury claims among more than sixteen liability insurers and thirty-four asbestos manufacturers in intertwined insurance coverage disputes that involve shifting insurance carriers and coverages over a fifty year period and finite resources?[9] If all the negotiators in such a "mega-negotiation" simply extrapolate from ordinary negotiation tactics, the process often is doomed to end in confusion or stalemate. Scores of separate initial proposals, counterproposals and reactions to these proposals with arguments, threats and concessions—without any imposed structure—are unlikely to produce agreement.

Particularly when the number of participants becomes very large, multiple party negotiation requires consciously designed negotiation structures unnecessary in the two party context. At some point, negotiation among 160 nations or 50 insurance carriers and asbestos manufacturers resembles a legislature more than it does the more traditional negotiation dyad. These large negotiations require agreement on procedures for conducting the process—a "Robert's Rules of Order" for negotiation—and usually a chairperson or a similar facilitator to guide the deliberations.[10]

Even in multiple party negotiations involving smaller groups, structure also is required. The participants in these negotiations usually should designate an agenda and specify a process for reaching agreement. Often, it is desirable to designate one person to serve as a facilitator of the negotiation. This individual can be either a *mediator*—a neutral third party—or one of the negotiators herself. The use of *mediators* as neutral third party facilitators is even more helpful in multiple party negotiation than it is in two party negotiation because of the mediator's ability to structure the negotiation process. Further, mediators facilitate the use of *problem-solving* tactics, and the complexity of multiple party negotiation usually necessitates the use of *problem-solving* tactics. *Mediation* and its effect on the negotiation process are discussed more fully in Chapter Twelve.

When a mediator is not available, one of the negotiators sometimes serves as a chairperson or facilitator of negotiation discussions. In most cases, the individual chosen should have moderate views, understand the conflicting interests of the different parties and represent a party with only a minor role in the negotiation. In other cases, the respect shared by the parties for a particular lawyer or other negotiator

8. *See* H. Raiffa, *supra* note 1, at 275–87.

9. From October 1982 through June 1985, Dean Henry Wellington of the Yale Law School facilitated negotiations among asbestos manufacturers, liability insurers and plaintiffs' attorneys. The resulting agreement, the Wellington Plan, established a voluntary nonprofit asbestos-claims facility for settling and arbitrating asbestosis claims, at the same time that it preserved the claimant's right to a jury trial. P. Brodeur, Outrageous Misconduct 293, 335–36 (1985).

10. For discussion of how similar problems are handled in complex litigation, *see generally* Manual for Complex Litigation, Second (1985). Among the procedures used to structure multi-party litigation are appointment of lead counsel, *id.* at section 20.22; and assignment of related lawsuits to a single judge, *id.* at section 20.12.

makes her an appropriate choice as facilitator. Even though the attorney for Omigosh had more than a minor interest in negotiating the intercreditors' agreement, he was an obvious choice to facilitate the discussion because of his role as a "stakeholder" and his impartiality among the interests of the various creditors.

D. SINGLE NEGOTIATION TEXT

One other technique for structuring multiple party negotiations, the so called "*single negotiation text*", deserves special attention. The *single negotiation text* is a problem-solving negotiation procedure of particular value in multiple party negotiations.[11] In this process, one of the negotiating parties or their lawyers, or a neutral third party, drafts a proposed agreement and asks the other negotiators for their suggestions and criticisms. At this point, the other negotiators are not requested to accept the proposal or to evaluate its overall desirability. After receiving specific suggestions and criticisms from the other negotiators, the original author redrafts the proposal, taking into account the feedback she received and incorporating the other parties' suggestions. Then she submits the revised draft to the parties. The process of soliciting criticism and redrafting begins again, and may recur three or four times—or even twenty or thirty times.

No single negotiator usually perceives the *single negotiation text* as becoming a better document at every step of the process. It is more likely that a negotiator finds that one round of modifications to the text result in a substantial improvement for her client's interests—sometimes at the expense of other parties—but that the next set of changes benefit other parties, perhaps to her client's detriment. Because the negotiators all desire to reach agreement, however, they probably tolerate changes that modestly diminish their clients' level of satisfaction as the process moves along. Eventually the drafter believes that the current draft does the best possible job of addressing the parties' interests. Accordingly, she submits it to the parties for their possible acceptance.

The *single negotiation text,* of course, can be used even in two party negotiation. When multiple parties negotiate, however, some type of a focal point is required, and the *single negotiation text* is a desirable alternative.

Probably the most famous use of the *single negotiation text* occurred during the negotiation between President Sadat of Egypt and Prime Minister Begin of Israel at Camp David during 1978.[12] Representatives of the United States, after listening to the Egyptian and Israeli delegations, prepared an initial *single negotiation text* which

---

11. *See* R. Fisher & W. Ury, *supra* note 2, at 118–22; D. Lax & J. Sebenius, The Manager as Negotiator: Bargaining for Cooperation and Competitive Gain 176–78 (1986); H. Raiffa, *supra* note 1, at 253–55.

12. R. Fisher & W. Ury, *supra* note 2, at 121.

then went through twenty-three more drafts during the next thirteen days. At that point, the American facilitators believed that no further improvement was possible, and they recommended adoption of the text. Both Egypt and Israel agreed.

The use of the *single negotiation text,* however, is not limited to international diplomacy. Typically committee chairpersons circulate a draft of a proposal or report to members of the committee and invite their feedback either prior to or during the next committee meeting. After receiving the comments of other committee members, the chair or committee staff makes revisions. For example, consider a state legislature driven to address the medical malpractice crisis by public outcry about dramatically increased medical malpractice premiums. Staff of the legislature's judiciary committee, working together with representatives of a state study commission who have been investigating the malpractice crisis, draft a comprehensive reform proposal. This initial draft legislation is widely circulated among key legislators, the governor's office, staff from other affected legislative committees, and representatives of various interest groups including physicians, hospitals, lawyers, insurance companies and consumer groups. As in other *single negotiation text* proceedings, changes are made as a result of feedback, and the process is repeated. In most instances in the political arena, it is not possible to achieve the support of all the affected interest groups; some end up opposing the legislation. Eventually, however, after many drafts and modifications, the proposal attracts support from enough of the key legislators and interest groups, whose suggestions are now incorporated into the draft legislation, to be enacted into law.

The *single negotiation text* process is most effective if the individual drafting the proposal, soliciting criticism and redrafting the agreement is a mediator or other third party. Under these circumstances, the initial proposal is likely to be an honest attempt to reconcile the conflicting parties' interests, and not a document drafted to manipulate the negotiating process. Moreover, when the initial proposal is drafted by a neutral mediator, the negotiators often feel more willing to offer honest criticisms and suggestions. It is understood by the participants that no one, not even the mediator hired to facilitate negotiation with techniques such as the *single negotiation text,* is committed to the initial draft.

The *single negotiation text* procedure does not require the negotiator to make any concessions until the final stage of the process when she is asked to accept the final version of the text. Instead, she is asked only for her input, suggestions and criticisms. With her reaction to each successive draft, this procedure allows the negotiator to communicate effectively her client's priorities and his level of resistance to acquiescence on particular issues. This is accomplished, however, without any image loss; the negotiator's response or lack of response to any particular provision of the *single negotiation text* does not communicate to the other negotiators that her bargaining resolve is being weakened or that their competitive bargaining tactics are working.

The *single negotiation text* can be used as a means of structuring complex multiple party negotiation even when a neutral facilitator is not available and one of the negotiators drafts the text. Under these circumstances, the negotiators should choose one among them whom they perceive to be capable of acting somewhat impartially and of appreciating other parties' interests. During the *single negotiation text* procedure, the other negotiators should evaluate carefully if the draft proposal prepared by their counterpart is a good faith attempt to provide a reasonable basis from which to bargain or whether it is so one-sided that it is intentionally drafted to gain a substantial initial negotiating advantage.

Just as the negotiator drafting a *single negotiation text* sometimes seeks to use the process to gain an unfair competitive advantage, the other participants also may seek to manipulate the process. Negotiators criticizing the *single negotiation text* and making suggestions may intentionally overstate their requirements or objections to a draft. Thus, they employ a *false demand* tactic, predicting that subsequent acquiescence on issues previously criticized, but of little concern, will result in other negotiators' reciprocal flexibility. Like all competitive tactics, however, this attempted manipulation can be dangerous because it risks negotiation stalemate. This chance is greater in multiple party negotiation where it is more difficult reaching an agreement acceptable to the various parties. The competitive negotiator also risks the possibility that the other parties will reach an agreement that excludes her.

The *single negotiation text* is only one problem-solving tactic particularly suited for multiple party negotiation. The complexity of multiple party negotiation means that competitive negotiating tactics such as extreme proposals, bluffing, and information concealment usually result in frustration and stalement, at least in those negotiations in which the parties do not readily divide into two bargaining coalitions. The most important difference between multiple party and two party negotiation remains the increased use of various problem-solving tactics to determine whether there is a zone of agreement that satisfies the underlying interests of the many participants.

Chapter Eleven

NEGOTIATION COUNSELING

A. INTRODUCTION

Legal negotiation is representative negotiation. It involves not only a relationship between the two negotiating attorneys, but also relationships between each lawyer and her respective client. In order to achieve the best possible negotiated agreement, the lawyer's ability as a counselor is at least as important as her negotiation skills. If the lawyer's effectiveness as a negotiator is measured by the extent to which the negotiated agreement serves the client's interests, the lawyer's ability to understand those interests is critical.

Counseling can be defined as the interaction between the lawyer and the client as they decide how to achieve the client's best interests. Chapter Four, *Negotiation Planning,* describes the planning process preceding negotiation as a joint one between the attorney and her client. Thus, the first opportunity in the negotiation process for client counseling occurs when the attorney and client prepare for the negotiation.

Whether to pursue or forgo the option of negotiating with a particular party is the most important decision during the initial client counseling session. Banana Computers, for example, might decide not to negotiate with the Chestnut Development Corporation, but to substitute negotiation with another shopping center or retail location. Another possible alternative is to build its own store. Similarly, Patrick Finney chooses between settlement of his claim and other options. After conferring with his attorney, if the facts indicate a slim possibility of recovery, Patrick Finney might decide to forgo his claim against the Baltimore and Western Railroad. It is possible with different facts that Patrick would feel such anger toward the defendant he would vehemently oppose any settlement talks and insist on a trial as soon as possible.

As suggested in Chapter Four, other decisions are made during client counseling conference prior to negotiation. The attorney and client decide the content of initial proposals, and settle upon which of the client's more important interests should be stressed during the negotiation. Optimally, the attorney and client discuss possible negotiating tactics and evaluate their effectiveness in achieving agreement and their impact on the client's ongoing relationship with the other party.

At the other end of the negotiation process, when the attorney concludes that she has received the best possible deal that this negotiation can produce, she and the client then engage in the "final" client counseling conference. During this conference, they together decide whether to accept the negotiated agreement or pursue other alternatives such as litigation or negotiation with other parties.

Client counseling does not end with the beginning of negotiation, however, only to be resumed after the bargaining is completed. Instead, client counseling conferences should be interspersed throughout the negotiation process. The lawyer should confer often with her client during the course of the negotiation and report to him on proposals advanced by the other party and new information gained during the bargaining process. Model Rule of Professional Conduct 1.4 includes precisely these requirements.[1] This new information and the negotiating behavior of the other party often cause the attorney and client to change their assessment of how to achieve the client's best interests.

The next part of this chapter considers the conflict between client-centered advocacy and the tendency of many attorneys to dominate the client counseling process. Part C of this chapter then discusses the client counseling conference following negotiation in which the client chooses between the negotiated agreement and other alternatives. Finally, Part D analyzes client counseling conferences that occur during the ongoing negotiation. This order of presentation—in which the counseling conference following negotiation is analyzed prior to counseling sessions during negotiation—although not chronological, allows consideration first of the basic structure of client counseling in which the lawyer assists the client in making decisions. The content and structure of counseling conferences during the negotiation itself are more varied. Further, these counseling sessions involve a greater mixture of issues relating to both the substance of the negotiation proposals and the negotiation process itself.

Note that this clear distinction between the client counseling conference that occurs after negotiation and client counseling sessions during negotiation is oversimplified in at least two ways. First, in many negotiations the client gives the attorney authority to accept a proposal containing certain terms before the attorneys reach agreement on such a proposal. In these cases, there is no "post-negotiation" client

---

1. Model Rule of Professional Conduct 1.4 provides:

(a) A lawyer shall keep a client reasonably informed about the status of a matter and promptly comply with reasonable requests for information.

(b) A lawyer shall explain a matter to the extent reasonably necessary to permit the client to make informed decisions regarding the representation.

Model Rules of Professional Conduct Rule 1.4 (1983).

counseling session in which the client must make a "yes or no" decision on an agreement reached by the attorneys. Thus, the most significant client counseling session in these situations is the one during negotiation when the client gives his attorney authority to make a specific proposal or to accept a certain offer from the other party. In other words, the structure of client counseling sessions during negotiation changes substantially depending upon what type of bargaining authority the client grants his attorney.

The second oversimplification underlying the notion of a separate and distinct client counseling conference following negotiation is the illusion that the attorney and client always will know when the negotiation is finished. If the client grants his attorney authority to enter into an agreement on given terms, then it is always possible that the other party will accept those terms during the next round of negotiation. Accordingly, a conference perceived by the attorney and client to be an intra-negotiation counseling session may in fact be the final counseling session when a *de facto* decision to accept a negotiated agreement is made. Conversely, there may be subsequent rounds of negotiation even following a counseling conference that at the time, the attorney and client believe is the final one. As previously discussed, although the other negotiator may claim that he can concede no further in a negotiation, he often finds a way to reopen a stalemated negotiation following the client's rejection of his final offer. A client counseling conference in which the client decides to reject the negotiated agreement, therefore, may turn out to be only an intra-negotiation counseling conference.

In any of these client counseling contexts, decision-making is the focus. Should Banana Computer begin negotiation with Chestnut Development Corporation? What proposals should be made to the other party? Which of the client's interests are most important? Which negotiating tactics should be used? Should the negotiated agreement be rejected or accepted?

Negotiated agreements that maximize the satisfaction of the client depend as much upon understanding the client's interests and in assuring that these agreements meet these interests as they do on any single lawyering skill. Because of this, and because client counseling assumes a few interesting wrinkles in the negotiation context, counseling is presented as an integral part of this text.[2] The basic structure of the client counseling session outlined in this chapter, with a few

---

2. The decision whether to address the vagaries of client counseling in a legal negotiation text is a difficult one. A single chapter on client counseling does justice to neither the importance nor the difficulty of effective client counseling. Separate law school courses and distinct law school texts are devoted exclusively to client counseling. The law student or lawyer is referred specifically to D. Binder & S. Price, Legal Interviewing and Counseling: A Client-Centered Approach (1977). To omit discussion of the counseling process in a negotiation text, however, risks that some law students and lawyers who study legal negotiation will not study legal counseling. The importance of client counseling to effective negotiation would make such an omission critical.

embellishments, is derived from the client-centered counseling model presented by Professors Binder and Price in their leading text, *Legal Interviewing and Counseling: A Client–Centered Approach.*[3]

B. THE LAWYER'S TENDENCY TO DOMINATE NEGOTIATION COUNSELING

The Model Rules of Professional Conduct explicitly provide that the decision to accept a negotiated agreement is to be made by the client, not the lawyer.[4] Further, under the Model Rules, lawyers are required to consult with clients about the means of their representation.[5] There is nothing surprising about these professional norms. The essence of the lawyer's role is to represent the client's interests. In the context of negotiation, the quality of the lawyer's role as a hired professional negotiator should be judged only by how well the agreement serves such interests.

Client counseling is fundamentally a process of identifying all available alternatives, considering the advantages and disadvantages of each alternative, and reaching a decision that maximizes the client's interests. It is an interactive process between attorney and client. Only the client knows his own underlying interests, and how he weighs the importance of various issues. Accordingly, only he can make the decision to accept or reject a negotiated agreement. On the other hand, the lawyer contributes her legal and practical expertise to the client's decision-making process. Her expertise is supplemented by the information and insights gained in her professional role as the client's representative during the negotiation itself.

Unfortunately, lawyers sometimes exceed their proper roles of informing and facilitating the client's decision-making process. They dominate counseling conferences in ways that contravene the lawyer's proper professional role and jeopardize the chances for a negotiated agreement that actually serves the client's underlying interests. Many attorneys in the past *told* their clients to accept or reject settlement offers, and some probably continue to do so. This arrogant and erroneous conception of the lawyer's professional role often results from the belief that the lawyer knows better than the client what is in his best interests. Clients often willingly abet this domination because they are reluctant to take responsibility for their own decisions.

Frequently the lawyer undermines the client's decision-making process more subtlely. At the beginning of the litigation, the lawyer paints a grim picture of the prospects at trial. Gary Gerstein tells Patrick that based upon his considerable experience, the jury is almost certain to find that he was comparatively negligent and reduce his damages appreciably, and that the question of the railroad's negligence

3. D. Binder & S. Price, *supra* note 2.   5. *Id.*

4. Model Rules of Professional Conduct Rule 1.2(a) (1983).

is a "real gamble." When the Baltimore and Western Railroad makes an offer to settle Patrick's case—any offer—Gary is in the position of presenting the offer as a minor miracle, pulled out of the hat by a terrific lawyer-negotiator. From the lawyer's perspective, the manipulation produces a great result. His client is ecstatic with his representation, and the manner in which Gary presents the offer to his client allows him to engineer substantially his client's acceptance of the offer. From the client's perspective, however, the situation is tragic. Patrick probably decides to accept the offer without knowing that he has a substantial chance of doing much better at trial. Client-centered advocacy requires unbiased and accurate information about each of the available alternatives.

Even lawyers who believe that the client should make the final settlement decision often experience the urge to dominate the client's decision-making process. The lawyer may sense that she knows more about the litigation or the transaction than the client, and is in a better position to make a decision. She also understands the negotiation process better than the client. Therefore, she believes that she is in a better position to decide what to include in a negotiation proposal because she knows what the other party is likely to accept or reject.

Participating in the negotiation process often psychologically encourages the lawyer to seize control of the client counseling process. On one hand, it is the lawyer who actively competes in the negotiation process. It is difficult for most lawyers to report back to clients after an ego-involving negotiation session, only to have their clients tell them that they wish to pursue a different proposal or negotiation strategy. In other cases, ironically, the lawyer's anxiety about her inability to control the uncertainties of the negotiation process compels her to establish control wherever she can—such as over her client during counseling sessions.

Choices regarding the substance of a negotiated agreement and negotiation tactics must be the client's, however, if the agreement is to effectively serve his interests. Attorney Gary Gerstein goes on to represent another client; Patrick Finney remains a paraplegic. If Gary believes there is an eighty percent chance of realizing a verdict in excess of $1.2 million dollars, a utilitarian calculation therefore suggests that any offer less than $960,000 should be rejected. Is Patrick "wrong" to decide to accept an offer of $785,000? Is anyone else really in Gary's position to choose between a certain $785,000 and a good chance—but still a chance—of a verdict in excess of $1.2 million? Also, could Gary's desire to try the case be influenced by extraneous factors such as the valuable publicity of achieving a million dollar verdict for his client?

The counseling model outlined here is designed to allow the client the greatest possible autonomy in making his own decisions about accepting or rejecting a negotiated agreement and other aspects of the negotiation process. There are limits, however, to the impact that any counseling model or structure can have on the allocation of decision-making authority between the attorney and the clients. Being aware of the importance of client-centered advocacy and the tendencies that push lawyers to dominate their clients probably is more important to facilitating negotiated agreements that actually serve the client's interests than is a recommended structure for counseling sessions. Does the lawyer best serve her client's interests by communicating frequently with her client, contributing her expertise and experience to the collaborative relationship and seeking agreements that stress the client's articulated interests? Or is the lawyer's proper professional role to decide what is best for the clients she serves, pursue such agreements during the negotiation, and then give clear unambiguous "advice" to the client as to what that person should do? What *is* the lawyer's proper professional role?

C. CLIENT COUNSELING FOLLOWING NEGOTIATION

1. TIMING OF THE DECISIVE CLIENT COUNSELING SESSION

Following the negotiation or late in the negotiation process, the attorney and her client confer about the choice between the negotiated agreement and other options. In reality, this primary decision-making conference may occur in a variety of contexts:

(1) the attorneys have reached a tentative agreement that the client must decide whether to accept and ratify;

(2) the client has received a final offer that he must accept or reject;

(3) the attorney has advised her client regarding the the best possible agreement that she believes can be achieved; or

(4) the attorney and client are considering the terms of one last final offer in an effort to reach an agreement.

Only in the first context has negotiation actually concluded. In the third and fourth situations, it is not even clear that an agreement can be reached or what the exact terms of such an agreement will be. Nevertheless, in most negotiations—those involving multiple bargaining sessions between the attorneys—prior to the final conclusion of bargaining, the client often makes the critical choice between a negotiated agreement and other alternatives. After repeated negotiation sessions, the attorney usually can predict the major terms of an eventual agreement with sufficient clarity to present the client with the choice between an agreement on those terms and the other available alternatives. Unless the attorney poses this choice to her client before proposing a "final offer" to the other negotiator, she leaves herself vulnerable to the awkward possibility that she will make a final proposal, the other negotiator will accept it, and then her own client will disavow the agreement.

2. DIFFERENCES BETWEEN CLIENT COUNSELING IN THE DISPUTE RESOLUTION AND TRANSACTIONAL CONTEXTS

The exact structure of the client counseling session depends upon the nature of the ongoing relationship between the attorney and the client and the posture of the negotiation, *i.e.,* is it completed or only nearing the critical phase? The format of the counseling conference is also different in a *dispute resolution* or litigation case than it is in a business or other *transactional* negotiation. In a litigated case, the counseling session following the negotiation usually involves a choice between two clearly delineated alternatives: an agreement, the terms of which either already have been negotiated or will be concluded in the near future, and the probable outcome of a trial.

Critical counseling sessions in *transactional* negotiations often occur at an earlier point when the terms of an agreement are less solidified. At a stage in the negotiation substantially in advance of the resolution of all issues, Chestnut Development Corporation and Banana Computers probably both decide that they are going to enter an agreement with each other on terms to be negotiated. Banana does not wait until agreement on all issues with Chestnut to evaluate how well acceptance of this commercial lease satisfies its interests when compared with other alternatives such as locating its store in a nearby shopping center or constructing its own building. Once agreement on major issues is reached, or it is perceived that agreement will be reached eventually by the parties acting in good faith, each corporation effectively decides to pursue negotiation with the other to the exclusion of other alternatives. Occasionally such a negotiation breaks down, but it is not realistic—after an initial commitment to negotiate with a certain party is reached—to view the negotiation as just another alternative. It represents the client's presumptive decision how to proceed unless he is surprised by subsequent events during the negotiation. To put it another way, most clients do not proceed with parallel negotiations with all available potential partners on a equal footing and then pick and choose which agreement is best.

This description of transactional negotiation suggests that in most cases there will be, in fact, two critical negotiation conferences. The first client counseling session usually occurs early in the negotiation after minimal contact with possible transaction partners. The probable terms of agreement on major issues to be negotiated can be tentatively predicted, if somewhat inaccurately. At this point, the client decides with which of the potential partners he wishes to negotiate. This initial counseling conference includes consideration of the advantages of a deal with any of the potential negotiation partners and predictions of the eventual terms of an agreement with each of them.

Once the client decides to pursue negotiation with a particular party, and the negotiation has proceeded—interspersed with intra-negotiation counseling sessions between lawyer and client—there will be another important client counseling conference at the conclusion of the negotiation. At this point, the client is asked to consider the detailed provisions of the agreement that has been negotiated and to accept or reject them. If the client finds some terms unacceptable, his alternative in most instances is not to reject the entire agreement, throw it in the wastebasket, and begin negotiation with another party. Instead, he is likely to return to the bargaining table with the same party and inform him of the unacceptable provision.

3. STRUCTURE OF CLIENT COUNSELING CONFERENCES

In any of these contexts, the client counseling conference follows essentially the same structure. The attorney and client together undertake a cost-benefit analysis to compare the various alternatives available to the client. To what extent does the negotiated agreement meet the client's interests? How would the client's level of satisfaction that would result from accepting the agreement compare with his probable satisfaction if he choose one of the other options instead? This process requires the attorney to outline the terms of the negotiated agreement, identify the client's alternative courses of action, consider with the client how each alternative addresses the client's interests, and solicit a decision from the client.

Often it is appropriate for the lawyer to begin a counseling conference with a *preparatory explanation* describing for the client what she expects will occur during the session. Suppose Gary Gerstein has concluded his negotiation on behalf of Patrick Finney with the attorney for the Baltimore and Western Railroad. He has received an offer of $850,000, that was described by Roberta Martinez, Baltimore and Western's attorney, as "final." Gary, in fact, believes it is a final offer. He probably should begin the counseling session with a brief explanation of the purposes of the meeting and how he intends to conduct the conference. For example, Patrick might expect, as many clients do, that Gary will "tell" Patrick what is the best decision. Assuming Gary is committed to client-centered advocacy, one purpose of the *preparatory explanation* is to counteract the client's notion that the attorney and not the client should make the decision. Accordingly, Gary might begin with the following *preparatory explanation:*

1—Gary: As you know, Patrick, we're scheduled to take your case to trial next Tuesday. I have talked again with Roberta Martinez, Baltimore and Western's attorney, and she has made one last offer to settle this case. I thought we should talk about that before we talk about the possibility of your testifying next week. Does that make sense to you?

2—Patrick: Sure. Does this mean we won't be going to trial?

3—Gary: That's possible. It will be up to you. Here's what I
             suggest we do. Let's try to list the choices available
             to you: going to trial, settling—there may be others.
             We can consider together how each alternative meets
             your interests. Then you will need to make a deci-
             sion on how we will proceed.

Gary's *preparatory explanation* tells Patrick that he needs to make his
own decision and outlines a structure for the counseling session consisting of three parts: identification of alternatives, consideration of how
well each alternative meets the client's interests, and making a decision.

The post-negotiation counseling conference should not be the first
time that the lawyer and client have considered all available alternatives. Counseling is an ongoing process that begins prior to the
negotiation. During the pre-negotiation counseling session described in
Chapter Four, *Negotiation Planning,* the lawyer and client necessarily
identify the alternatives available to the client when they determine
the client's Best Alternative to a Negotiated Agreement. From the
client's feedback during that negotiation planning session, the lawyer
knows which alternatives the client considers most viable or attractive
at that stage. Additional alternatives might have been suggested
during the negotiation or may have become apparent from other
sources since negotiation began.

In identifying options for consideration by the client, the lawyer
should list the alternatives discussed prior to negotiation and any
others that he has become aware of during the intervening period of
time. Generally, the lawyer should neither describe in detail the
alternatives during this listing process nor indicate her personal opinion of the various options. Either form of embellishment by the lawyer
might exert too much influence on the client's decision-making process.
It is appropriate, however, for the lawyer to summarize any conclusions
that she and her client reached during the negotiation planning session
regarding the viability of potential options. It is not usually advantageous to reopen a discussion of an option that the client rejected
previously. Because alternatives that the lawyer and client previously
decided were not viable need not be reconsidered from scratch, the post-
negotiation conference becomes more manageable in scope. Before
discarding an option, however, the lawyer should check briefly to
assure that the client still rejects an alternative and that his earlier
evaluation has not been changed by the negotiation process or other
events occurring in the meantime.

In the case of Patrick Finney's lawsuit against the railroad, the two
readily apparent alternatives are to accept a settlement in the amount
of $850,000 or to proceed to trial during the next week. There may be
others, however. For example, depending upon Gary Gerstein's past
experience with opposing counsel and the court, he might suggest as an
option that he seek a further continuance—on the premise that the

negotiation is not actually concluded and agreement could be reached with a little more time. Another possibility might be for the parties to agree that Baltimore and Western is seventy percent "at fault." The parties would agree to litigate only the amount of damages, and Baltimore and Western would pay seventy percent of the jury's verdict on damages.

Once the lawyer and client agree upon a list of alternatives to consider, they evaluate the extent to which each alternative meets the client's underlying interests. The consequences of each alternative include not only their effects on legal and economic interests, but on social and psychological ones as well. The lawyer, because of her expertise, takes primary responsibility for predicting the legal consequences of the client's decision. For example, Gary Gerstein would predict the probable results of taking Patrick's case to trial.

Predicting trial outcomes is a difficult process involving assessing the facts, the law, the credibility of witnesses, and how the judge will exercise his discretion. Trial outcome prediction was previously described in Chapter Four, *Negotiation Planning.*[6] The uncertainties of the trial process mean that the lawyer treads a delicate line between making trial outcome guarantees with an unrealistic degree of confidence and failing to offer the client any useful prediction at all by telling him that trial "is always a gamble."

Both the lawyer and the client may contribute substantially to an evaluation of the economic consequences of an alternative. For example, Bev Bailey and Jeff Walton, the manager of Banana Computers, jointly evaluate a proposal that provides for a base rent of $25 per square foot, additional rent equal to six percent of all gross revenues in excess of $500,000 and an additional charge of $8 per square foot for maintenance, utility and other common expenses.

The *social* or *psychological* consequences of a negotiation proposal are usually best identified by the client. For example, Chestnut's relationships with its other tenants might be impaired if the Chestnut Development Corporation yielded to Banana's request for a lower rental during the initial year of its operations, and did not insist upon a confidentiality clause. This is a *social* consequence of a proposed alternative, and Chestnut's employees are probably in a better position to evaluate it than the attorney. An example of a *psychological* consequence of an alternative is the great anxiety that Patrick Finney anticipates regarding cross-examination if he elects to go to trial. Although the client usually makes most of the contributions to the discussion of *social* and *psychological* factors, the lawyer can guide the inquiry by raising specific questions about concerns that other clients have had when faced with similar choices. However, the lawyer also should ask her client open-ended questions about the advantages or disadvantages of each option or how he feels about settling or proceed-

---

6. *See supra* Chapter Four, *Negotiation Planning,* at 51–4.

ing to trial. Unless she asks such open-ended questions, her client's responses to her narrowly focused questions may never reveal additional considerations not specifically identified by the lawyer.

Once again, any discussions conducted by the lawyer and her client prior to negotiation make the post-negotiation counseling conference easier. During the earlier session, the lawyer and her client should have discussed the client's interests as a part of the negotiation planning process. Because the lawyer gained an awareness of the client's underlying interests during the earlier session, she conducts the post-negotiation conference more effectively by referring back to the client's previously articulated interests. Of course, new facts gleaned from the negotiation process itself, or from other sources in the meantime, will affect the evaluation of how well each alternative meets the client's underlying needs. For example, after he learns Roberta Martinez's evaluation of probable trial outcome and some suggestion of her trial strategy, Gary Gerstein can offer a better explanation of the trial alternative. In addition, even without new factual disclosures, the client may evaluate other issues in a new and different light. For example, as trial approaches, Patrick may be more aware of his own anxiety associated with trial than he was two years earlier when negotiation began.

The amount of information available to the lawyer and her client in assessing the consequences of the negotiation alternative obviously depends upon how far the negotiation has proceeded. The specific consequences of a negotiated agreement can be detailed more effectively after the attorneys agree on a draft document that requires only the clients' ratification. When a counseling session occurs much earlier in the negotiation process, the lawyer can only describe the current negotiation proposals offered by the other side and her estimates as to the terms of an eventual agreement. Nevertheless, it is often at this earlier juncture that the critical decision is reached to pursue actively a negotiated agreement with a particular business partner. To be sure, the client can always reject the negotiated agreement once its terms are negotiated by the two lawyers. Neither the attorney nor her client is well-served, however, by a string of negotiations that proceed for a substantial period of time and then break down. A client, such as Banana Computers, does not want to pay a lawyer to negotiate on parallel tracks with every available shopping mall, shopping center, or other retail location. Banana probably decides fairly early in the negotiation process to bargain with Chestnut to the exclusion of other possible commercial landlords. It makes this decision prior to the time that it knows all the terms of its eventual lease with Chestnut.

At some stage in the negotiation process, the client chooses between the available alternatives—including the negotiated agreement and other options—after considering how his interests are affected by each one. The client, and not the attorney, is in the best position to make this choice. Only the client knows the depth of the anxiety he feels when faced with going to trial and how to weigh this fear in his decision making process. Further, individuals possess varying levels of risk adverseness—some will gamble on a greater award at trial, others prefer a smaller, but more certain, payment even if a strictly utilitarian calculation suggests a more lucrative probable trial outcome. Thus, proper understanding of the lawyer's role as a professional—and commitment to client autonomy—means that only the client should make the choice between a negotiated agreement and the other alternatives. The lawyer can, and should, however, use her expertise and experience to assist the client in making an informed decision.

Once the lawyer and client have identified the alternatives and considered the consequences of each one, the client reaches a decision. In her role in the client's decision making, the lawyer assists him by summarizing the possible options and the consequences of each option. Sometimes she can do this best by listing the consequences of each option on paper. The client may require additional time, perhaps overnight, to think about his decision.

Clients frequently ask their lawyers if they should accept a negotiated agreement or pursue other options. In many cases, such a request poses no ethical dilemma for the lawyer. If the client is a sophisticated businessperson who customarily makes his own decisions without hesitation, then he probably is simply requesting additional input before making his own decision. In some cases, a client simply turns over an entire matter to an attorney. Examples of this practice include a business which turns over a series of collection actions to an attorney, or a large commercial real estate developer who asks an attorney to acquire several parcels of property at the best available price. In these cases, the attorney should not hesitate to make a recommendation to the client regarding the advisability of a negotiated agreement.

More troublesome is a request for advice on whether a negotiated agreement should be accepted or rejected from a client who is not a "regular player" in the legal system. Many people still believe an attorney should make their decisions for them because of the attorney's supposedly greater experience in legal and worldly matters. If the attorney responds to the client's request for a recommendation, the client often finds it difficult to make his own decision regarding what is best for his own interests—given his particular value system and level of risk adverseness—in the face of potentially conflicting advice from his lawyer. Under these circumstances, the lawyer should refrain from making a recommendation and instead reiterate the reasons why it is important for the client to make his own decision.[7]

7. Under some circumstances, the attorney should advise her client in writing of the alternatives available to him and the consequences of accepting each alternative. This letter should clearly state that the decision whether to accept a settlement offer is the client's. Besides confirming that the client understands his choices, this procedure protects the lawyer from a subsequent claim she did not accurately inform him of the alternatives or coerced him into making his choice. For example, a defendant who pleads guilty sometimes later alleges that counsel did not accurately inform him about his choices. Therefore, he argues, his plea violates due pro-

Suppose Patrick Finney feels unable to decide whether to accept or reject a $850,000 settlement offer and asks Gary Gerstein what he should do. Consider the following response from Gary:

1—Gary: I know you are finding this a difficult decision. The stakes are very high. You think that you're entitled to more than the $850,000 without the risks that you would face at trial. After all, they were negligent.

2—Patrick: You got that right.

3—Gary: The trouble is, I don't know what's the right decision for you. I can help you out by giving you some predictions about what's going to happen at trial. We can review the various consequences about going to trial and not going to trial. But I can't make your decision for you. You're the one who has to live with it. It sounds a little cold-hearted, but I'll go on to another case. There's a risk in going to trial and I don't know how much risk you're willing to take. I also don't know how bad you're going to feel if you settle for less than you think you're entitled to. Would it be helpful to you to go over the advantages and the disadvantages of settling one more time?

Gary answered Patrick's request for a recommendation in segment number 1 with an active listening response concerning the difficulty of making a decision and Patrick's sense that he is entitled to better and more clear-cut choices than he has. In the second and third segment, Gary then explains again why Patrick should make the decision instead of him. He offers to assist him by reviewing the alternatives and the consequences of each alternative again. Most of the time, this explanation—perhaps repeated more than once—leads the client to assume responsibility for his own decision.

The lawyer also should be more active in offering advice to the client when the client's decision to accept or reject a negotiated agreement is inconsistent with the client's previously articulated interests. For example, if Jeff Walton, manager of Banana Computers, had informed Bev Bailey during the negotiation planning session that Banana could not possibly afford to pay more than $20 per square foot during the initial start-up period, and Jeff is now prepared to accept a negotiated agreement calling for a base rent of $25 per square foot and additional charges for maintenance, insurance, utilities and other common expenses of $8 per square foot, Bev should call this discrepancy to Jeff's attention. Although there is often an explanation for this change in position, it is important for the lawyer to highlight this inconsistency and inquire about its causes.

cess because he received ineffective assistance of counsel. *See e.g., Hill v.* *Lockhart,* 474 U.S. 52, 106 S.Ct. 366, 88 L.Ed.2d 203 (1985).

D. CLIENT COUNSELING CONFERENCES DURING NEGOTIATION

If the lawyer is to negotiate an agreement that serves her client's interests and is to facilitate client-centered advocacy, client counseling sessions with the client prior to the negotiation and at the conclusion of the bargaining are not sufficient. The lawyer should confer frequently with the client during the negotiation itself, preferably after each contact with the other lawyer. Frequent client contacts between negotiation sessions facilitate both negotiation results which maximize the interests of the client and client-centered advocacy. Often these client conferences may be brief; in some instances, either a telephone call or even an exchange of correspondence may suffice.

During these intra-negotiation counseling sessions, the lawyer should report on the progress of the negotiation and solicit input from the client on what steps to take during the next bargaining session. This level of consultation is required by Model Rule of Professional Conduct 1.4 which requires the lawyer both to keep the client reasonably informed on an ongoing basis and to offer the information necessary for the client to make an informed decision about whether to accept or reject a settlement offer.[8] The client counseling process outlined here is a suggested model for implementing the requirements of Rule 1.4.

In reporting to her client on the progress of the negotiation, the lawyer should discuss the proposals that have been made by both negotiators during the bargaining. She also should inform the client about any new information obtained from the other side that was previously unknown to the client. Particularly in transactional negotiations where discovery is not available, much of the client's information about the matter being negotiated will come from the negotiation itself. The negotiator also learns something about how the other party views a potential business relationship with her client and what the probable terms of the arrangement will be. During the initial stages of many negotiations, the client only vaguely understands how the other party sees the situation and has incomplete information about the facts. The lawyer, therefore, needs to correct any earlier errors in assessing the other party, as well as to relate any new information which emerges during the negotiation.

After the lawyer has reported to her client, she should seek input from the client on several issues:

(1) decisions as to whether proposed agreements on specific issues are acceptable to the client;

(2) the client's relative preference among the various issues being negotiated;

---

8. Model Rules of Professional Conduct Rule 1.4 (1983).

(3) approval of various proposals or concessions which the lawyer recommends as part of the negotiating process;

(4) changes in the client's minimum disposition or evaluation of her Best Alternative to a Negotiated Agreement as a result of new information received; and

(5) any changes in negotiating tactics or strategy and their potential implications for the client's ongoing relationship with the other party.

Most negotiations are multiple issue negotiations, and the client seldom approves agreement on all issues in a single counseling session. More likely, agreements on various issues are reached at different stages of the negotiation process. For example, Jeff Walton, manager of Banana Computers, begins with an initial decision to enter into serious negotiations with the Chestnut Development Corporation. At this point, the lawyers for the two parties would be brought into the bargaining process. The subsequent negotiating session might include both clients and lawyers and reach agreement on which of the available locations Banana will be leasing. During the next meeting between the lawyers, the basic rental structure—base rent plus a percentage of gross sales plus common expenses—may be agreed upon. If each of the clients approves agreement on this rent provision during separate counseling sessions, the lawyers then might proceed to negotiate about the possibility of a lower base rental during an additional start-up period, as well as the specific amounts for the various components of the rental.

At each step of the bargaining process, the client should approve agreement on each significant specific issue. Perhaps the technical requirements of Model Rule of Professional Conduct 1.2 would be satisfied by a blanket ratification of the entire agreement by the client following negotiations. Such an "up or down" decision by the client, however, is less likely to yield an agreement that serves the client's underlying interests to the greatest possible extent.

As the issues become more clearly defined during the negotiation, the lawyer also should inquire as to the relative degree of importance the client attaches to each issue. Recall that one problem-solving tactic, logrolling, consists of conceding on some issues in exchange for the other party's concessions on other issues. If logrolling is to result in an agreement that maximizes the client's level of satisfaction, then the lawyer needs to be acutely aware of how much the client values each issue. Bev Bailey needs to know, for example, whether Banana Computer is more concerned with having a lower base rent during the initial start-up period or if store location is the most important consideration. Prior to the negotiation, the client typically "wants it all" and cannot tell his lawyer which issues he is willing to concede and trade for concessions on other issues. These decisions often must wait until the client learns during the negotiation process itself how highly the other party values each issue. In other words, the client's willingness to concede on a particular issue is influenced by the concessions he may be able to extract from the other party in exchange for his concession.

The lawyer and client also should consider what proposals or concessions the lawyer should make during the next round of bargaining. Often it is advantageous for the lawyer to make a proposal knowing that if it is accepted by the other negotiator then the parties have reached a binding agreement on that particular issue. This requires the lawyer to have authority to bind her client on a specific issue prior to bargaining on that issue. The lawyer's request for this authority from her client should be preceded by a discussion of the advantages and disadvantages to the client of the agreement that would result if the proposal is accepted by the other party. In other words, if the lawyer intends to make a proposal that conceivably could lead to agreement and to do so with authority to bind her client, her proposal should be proceeded by the complete counseling process described in the previous section.

If the lawyer learns facts during the bargaining that are significantly different than the information previously available, the lawyer and client should reconsider the possible use of problem-solving tactics. With greater understanding of the other party's specific interests, they may be able to use brainstorming or other solution-generating techniques to devise proposals that meet both parties' underlying interests. Further, the new information may suggest additional forms of *compensation* for the other party in exchange for his making concessions that the client needs in order to reach agreement. Finally, greater understanding of the other party's interests may suggest additional opportunities for employing *cost-cutting* techniques, that is, new methods of reducing the other party's costs in making necessary concessions.

The client's perception of his alternatives to negotiated agreement and his minimum disposition also may change as the lawyer and client receive new input during the negotiation itself. For example, during the bargaining, Roberta Martinez will offer Gary her strategically biased assessments of the probable trial outcome in Patrick Finney's case, as well as her opinion of the credibility of the expert witnesses who will be testifying for Baltimore and Western. Her arguments on these points may yield new information for Gary Gerstein affecting his assessment of the probable trial outcome. Patrick and Gary may decide together that the prospects for trial are not as rosy as they once perceived. Accordingly, Patrick might change his minimum requirements for a negotiated settlement.

Finally, the lawyer and client, during counseling conferences interspersed between bargaining sessions, should discuss potential changes in their negotiation tactics or strategy. As discussed in Chapter Three, *Choosing Effective Negotiation Tactics,* the other negotiator's strategy is a primary factor to be considered in choosing effective negotiation tactics. For example, if the other negotiator is using predominantly competitive tactics early in the negotiation, this probably suggests that the negotiator should respond with competitive tactics unless she has reason to believe that her more collaborative tactics would be reciprocated. Any change to more competitive tactics during the bargaining process after the negotiator has begun with collaborative tactics, however, risks impairing the client's ongoing relationship with the other party. Accordingly, when the lawyer decides that her negotiation strategy needs to be substantially altered, this decision should be evaluated jointly by the lawyer and client.

The alternation of bargaining sessions and counseling conferences may repeat itself any number of times during the negotiation. The most important recommendation for the lawyer is that she confer regularly with the client during the negotiation process. These conferences enable the lawyer to use all the information available to the client, as well as an accurate reading of the client's interests, in pursuing the best possible negotiated agreement. In addition, continuing contact between the client and his lawyer usually results in greater client satisfaction with the lawyer's representation.

Chapter Twelve

ALTERNATIVE DISPUTE RESOLUTION AND NEGOTIATION

A. EMERGENCE OF THE ALTERNATIVE DISPUTE RESOLUTION MOVEMENT

The last fifteen years have witnessed the burgeoning use of dispute resolution techniques other than adjudication by courts. This expanded use of mediation, arbitration and other forms of alternative dispute resolution was prompted largely by concerns about crowded court dockets and the delay and costs involved in litigation, as well as by a desire to provide a less formal and more accessible means of resolving disputes.[1] This recent proliferation of non-litigation dispute resolution, however, should not overshadow the long history of alternative methods for resolving disputes in this country,[2] particularly in the fields of labor [3] and commercial arbitration.[4]

From society's perspective, the argument in favor of the use of alternative dispute resolution methods is compelling. The delay and cost involved in traditional litigation are immense. Looking only at tort claims, Kahalik and Pace estimate that in 1985, plaintiffs spent between $2.5 billion and $3.8 billion on attorneys' fees and other legal expenses for automobile claims, and between $3.78 billion and $3.84 billion on other tort claims.[5] These figures were somewhat higher than the $2.26 billion spent by defendants in automobile cases and the $3.68 billion defense fees and expenses in other claims, according to Kahalik

---

1. *See* E. Johnson, Jr., A Preliminary Analysis of Alternative Strategies for Processing Civil Disputes 2 (1978).

2. For a general overview of the history of "informal justice," including alternative dispute resolution, *see* J. Auerbach, Justice Without Law? Resolving Disputes Without Lawyers (1983).

3. *See* F. Elkouri & E. Elkouri, How Arbitration Works 2–3 (4th ed. 1985); No-

lan & Adams, *American Labor Arbitration: The Early Years*, 35 U.Fla.L.Rev. 373 (1983).

4. *See* Mentschikoff, *Commercial Arbitration*, 61 Colum.L.Rev. 846, 854–855 (1961).

5. J. Kahalik & N. Pace, Costs and Compensation Paid in Tort Litigation 40–41 (1986).

and Pace. For every dollar spent by insurance companies for claims payments, between 38 and 50 cents goes to lawyers.[6] Delay is also a problem in tort cases and other types of litigation. Less than forty percent of all tort cases are disposed of within a year after the complaint is filed, and a significant portion of cases take more than four years, according to a survey of more than 800 plaintiffs' personal injury attorneys and defense counsel in Florida conducted by the author in 1987.[7]

The purpose behind most forms of alternative dispute resolution techniques is to expedite the prompt and efficient negotiation of claims. Alternative dispute resolution processes also strive to achieve agreements that more adequately satisfy the parties' underlying interests. These methods work by facilitating the negotiation process, and by eliminating the factors that typically impede successful negotiation of disputes. The 1987 survey of 800 tort lawyers practicing in Florida sought to uncover what factors were most significant in delaying settlement in tort cases. The results of that survey are reported in the following table:

TABLE 12–1
FACTORS DELAYING NEGOTIATED AGREEMENTS: PERCENTAGE OF CASES IN WHICH EACH FACTOR PLAYS A SUBSTANTIAL ROLE

	Percentage of Attorneys Identifying Factor	
Reason for Delay	*Plaintiffs'*	*Defense*
Opposing counsel's lack of preparation	21.1%	19.1%
Own lack of preparation	10.3%	10.3%
Opponent's sense he can get better deal later	22.8%	25.0%
Respondent's own sense that she can get better deal later	21.8%	11.0%
Client's recalcitrance	11.3%	15.7%
Other party's recalcitrance	18.8%	17.5%
Waiting for further events to clarify amount of damages	20.6%	21.1%
"Time-value" of money to defendant and lack of pre-judgment interest rule	35.6%	4.7%

Source: Survey of Florida Tort Lawyers (1987).

Most of the alternative dispute resolution processes described in this chapter operate by overcoming these impediments to negotiation.

6. Academic Task Force for Review of the Insurance and Tort Systems, Final Fact–Finding Report on Insurance and Tort Systems 405 (Florida Executive Office of the Governor, 1988) (copy on file with author).

7. *Id.; see also* T. Church, A. Carlson, J. Lee, T. Tan, K. Chantry & L. Sipes, Justice Delayed: The Pace of Litigation in Urban Trial Courts 10–11 (1978).

Consider, for example, an arbitration procedure in which the parties informally present their cases to a neutral arbitrator who then issues a non-binding judgment. Although not dispositive of the claim, the arbitrator's decision serves as a focal point for further negotiation. The arbitrator's award suggests to the lawyer's own client and to the other party that they will not receive a substantially different result if the case is subsequently heard by a judge or jury, thus causing both parties to view the claim more realistically. Further, by forcing both parties to prepare for a hearing, the non-binding arbitration procedure reduces the likelihood that a lack of preparation or prompt case evaluation by either lawyer is preventing settlement.

The next part of this chapter describes *mediation*, perhaps the most important of the alternative dispute resolution processes. *Mediation* is typically defined as a process in which a neutral third party assists negotiators in reaching an agreement.[8] It thus consists of a rather broad array of negotiation facilitation techniques. The remainder of the chapter describes other alternative dispute resolution techniques including binding arbitration, final offer arbitration, court-annexed or other non-binding arbitration, summary jury trials and mini-trials. In contrast to the diversity of mediation techniques, most of these specific dispute resolution processes, in order to assist the negotiators in reaching agreement, rely upon a non-binding substantive evaluation of the case by a neutral third party.

B. MEDIATION

1. INTRODUCTION

Mediation has emerged during the past decade as a significant alternative to litigation for resolving disputes in a wide variety of cases. Family and divorce mediation programs,[9] as well as mediation programs designed to avert the filing of criminal complaints in minor disputes,[10] have proliferated throughout the country. At the same time, mediation increasingly has been used on a more selective basis to resolve major public interest, environmental and corporate disputes.[11]

---

8. More comprehensive descriptions of mediation in legal negotiation are included in L. Riskin & J. Westbrook, Dispute Resolution and Lawyers (1987), particularly 196–249, and N. Rogers & R. Salem, A Student's Guide to Mediation and the Law (1987), particularly 7–39; *see also* D. Pruitt, Negotiation Behavior 201–218 (1981).

9. For a partial listing of family and divorce mediation programs, *see* ABA, Dispute Resolution Program Directory 315–22 (1986–1987). [hereinafter cited as Directory].

10. The use of mediators to resolve disputes involving crime is discussed in N.

Rogers & R. Salem, *supra* note 8, at 187–222. Programs providing such services are identified in Directory, *supra* note 9.

11. Among the major mediations described by Rogers and Salem is a case of racial unrest in a midwest state reformatory. N. Rogers & R. Salem, *supra* note 8, at 16–17. In another case, a mediator facilitated resolution of a disagreement between neo-nazis and Chicago city officials over the neo-nazis' right to conduct demonstrations. *Id.* at 35–36. The *ABA's Dispute Resolution Directory* identifies mediators providing services in environmental cases, *see* Directory, *supra* note 9, at 327–29, and in corporate disputes. *See id.,* at 331–32.

In the context of this book, mediation can be analyzed as the efforts of a neutral party to facilitate the use by the negotiators of *problem-solving* and *cooperative* negotiation tactics. Many of the techniques described in this section as tools of the mediator, such as *active listening, brainstorming* and *cost-cutting,* already have been considered as tactics employed by the negotiators themselves.

Just as negotiators often do not successfully engage in joint problem-solving until after an unproductive competitive phase of negotiation, parties often do not begin mediating until they acknowledge mutual frustration. When a party merely expresses a willingness to mediate, this should be recognized as a problem-solving tactic inviting reciprocal problem-solving or cooperative behaviors by the other party. On the other hand, a competitive negotiator sometimes views a willingness to mediate as a sign of weakness.[12]

Section 2 surveys the variety of functions that a mediator can perform during the negotiation process. Section 3 outlines a typical format for a mediation.

2. THE FUNCTIONS OF A MEDIATOR

Virtually any technique used by a neutral third party to facilitate negotiation can be regarded as mediation. Most mediation techniques, however, fulfill one or more of the following goals:

(1) to improve communication between the negotiating parties;

(2) to improve the attitudes of the parties toward each other;

(3) to educate the parties or their attorneys about the negotiation process;

(4) to inject a dose of reality when one party is viewing his situation in an unrealistically favorable light; or

(5) to generate new proposals the parties have not identified.

The goals of improving communication between the parties and improving the attitudes of the parties toward each other are intertwined. The willingness of parties to share information with each other, and to engage in *cooperative* or *problem-solving* tactics, often is understandably constrained by the negotiator's realization that she will weaken her position unless the other party reciprocates her collaborative moves. Cooperation and problem-solving require trust, and generally the parties in a lawsuit or other dispute are mistrustful and feel angry with each other.

The mediator attempts to create an ambience conducive to *cooperative* and *problem-solving* tactics. The mere presence of the mediator will affect the behavior of some negotiators; they are less likely to use verbal abuse or extremely competitive tactics in the presence of someone perceived to have influence over the outcome of the negotiation.

---

12. In most labor mediation, the potential implications of a willingness to mediate as a cooperative tactic are avoided because mediation is mandated as part of the grievance process. *See generally* F. Elkouri & E. Elkouri, *supra* note 3, at 153–211.

Further, mediators frequently use *active listening* to convince the parties that someone has listened to their versions of the dispute and has understood their concerns. *Active listening* contributes to the parties' trust in the mediator. Their sense that someone is listening to them increases the parties' willingness to explore new alternatives. Mediators also encourage each party to vent his underlying anger or fear, usually without the other party present, so that these hidden emotions do not subtly undermine the party's ability to pursue a negotiated agreement which serves his best interests.

The mediator facilitates the *information disclosure* by the parties necessary for *cooperative* or *problem-solving* tactics to work. She can monitor the information sharing process to assure that it is not one-sided, and can pressure a party concealing information into reciprocating the other party's information disclosure. Once a party agrees to mediate, there is considerable pressure on him to answer a specific question from a mediator. Under many circumstances, the mediator asks questions of one of the parties in a *caucus* or a private meeting that excludes the other party. The mediator can agree not to share the information with the other party or only to do so when the other party reveals similar information.

As a professional specializing in the negotiation process, the mediator also educates the parties about negotiation. One party may be overly competitive, thus risking retaliatory competitive tactics, ill will, or even negotiation stalemate or breakdown. Another party might be too cooperative, subjecting himself to exploitation. The mediator can suggest cooperative or problem-solving tactics where appropriate, or even urge a slower concession pattern if the negotiator concedes too rapidly and may be left with no room to maneuver in the final stages of bargaining.[13] The mediator's function as an educator is particularly valuable in facilitating *problem-solving* negotiation tactics. Restated briefly, these are: encouraging the parties to discuss underlying interests, generating multiple solutions and facilitating the use of logrolling, cost-cutting and compensation techniques.

Under some circumstances, the mediator makes suggestions regarding the substance of the negotiated agreement, as well as the negotia-

---

13. A more difficult ethical question is whether or not the mediator should intervene substantively to prevent a negotiator from "giving away the family farm" and conceding more than is necessary to reach an agreement. In other words, is the mediator's ethical obligation solely one of *impartiality* or does the mediator also have a role in monitoring the *fairness* of the agreement? In the traditional mediation process in labor grievance proceedings, mediators rarely need to be concerned about fairness because both parties are represented by experienced negotiators. Thus, the mediator's role as a neutral is enshrined in various ethical codes for mediators. *See e.g.*, Society of Professionals in Dispute Resolution, Ethical Standards of Professional Responsibility (1986). As mediation has expanded to other kinds of cases, however, particularly family disputes, some commentators suggest that mediators have an ethical obligation to protect against "unfair" agreements, even when this obligation requires a breach of the mediator's neutral role. *See e.g.*, Susskind & Ozawa, *Mediated Negotiation in the Public Sector*, 27 Am.Behav.Scientist 255, 267–68 (1983).

tion *process*. When the mediator has listened to the parties and understood their interests, she may be in a position herself to suggest consideration of proposals or ideas that the parties have not identified. Usually the mediator offers her own proposals only as a last resort, preferring that the parties themselves identify possible resolutions. Even when she advances her own proposal, the mediator is often most effective when one of the negotiators believes that the suggestion was "her idea." Similarly, if one party has unrealistic expectations regarding either the negotiation process, or the trial or other alternative to a negotiated agreement, the mediator can offer her own realistic assessment. Finally, the mediator protects a party less experienced in the bargaining process by urging patience in making concessions, instilling poise and occasionally blunting the fury of extremely competitive tactics from the other negotiator.

In any of these roles—suggesting her own proposals, injecting a dose of reality or protecting a weaker negotiator—the mediator risks becoming too involved in the substance of the agreement instead of serving only as a facilitator. For some parties, the mediator's influence on their decisions will be considerable. If the mediator intrudes excessively into the substantive content of the negotiated agreement, she virtually becomes an adjudicator and not a mediator. The final agreement may not serve the interests of the parties, and either side may resent the agreement because of his sense that it was imposed upon him.

3. THE STRUCTURE OF THE MEDIATION PROCESS

The mediation session typically begins with the mediator introducing herself to the parties and their attorneys. This step is more than a formality, because the parties' trust in the mediator is essential to achieving a successful resolution. A brief opening statement by the mediator outlines the procedures to be followed during the mediation process, the mediator's role, and what is expected of the parties.[14] The mediator should stress that the process is a voluntary one, that a dissatisfied party can walk away from the mediation at any point, and that the mediator has no power to impose an agreement. She also should stress her impartiality, including her lack of prior relationships with either party.

The mediator then should describe the procedures she intends to follow, including opening statements by both parties and possibly *caucuses* in which the mediator will meet individually and confidentially with one of the parties. An early explanation of the caucus procedure is important so that the party not included in the caucus understands its purpose and does not believe that the mediator and the other party are "conspiring," or that the caucus procedure jeopardizes the mediator's impartiality. Finally, the mediator should informally pro-

---

14. *See* L. Riskin & J. Westbrook, *supra* note 8, at 222–24; N. Rogers & R. Salem, *supra* note 8, at 22–27.

vide behavioral guidelines suggesting how the parties should treat each other during the mediation process.

Each party participating in the mediation has an opportunity to present an opening statement, including its version of the dispute and a description of its underlying interests. Obviously, this opening presentation often serves as an opportunity to vent frustration and gives the client the sense that someone hears his grievance. The opening statement also reduces misunderstandings between the parties, allows each party to learn about the other's actual interests, and identifies those areas where a genuine factual disagreement exists.

The mediator performs a variety of subtle functions during opening presentations. She asks questions to elicit further information about topics she believes are important or that may suggest a commonality of interests between the parties. She *"active listens"* to build rapport, and to be empathetic without casting value judgments on the strong emotions often expressed in opening statements. She restates the parties' descriptions of historical facts and their interests, in order to clarify them. Often she paraphrases, in more neutral terms, pejorative or value-laden language so that the statements do not create anger or defensiveness. She prevents interruptions by the other party during the presentation, and verbal attacks by either participant.

The next, and probably most important, phase of the mediation process is analogous to the "narrowing of differences" component of the negotiation process described in Chapter Eight. During this stage of mediation, the mediator encourages and facilitates the use of both *cooperative* and *problem-solving* negotiation tactics. This text first describes the mediator's role in encouraging *cooperative* tactics; then it addresses the mediator's facilitation of *problem-solving* tactics.

The mediator uses a variety of approaches to encourage the parties to make concessions or use other *cooperative* negotiation tactics, depending upon what factors are inhibiting these approaches.[15] In some cases, one of the negotiators refuses to concede because she believes that if she continues to use *competitive* tactics, the other party eventually will make most of the concessions. Here the mediator performs as an "agent of reality," offering the competitive negotiator a more realistic estimate of the other party's *minimum disposition* and the content of the final agreement.

In other negotiations, a lawyer or her client fears that concessions will lead to *image loss,* that is, her concessions will be seen as a sign of weakness and will encourage renewed competitive tactics by the other party instead of reciprocation. The mediator can mitigate *image loss,* under these circumstances, in any of several ways. Most importantly, she can use a series of private meetings, or *caucuses,* with the parties and their lawyers, to transmit concessions between them in ways that avoid image loss. For example, during the mediator's session with

15. *See* D. Pruitt, *supra* note 8, at 207–215.

Patrick Finney and Gary Gerstein, they might communicate to the mediator a willingness to settle for $875,000 that they would not be willing to express in an open negotiating session with Roberta Martinez, the lawyer for the Baltimore and Western Railroad. They fear that if during a bargaining session they openly express this concession, Roberta would see it as a sign of weakness and she would refuse to concede further. In a subsequent *caucus* with Roberta Martinez and the railroad claims manager, however, the mediator might present the $875,000 figure as her own estimate of where an agreement with Patrick is possible. Because it is never attributed to Patrick, this "disguised" concession produces neither *image loss* nor any loss of room to maneuver within the bargaining range if Baltimore and Western rejects it. Conversely, where the mediator becomes convinced during a *caucus* that one party sincerely has reached its limits and can concede no further, this information also can be communicated to the other party. The other party then knows it must make concessions to avoid negotiation stalemate or breakdown.

Some lawyers and clients obviously will not tell the mediator their true bottom line, certainly not at the beginning of the mediation process. When the mediator makes it clearly understood that indications of *minimum disposition* are not to be shared with the other party, however, it is likely that parties will be more open and flexible with a mediator than with the other party in the negotiation.[16] Further, as the mediator gains the trust of the lawyer and her client during the negotiation and succeeds in delivering concessions and other indications of flexibility from the other party—who had been unyielding prior to the mediator's involvement—the lawyer and client are more likely to be flexible and to reveal their true interests.

The mediator also facilitates *cooperative* tactics by assisting negotiators in releasing themselves from *positional commitments* they have made during the bargaining process. Ordinarily, if a lawyer has stated that her client "could not possibly accept a settlement of $100,000," she sustains a substantial *image loss* or loss of credibility if she then concedes to such a figure, even if her client's best interests indicate that such a concession is warranted. On some occasions, particularly late in the negotiation, the mediator's direct suggestion that a party retreat from an earlier positional commitment may be all that is required. In other cases, the mediator assists in developing a rationale for why the *commitment* no longer applies to current circumstances. For example, recall Israel's commitment that the Sinai could not be returned to Egyptian sovereignty because of Israel's security concerns about having the Egyptian Army positioned in the Sinai within striking distance of Israel. The suggestion of the American mediators that the Sinai be returned to Egypt, but remain demilitarized, released Israel from its earlier negotiating commitment to retain sovereignty over the Sinai.

16. As one mediator told the author, "both parties lie, but they lie less to the mediator."

Finally, the mediator herself may make a substantive proposal that she knows satisfies both parties' requirements for an agreement. Little or no *image loss* occurs when a party "concedes" to the proposal of the neutral facilitator. However, the mediator should advance her own proposal with reluctance and only during the last stages of mediation. If the parties reject such a proposal, both the mediator's credibility and her image as an impartial facilitator are impaired.

In many negotiations, the most important role for the mediator is to facilitate the use of *problem-solving* negotiation tactics. Many of the *problem-solving* tactics described elsewhere in this text—brainstorming, the use of the single negotiation text, logrolling, compensation and cost-cutting [17]—may not be familiar to many lawyers. The mediator's role and experience make her particularly qualified to educate the negotiators about these procedures and to introduce them into the negotiation process.

A well qualified mediator has had special training and experience in encouraging parties to reveal their underlying interests, in facilitating the identification of alternatives (sometimes during a brainstorming process), and in evaluating each of these alternatives. In addition to her expertise, the mediator's neutrality makes it easier for her to conduct a brainstorming or other solution-generating session, because her leadership during the process does not threaten any of the other participants. Mediators also can suggest, either during negotiation sessions or during private *caucuses,* appropriate specific applications of the logrolling, cost-cutting and compensation techniques. The mediator's better understanding of both the parties' interests and the relative importance of various issues to each of them makes her particularly able to guide the logrolling process.

The role of the mediator as a facilitator of *problem-solving* tactics is particularly valuable in multiple party negotiations. As previously described, the complexity of these negotiations often makes it difficult to reach agreement through the exchange of concessions, thereby increasing the importance of *problem-solving* tactics. Further, as discussed in Chapter Ten, the mediator is uniquely capable of using the *single negotiation text* as a *problem-solving* tool. When a mediator drafts the text, the parties are more likely to view it as a neutral document. The mediator does not face the same conflict as the negotiator preparing a *single negotiation text.* The negotiator must choose between a balanced text that clearly indicates her willingness to make concessions, and a text so favorable to her client that the other parties

---

17. For a description of those problem-solving tactics, *see supra* Chapter Four, *Negotiation Planning,* at 55–60, for brainstorming. For logrolling, *see supra* Chapter Three, *Choosing Effective Negotiation Tactics,* at 32; Chapter Four, *Negotiation Planning,* at 55, 60; Chapter Five, *The Relationship Between the Negotiators: The Initial Orientation,* at 77–8; Chapter Nine, *Closure,* at 170–1. For compensation, *see supra* Chapter Four, *Negotiation Planning,* at 60–1; Chapter Nine, *Closure,* at 172. For cost-cutting, *see supra* Chapter Four, *Negotiation Planning,* at 60; Chapter Nine, *Closure,* at 171–2. For single negotiation text, *see supra* Chapter Ten, *Multiple Party Negotiation,* at 181–3.

will not view it as a credible starting point for serious bargaining. The mediator also can serve the role of chairperson or facilitator in multiple party negotiations and thus provides the necessary structure for these complex interpersonal interactions.

In the concluding phases of the negotiation process, the mediator often restates agreements reached between the parties.[18] As agreement is achieved on individual issues, the mediator's summary both assures that the resolution is understood by all parties and also spurs the negotiators in their efforts to resolve remaining issues. Mediators frequently are involved in drafting the written agreement with the parties' lawyers.

4. THE APPROPRIATE USE OF MEDIATION

When should the lawyer encourage her client and the other negotiating parties to employ a mediator? It is impossible to define categories or rules for determining what cases should be mediated. Generally, mediation is appropriate when both parties share high aspirations and therefore are reluctant to concede, but continue to believe that a negotiated agreement is preferable to the other alternatives. Often the parties only understand the need for mediation late in the negotiation process. By this time, they recognize that their *competitive* tactics are not succeeding, and that the level of frustration between the negotiators make it difficult for them to employ *problem-solving* or *cooperative* tactics without outside intervention. Specifically, mediation is suggested when there is a recognition that the negotiation situation offers *integrative* potential the negotiators have failed to develop. Mediation can also be fruitful in a predominantly *distributive* negotiation context if the lawyer's client or the other party has unrealistic expectations.

Usually, the lawyer has a role in selecting the mediator. No decision is as important to the client pursuing a satisfactory negotiated agreement except perhaps the initial decision regarding which lawyer to retain. A poorly trained or inexperienced mediator may pressure a client into an agreement that does not meet her interests and may miss opportunities for substantially better agreements. Unfortunately, the range of abilities of those in the expanding profession of mediation varies widely. It is incumbent upon the lawyer to check carefully the experience, training and references of a mediator.

C. OTHER DISPUTE RESOLUTION PROCESSES

This section defines each of the important alternative dispute resolution processes other than mediation, briefly describes its operation and analyzes how it facilitates the negotiation process.

18. *See* N. Rogers & R. Salem, *supra* note 8, at 39.

1. BINDING ARBITRATION

Arbitration is a process in which the disputants submit a controversy to a neutral party, or sometimes a panel of neutral parties, to hear arguments, consider evidence, and render a decision.[19] The arbitration decision may be either binding or non-binding on the parties. Binding arbitration is functionally a substitute form of adjudication by a third party, replacing adjudication by a court. On the other hand, non-binding arbitration requires the parties to agree to the award for it to be dispositive. Therefore, it is not as a substitute form of adjudication, but rather a facilitator of negotiated agreements. Referring to both the binding and non-binding types of this process as "arbitration" is misleading. It will be apparent during further consideration of alternative dispute resolution processes that non-binding arbitration functions more like mediation, summary jury trials and mini-trials, than it does binding arbitration. These kinds of dispute resolution techniques facilitate negotiation, and unlike binding arbitration, do not involve a binding decision by a third party.

Most often, parties voluntarily agree to binding arbitration as a dispute resolution mechanism either as part of a contractual provision governing disputes that might happen in the future or after a dispute occurs. Binding arbitration has been used extensively for many years in grievance proceedings and other labor disputes. Increasingly, construction and other commercial contracts also provide for binding arbitration as a process to resolve disputes. The voluntary nature of most binding arbitration enables the parties to stipulate to the procedural and evidentiary rules used during arbitration and the process for selecting the arbitrator.[20] Because the parties usually control the selection of the arbitrator, they are able to choose someone with the expertise necessary to understand the dispute.

Arbitration proceedings usually are more informal than court hearings and the rules of evidence are applied flexibly. Discovery prior to the hearing is usually minimal.[21] In simple cases, the arbitrator renders his decision orally at the conclusion of the hearing, but most often the arbitrator issues his decision in writing, accompanied by a short written opinion, only after he has had adequate opportunity to review written documents and other testimony presented at the hearing.

Binding arbitration offers several advantages when compared with court proceedings. It is generally speedier and more informal, and it

---

19. *See generally* F. Elkouri & E. Elkouri, *supra* note 3.

20. The procedural rules governing an arbitration come from a variety of sources including contract provisions, applicable statutes and informal agreements among the parties, often including an agreement to arbitrate under the rules of the American Arbitration Association. *See id.,* at 222–23.

21. In labor arbitration, the parties typically discover the other side's evidence during the grievance procedure. In addition, arbitrators frequently possess *subpoena* power, and even when they do not, a request from an arbitrator for evidence is usually honored. *See id.,* at 304–310.

usually avoids the series of motion hearings, extensive discovery and the protracted wait for a trial date that is now typical in civil litigation. At the same time, each disputant, such as a union member who believes that his rights have been violated under a collective bargaining agreement, retains his "day in court" and an opportunity to air his grievance. By avoiding litigation, parties often preserve their ongoing accommodative relationship. For example, in some areas such as labor or commercial grievances, arbitration is viewed as part of doing business, while initiating litigation is viewed as an extremely adversarial act.

Parties also may agree that unlike trials, arbitration proceedings are confidential. Confidentiality may be an important incentive for a party concerned about adverse publicity, or the disclosure of trade secrets involved in a dispute. Other defendants find binding arbitration an attractive alternative in cases where they fear that an adverse precedent would be set in a court case. It is precisely these factors that have led some critics to attack arbitration for its ability to hide from the public eye grievances that require societal attention and to avoid setting legal precedents protecting the rights of others who are similarly situated.[22]

Unlike the other processes discussed in this chapter, binding arbitration does not necessarily facilitate the negotiation process. In fact, a strong argument can be made that the availability of binding arbitration procedures—at least in areas other than labor grievances—reduces the incentives to reach a negotiated agreement.[23] In the absence of arbitration, one of the incentives to settle a dispute is to avoid the cost and delay involved in pursuing litigation. As those costs in money and time are reduced by substituting arbitration for litigation, more disputants probably seek an adjudication by a third party instead of a negotiated agreement. Particularly with smaller claims, easy access to binding arbitration actually may reduce settlement rates.[24] However, the other advantages to having arbitration available as an alternative—particularly savings in time and expense at the same time the disputants retain their rights to a hearing—usually outweigh the importance of reduced settlement rates.

2. FINAL OFFER ARBITRATION

One variation of binding arbitration is designed specifically to facilitate the negotiation process and not to impede it. In *final offer*

---

22. *E.g.,* Brunet, *Questioning the Quality of Alternative Dispute Resolution,* 62 Tulane L.Rev. 1, 15–31 (1987); Fiss, *Against Settlement,* 93 Yale L.J. 1073, 1085 (1984).

23. In the labor field, a well defined grievance procedure generally is available under the collective bargaining agreement. *See* F. Elkouri & E. Elkouri, *supra* note 3, at 153–211. Such grievance procedures fa-

cilitate a negotiated resolution. The combination of grievance and arbitration processes in labor grievances thus probably increases, rather than decreases, the rate of negotiated resolutions.

24. *See* J. Adler, D. Hensler, C. Nelson, Simple Justice: How Litigants Fare in the Pittsburgh Court Arbitration Program 95 (1983).

arbitration, the parties submit their last, best negotiating offers to the arbitrator prior to the hearing. After hearing the evidence, the arbitrator is restricted to choosing one or the other of the final proposals.

The most widely publicized use of *final offer arbitration* is in the collective bargaining provision governing salary disputes between major league baseball players and team owners. Public employee bargaining statutes [25] also frequently provide for *final offer arbitration,* and sometimes is used in other contracts to resolve disputes over compensation. When a baseball player and team owner cannot agree on a salary, each submits a last, best proposal. Casey Jones insists that his salary should be $900,000 for the next year, and the owners of the Mudville team insist that a fair salary for Casey is only $500,000. The arbitrator, after hearing testimony of Casey's exploits, perhaps in lyrical form, and evidence of the salaries paid to comparable players, must choose either the $900,000 figure submitted by Casey or the $500,000 figure submitted by the team owners. The arbitrator has no discretion to select a number between the two proposals or any other figure.

The effect of final offer arbitration is to encourage concessions during negotiation. The less that Casey demands, the more reasonable his demand looks to the arbitrator. Conversely, the greater the offer by the team owners, the more likely that their proposal will be chosen. As each party strives to appear reasonable to the arbitrator, concessions are made on both sides, thus narrowing the differences between the parties. It is likely that they ultimately will reach agreement themselves in order to avoid the expense and the risk involved in a decision by a third party.

The available empirical evidence supports the assertion that *final offer arbitration* leads to more concessions and negotiated agreements than other forms of final arbitration.[26] Although the results of this process may be "reasonable" compromises, however, they are not necessarily "correct." For example, *final offer arbitration* would not be an appropriate system for resolving all personal injury or medical malpractice claims. It would entice the parties to negotiate seriously, thus reducing attorneys' fees and other litigation costs. However, an insurance company or uninsured defendant probably would be reluctant to refuse to make any payment whatsoever to a plaintiff, even if it believed the claim was utterly without merit. Even if the refusal to pay were correct, such a harsh stance might appear "unreasonable" to the arbitrators. Accordingly, the use of *final offer arbitration* in this context probably would lead to more payments in frivolous cases.

25. These statutes often grant public employees the right to seek final arbitration when they are prohibited from striking. *See e.g.* Iowa Code Ann. §§ 20.12 and 20.22 (West 1978); Mich.Comp.Laws §§ 423.231–423.238 (1978); N.J.Stat.Ann. § 34:13A–16 (West 1988); Wis.Stat.Ann § 111.77 (West 1988).

26. *See* D. Pruitt, *supra* note 8, at 224.

3. COURT ANNEXED ARBITRATION AND OTHER TYPES OF NON–BINDING ARBITRATION

Binding arbitration produces a final resolution of the claim. Non-binding arbitration, on the other hand, promotes the negotiation process. The decision of the third party arbitrator, although non-binding, assists the lawyers and their clients in realistically valuing the case, and thus provides a focal point for settlement discussions.

Non-binding arbitration typically is "court-annexed" arbitration, as contrasted with arbitration voluntarily agreed to by the parties. Statutes or local court rules authorize trial courts to require disputants in specified cases, such as all cases in which the amount in controversy is less than $10,000 or all medical malpractice cases, to participate in non-binding arbitration prior to taking their cases to trial. The arbitration program is administered by the court. Hearings are informal and involve abbreviated presentations of cases by the litigants. If the arbitrator's award is accepted by both parties, it is entered as the judgment of the court. If either party rejects the award, the case is set for a trial *de novo*. In most programs, the arbitration award is not admissible at trial. Usually, however, if the party rejecting the arbitrator's award fails to do better than the award at trial, it is forced to pay court costs, the other party's attorney's fees or some other specified penalty.[27]

Court-annexed arbitration programs usually require that certain categories of cases be submitted to non-binding arbitration. If non-binding arbitration is elective as opposed to mandatory, however, what factors should suggest to the lawyer that a case should be submitted to non-binding arbitration? The most important factor to consider is unrealistic case evaluation by the other party. When the opposing attorney or his client is not evaluating the settlement value of a case realistically, non-binding arbitration may be useful because its results tend to reduce inflated expectations. Conversely, non-binding arbitration also may be useful when an attorney believes that her own client has unrealistic expectations. Further, non-binding arbitration sometimes is helpful when the other attorney has not prepared the case fully enough to realistically evaluate it. The arbitration hearing requires the attorneys to focus on the case, and that sometimes is all that is necessary for settlement.

The lawyer should recognize the risk, however, that some opposing attorneys using competitive tactics will view a request for arbitration, or the use of other alternative dispute resolution processes to value a case, as a sign that the lawyer is overly anxious to settle the case and to avoid litigation. In some instances, this may lead to even greater use of competitive tactics. Further, some attorneys use non-binding arbitra-

---

27. *E.g.,* West's Ann.Cal.Civ.Proc. § 1141.21 (West 1988) (payment of court costs and experts' fees); Mich.Comp.Laws § 600.4921 (1987) (payment of court costs and reasonable attorney's fees).

tion as a form of inexpensive discovery, without any intent to be influenced by the results.

How well has court-annexed arbitration succeeded in reducing the delays and costs involved in litigation? The empirical answers to this inquiry are, at this point, either mixed or inconclusive.[28] On one hand, court-annexed arbitration programs have been very successful in reducing case disposition time, and also are viewed favorably by the litigants and attorneys who participate in them. The evidence as to whether non-binding arbitration reduces either the aggregate costs of the dispute resolution system or the costs of the litigants, however, is inconclusive.

The question of whether court-annexed arbitration reduces the total costs of dispute resolution, including both court costs and attorneys' fees, requires a comparison of:

(1) the total system-wide costs of handling cases without court-annexed arbitration, which equals the sum of the costs of:

(a) cases which are settled; and

(b) cases which are litigated; with

(2) the total cost of a system with court-annexed arbitration. This cost equals the sum of the costs of:

(a) cases settled without arbitration;

(b) cases that are arbitrated and then settled; and

(c) cases in which the parties fail to settle following arbitration and proceed to trial.

The cost effectiveness of court-annexed arbitration thus depends upon two factors:

(1) How much is spent on unnecessary arbitrations? In other words, what is the total cost added by arbitration hearings in those cases that would have settled without arbitration? and

(2) How much is spent for unsuccessful arbitrations? In other words, how often will one of the parties reject the arbitrated award and request a trial *de novo,* and how much expense is added by these unsuccessful arbitrations?

If court-annexed arbitration is to be cost effective, it must significantly reduce the number of litigants exercising their rights to trial. If a substantial number of litigants elect a trial *de novo,* a court-annexed arbitration system actually can be more expensive because of the cost added by the arbitration hearings. At this point, the empirical evidence is inconclusive.

The issue of whether the litigants themselves realize significant cost savings from court-annexed arbitration also depends upon how

28. *See e.g.,* J. Adler, D. Hensler, C. Nelson, *supra* note 24, at 86–96; D. Hensler, A. Lipson & E. Rolph, Judicial Arbitration in California: The First Year 24–91 (1981); Goldberg & Brett, *An Experiment in the Mediation of Grievances,* Monthly Labor Review 23–29 (March 1983).

attorneys' fees paid by the disputants are affected by arbitration proceedings. For example, it is not known whether plaintiffs' attorneys in personal injury cases, who typically use contingent fee arrangements, reduce their fees in cases resolved through arbitration instead of through litigation. Nor is it known if they increase their fees in cases involving arbitration that would have settled without arbitration.

The inconclusiveness of these answers regarding the system-wide impact of court-annexed arbitration should not discourage the lawyer from using this procedure in a particular case to facilitate the negotiation process to her client's benefit. Non-binding arbitration is an important tool when the other lawyer or her client is not negotiating reasonably because he has not fully prepared his case or because he lacks a realistic opinion of its settlement value. In some cases, non-binding arbitration also assists the lawyer in the counseling process by resolving a discrepancy between the differing case evaluations of the lawyer and the client.

4. SUMMARY JURY TRIAL

The *summary jury trial* is a second form of non-binding adjudication designed to assist the parties in the negotiation process.[29] The *summary jury trial* involves a brief summary presentation of evidence to a mock jury who issues an advisory opinion that becomes the focal point for further negotiation.

Judges using the *summary jury trial* procedure generally carefully select the cases to be heard in this format. Although not limited to complex cases, the *summary jury trial* procedure usually takes a full day for the judge and the mock jury, so there is little benefit in using the procedure for a trial expected to last only a day or two. Typically, its use has been limited to those cases where the parties have been frustrated in achieving a negotiated agreement. Proponents of the *summary jury trial* process believe that its use should not be restricted to any particular category of cases, but identify four specific factors that suggest its potential application:

(1) where there are substantial discrepancies between the opposing attorneys' evaluations of unliquidated damages such as "pain and suffering";

(2) where the lawyers disagree sharply as to how the jury will apply the facts to nebulous legal concepts such as "reasonableness";

(3) where one of the parties lacks a realistic view of the value of the case; or

29. The use of the *summary jury trial* was pioneered by federal district court Judge Thomas Lambros. *See* Lambros, *Summary Jury Trial: A Flexible Settlement Alternative,* 79–98 in ADR and the Courts: A Manual for Judges and Lawyers (E. Fine, ed. 1987); Lambros, *The Summary Jury Trial: An Alternative Method of Resolving Disputes,* 69 Judicature 286–290 (1986).

(4) where one of the parties strongly desires to have his "day in court" or to have his case heard by an impartial jury.

Several of these factors demonstrate the desirability of having a jury involved in the process of obtaining a non-binding adjudication for settlement purposes, as opposed to other neutral legal professionals such as arbitrators.

A judge can adapt the precise format of the *summary jury trial* proceeding to meet the circumstances of a particular case. Generally, a mock jury is drawn from the regular venire. Counsel for each party delivers an abbreviated presentation, usually no more than one hour, of what she expects the evidence at trial to prove. Counsel is limited to facts drawn from discovery or from her good faith representations of what witnesses have told her. In addition to this oral presentation, each lawyer may present documents or tangible exhibits to the jury. The attorney's presentation is limited to representations based upon evidence that will be admissible at trial; evidentiary objections by opposing counsel are allowed but discouraged. A judge or a magistrate presides over the hearing and gives an abbreviated charge at the conclusion of the hearing. He then provides the mock jury with a jury form containing specific interrogatories, as well as general inquiries regarding liability and damages, so that each lawyer is given considerable feedback about how the jury views the case.

A *summary jury trial* can facilitate the negotiation process at a variety of different stages. An agreement sometimes is reached during the final pre-trial conference prior to the *summary trial* because the lawyers have prepared their cases and evaluated the other side's case more carefully than before. Most judges require the parties themselves to attend the presentation of the case, and agreement may occur after the parties themselves have heard the summaries of the evidence, even before the jury renders its advisory verdict. When the jury returns, both the judge and counsel for the parties are given the chance to question the jurors about how they perceived the evidence, thus contributing further to achieving a realistic settlement. However, most negotiated agreements do not occur until several weeks following the *summary jury trial* when the lawyers and their clients have had an adequate opportunity to assess the meaning of the mock jury's verdict and other feedback from the jurors.

Judges who regularly employ the *summary jury trial* report considerable success in facilitating negotiation in those "difficult to settle" cases which otherwise result in protracted trials.[30] This success appears attributable both to the careful selection of cases which are heard in *summary jury trials* and to the strength of the message regarding the value of a case when it comes directly from a jury.

---

30. In *Strandell v. Jackson County, Ill.,* 838 F.2d 884 (7th Cir.1988), the Seventh Circuit Court of Appeals held that Rule 16 of the Federal Rules of Civil Procedure did not authorize a federal district court judge to *compel* litigants to participate in a summary jury trial against their will.

5. MINI–TRIAL

Mini-trials are voluntary and private proceedings in which both parties present evidence to assist them in reaching a negotiated agreement. The parties agree in advance about the rules and procedure for the conduct of the hearing. Generally, senior representatives of the disputing parties with settlement authority actively participate in the *mini-trial*. *Mini-trials* have been used primarily to resolve business disputes between parties with ongoing relationships.

The formats of *mini-trials* are extremely varied, reflecting whatever arrangements the disputing parties agree upon. Usually the procedures resemble those of a summary jury trial with neither a jury nor a non-binding decision from the neutral party. Each party presents a summary presentation of its facts. Usually a neutral advisor presides, but frequently she is joined "at the bench" by the senior representatives of the disputants. In other cases, the senior representatives preside without a neutral advisor. Placed in the role of listening to presentations of evidence, a senior representative often finds that he develops a more detached and neutral "judicial" view of the dispute that later aids negotiation.

After listening to the strengths and weaknesses of their respective cases, the senior representatives renew settlement negotiation. The neutral advisor does not issue a decision, but the senior representatives often ask her questions regarding her view of the case or about specific issues. Negotiation continues until either the parties agree, or they decide that they cannot agree.

Like non-binding arbitration and summary jury trials, mini-trials expose both the lawyers and the representatives of the parties possessing settlement authority to the strengths and the weaknesses of both sides of the case, and help show them how the dispute will look to a judge or jury. *Mini-trials* are probably most useful when there is a dispute of facts between the parties. The use of *mini-trials* has increased in recent years, and so have the participants' claims that mini-trials have saved millions of dollars in legal fees by avoiding protracted litigation.[31]

31. *See e.g.,* "Modified Mini–Trial Bridges Communications Gap in $2.4 Million Case." 4 Alternatives to the High Cost of Litigation, No. 6, 4, 14 (June 1986). When Sherwin–Williams sued a Chicago based corporation for non-payment under a contract for purchase of charcoal lighter cans, the purchaser counterclaimed for $2 million. After years of discovery and high legal fees, the parties used a mini-trial process to expedite settlement. Counsel for Sherwin–Williams reported saving "an incredible amount of money in legal fees." *Id.* at 14. Similarly, after using a hybrid mini-trial technique to settle a dispute between a publicly-traded company and one of its directors, a New York attorney reported that the total cost of the six week mini-trial was "a fraction—and I don't use the term loosely—of legal fees that would have been well in excess of $1 million." "The Hybrid Mini–Trial of a New York Lawyer," 4 Alternatives to the High Cost of Litigation, No. 6, 1, 8 (June 1986).

D. CONCLUSION

This book began at the *micro* level, introducing the negotiation process as a critical aspect of an individual lawyer's representation of her client. It has come full circle to a *macro* perspective; this last chapter addresses the legal culture's recent recognition that the negotiation process is an important form of dispute resolution and that institutional arrangements should be made to facilitate negotiation through mediation, arbitration and similar processes.

Ultimately, however, fulfillment of your client's interests depends heavily upon you, the lawyer. Your understanding of the negotiation process—as well as your knowledge of law, preparation and character—contributes to solving problems, settling disputes, and creating opportunities for your clients.

*

Index

†